MONARCHY

LOUIS XIV
*From the pastel by Charles le Brun
in the Louvre, Paris*

MONARCHY

A Study of Louis XIV

BY

HILAIRE BELLOC

Foreword by Roger Buck

AROUCA
PRESS

First published by Cassell and Company Ltd. 1938
Published by Arouca Press 2022

ISBN: 978-1-990685-06-4 (pbk)
ISBN: 978-1-990685-07-1 (hardcover)

Arouca Press
PO Box 55003
Bridgeport PO
Waterloo, ON N2J 3G0
Canada
www.aroucapress.com
Send inquiries to info@aroucapress.com

CONTENTS

FOREWORD

Roger Buck

HILAIRE BELLOC KNEW TWO worlds: France and England. Born in France to a French father in 1870, he was raised mostly in England by his mother, following his father's death. Despite this, Belloc never lost sight of the land of his birth, spending summer holidays there, even attending French school for a while, and serving in the French army. Only much later did he truly settle in England, finally accepting British nationality in his mid-thirties. Living in England, he participated in such eminent British institutions as Oxford University and the House of Commons, where he was twice elected as a Member of Parliament. Still, even then, France continually occupied his mind and heart. His Sussex home was close to the English Channel and from there he made countless excursions to the continent, even renting rooms in France and French Africa to write his works.

All this gave the man intimate insight into two profoundly different cultures. One might even say: *two different minds*. Because, as far as Belloc was concerned, there was a distinct English Protestant mentality, which could never really comprehend the very different Catholic mentality of the French. The same was just as true, if not more so, of the American mentality born of Britain's. All this, plus the fact he possessed extraordinary capacity for original insight—entailing true genius, I believe—means he left the Anglosphere a unique legacy.

For unlike Belloc, most of us will only ever know one culture *intimately*: the one that indelibly stamped us by birth and rearing. For most reading these pages, that culture means the Anglosphere, rooted in Protestant England and nearly everywhere (save Ireland), assuming subtly Protestant forms, even long after Protestantism has decayed into Secularism.

How rarely do we Anglophones fully appreciate this! The Anglosphere is the air that we breathe, an air deprived of the Real Presence of Christ since the Mass was stamped out by the English Reformation of the Sixteenth Century. True, the Mass and other Sacraments reentered the Anglo-American world in the Nineteenth century, due in large part to immigration from Ireland (and in America, from countries like Italy and Poland.) But the fact remains that for hundreds of years, the Anglosphere has been conditioned by a profoundly un-sacramental view of reality and its greatest thinkers, statesmen, cultural leaders—Hobbes, Locke, Hume, Smith, Franklin, Jefferson, amidst countless others—have been conditioned by the same.

But France, that great civilisation, was *different*. Despite the terror of the French Revolution which temporarily *interrupted* the Mass, the Holy Sacraments were never *eradicated* there. A distinct Catholic air still filled the France that Belloc knew and loved. And for Belloc that Catholic air had a direct result: he saw how France had never ventured as far down the Capitalist Road as Britain or America. Moreover, the French resisted the 1789 revolution with a *ferocity* unknown to their Anglophone counterparts. France—not England, nor America—gave birth to the Counter-Revolution. And that Counter-Revolution perdured, with generations of French ferociously protesting liberal, secular France.[1] All this contributed to the revival of the French Monarchy in the 1800s, *after* the Revolution. And, as we

---

[1]   I have explored this fierce, epic battle elsewhere. See Roger Buck, *Cor Jesu Sacratissimum: From Secularism and the New Age to Christendom Renewed* (Kettering, OH: Angelico Press, 2016), p. 343-368.

shall explore, a *right-wing* anti-Capitalist, monarchical spirit persists in France even today. The Counter-Revolution is still alive there! France is indisputably the cradle of the international movement to restore the Latin Mass and when the French Socialists passed same-sex "marriage" legislation in 2013, a million French took to the streets to protest. Nothing like this happened in the Anglosphere.[2]

Yes, even today, the French mentality remains strikingly different to that of the English-speaking world. Belloc got this. He *grokked* it in a way very few English or Americans have ever done. For him, France, for all its sins, represented "a road less travelled" in a world increasingly dominated by Protestant, Anglo-American values.

All this, I say, is key to Belloc's late 1938 book, *Monarchy*. For this great work represents both a profound meditation on Kingship and a profound comparison between the road taken by the Protestant, English (and also Dutch) mentality and that taken by the Catholic French mentality. Comparison, did I say? That word hardly suffices! For *Monarchy* is the extraordinary fruit of a *lifetime* contrasting, contemplating, probing, enquiring, desperately searching for answers and alternatives to the dreadnought of Anglosphere Capitalism, born of Anglosphere Protestantism.

At least, this is what deeply impressed itself on me over the long years I not only pondered Belloc's writings, but also numerous biographies of the man. This impression on my soul has been enhanced by the fact that I too have contrasted these two worlds, albeit to a far lesser extent than he did. For I have also lived in France and felt deeply struck, even today, by her *mentalité très différente* from that of my own sacramentally-starved British and American origins.

---

2   Consider: the American population is roughly five times that of France's. Had French attitudes been replicated in the USA, one might have expected five million protesters, centred in Washington D. C. *Mais non...*

I moved to France after decades of living in both the US and UK and the culture shock was highly instructive. It helps me understand the youthful Belloc, who, while staying in Paris in 1900, wrote frank and intimate letters to his wife in England with lines like this:

> It is horrible to be here and *realise* what a stench surrounds Protestantism & what a decaying corpse the society of England has become... Indeed [France] is the chosen instrument of God & without it the Devil would rule the world.[3]

Belloc himself emphasises the word "realise" here. This dramatic touch suggests something may have *jolted* him about France. Something *vibrant and living*—not corpse-like. Now, Belloc was perhaps not even thirty when these private words were posted home. And he was not without a love of England. However, my own research into his life and work suggests this early, jolting sense of difference between Protestant England and still-Catholic France would only mature over the course of his life, reaching literary culmination in his 1938 *Monarchy*.

This lies at the heart of this great book. For although the book certainly concerns Monarchy, it also addresses the rise of *a new mentality in the West* that eventually ruined Monarchy. For with the Reformation, Belloc saw a new spirit gripped the Western mind. That new spirit, born of Luther in 1517, forged ahead in 1534. In that year, King Henry VIII, breaking with Rome, declared himself head of a new national organ: the Church of England. The initial results entailed the harrowing destruction of the Monasteries, the elimination of the Sacraments, the wanton destruction of centuries of Catholic tradition, customs, and thinking. Yet the long-term results were even more extensive. They led to a liberal mindset that made Capitalism possible in Britain,

---

3   Quoted in A. N. Wilson, *Hilaire Belloc* (London: Hamish Hamilton, 1984), p. 93–94.

then America. This, in its turn, fostered the spoliation of Monarchy as two great Capitalist empires—first the British, then the American—spread Liberalism across the planet. (Capitalism is really only the economic variety of Liberalism, something the French see better than we do and why, to our surprise, they call economic "conservatives" like Reagan or Thatcher "ultra-liberals"...)

MONARCHY VERSUS MONEY

Yes, Belloc knew two worlds: that of the British Empire, still going strong in his day and that of France, which despite her 1789 revolution, never succumbed to Liberalism as thoroughly as England. France, he saw, still held a *different alternative spirit* to Anglo-dominated modernity.

This alternative is what this book is really about.

Only secondarily is it a biography of that very imperfect Catholic monarch, Louis XIV. For as Belloc tells us:

> The book which the reader has before him makes no pretence to be a life of Louis XIV. It is of a quite different sort from biography. It is a *study* of certain matters [related to] the principle of *Monarchy*. My book is no more than an attempt to give examples of how all the soul of this long life and its action, illustrate the character of Monarchy... 4

And elsewhere Belloc says of Louis:

> This man, who was to present the most perfect example of Monarchy in all its advantages and disadvantages, had a life exactly suitable for our examination of Kingship. 5

Belloc's primary concern, then, is exploring Monarchy in both its benefits *and* drawbacks! We will hear how the Sacred Power of Kingship, rightly used, can bring the

---

4   P. xlix in this book.
5   P. 11 in this book.

greatest blessings to the people. We will hear how, misused, it can bring the greatest evil. . .

The main focus then lies not with the famous *Roi de Soleil,* or Sun King (1638-1715)—though it does tell his tale— but rather in demonstrating the nature of Monarchy, as opposed to the emergent Capitalist systems in the Protestant Netherlands and Britain at that time. Thus Belloc tells us:

> The matter which I think is *central to this study* and which *I have particularly emphasised* is the natural con- flict between Monarchy and the Money-power. That is the political *core of the whole story,* from Fouquet to the struggle with the Dutch merchants (that is, with the Bank of Amsterdam), and on to the strug- gle with the City of London, its newly-established banking system, its brethren and allies, the big English landowners.
>
> This essential, this inevitable duel to the death between Monarchy and Money-power, must run through any appreciation of the time. Those who omit it . . . omit *the one thing salient,* the one thing omission of which renders their judgment worth- less. We shall see how Louis wrestled with the Money-power, however incomplete was his victory over it, and how, from first to last, over more than fifty years, *it fills all the business of the reign.*
>
> And that reign is but one chapter in the endless struggle between *Monarchy representing and defending the mass of men, their needs, their freedom, and Money-power working for the exploitation of mankind.*[6]

Now, Belloc considers this "central" to the book. But it is, as we shall see, hardly the only issue in this multifaceted work, which treats not only Monarchy's role in terms of protecting people from rapacious Capitalism, but also from the ruin of Catholic faith, arts, culture, and more. Though to appreciate all this, Belloc insists we must first appreciate the *different road* that Louis XIV took to the road taken

6   P. 1 in this book, emphasis added.

by the Protestant Netherlands and Britain—the route to
modern Plutocratic Globalism. Hence, his book contains
what might otherwise seem a bizarre diversion. For smack
in the middle of the story comes a chapter called: "What
is Banking?" Needless to say, one would hardly expect
this in a straightforward biography of a French king! No,
Belloc's intent is something altogether different. And so
he finds it necessary to digress:

> It is well, at this point, to make quite clear *the polit-
> ical menace*... of the new banking whereof Amster-
> dam was the pioneer in modern times.
>
> I have called it in general "the Money-power,"
> [which today entails] the special form of Money-
> power called Modern Banking, and lest a point
> not often defined should be misunderstood I will
> proceed to define it.
>
> The power of a banking system lies in three
> things: first that it is able to create currency uncon-
> trolled by the State, and in amounts not limited
> save by the bankers' own interest and convenience.
> It makes money "out of air" as it were.
>
> Secondly, this "money" is not real wealth as
> is land or crops or cattle, and can therefore be
> transferred, expanded or *concealed* without offering
> any hold to the sovereign Authority which should
> properly govern all society. In other words *a bank-
> ing system is a state within the State.*
>
> Thirdly, the bank-currency thus created out of
> nothing is what is called "liquid." The whole of it
> can be used for whatever purposes the bank pro-
> poses. It comes *to check industry at will, to bribe or
> subsidise whom it will or to penalise whom it will, to control
> as a money-lender the activities of the community and to
> drain the wealth of that community by the usury it demands.*[7]

Strong stuff! At least for those of us for whom banking, usury, Plutocratic subsidy (or bribery?) of the media,

---

7   P. 185 in this book, emphasis added.

universities, the arts and more is the air we are all long accustomed to breathe. What Belloc is saying is not only that this air is toxic—extremely hazardous to our individual and collective well-being—but that a Catholic Monarch, however imperfect, once *exemplified* a different way forward. Once again: "a road less travelled."

SOME BACKGROUND ON EUROPEAN HISTORY

All this, however, may need explaining for modern readers that are, alas, likely to be less educated regarding the European past than Belloc's audience in 1938. Moreover, though not over-long, *Monarchy* is a *big book*—a complex, controversial work, bursting with novel ideas, filled with strange, beautiful, numinous depths.

The book then is not as accessible as it could be. Hence this introduction. And to render this book more accessible, it seems necessary to back up—indeed back up several centuries to the world of Catholic France in 1638. We need to understand the very different universe that Louis was born into. And that universe is a European Christendom, *freshly* torn apart by the Reformation. For a hundred years, Europe has become increasingly divided, not only into two warring camps, but two warring *minds*. This is so much the case that Northern Europe has taken on, in Belloc's view, at least, a *new identity*, dangerous and hostile to its own past and to all the Catholic culture of the South.

Now the principal Northern actors here are Britain and Holland. And what of Lutheran Germany? Some readers may ask this neither realising, perhaps, that no united German state existed at this time, nor that the Thirty Years War (1618–1648)—which forms a backdrop to this tale—had first consumed, then ruined the German-speaking world.

Also, a word should be added here regarding Catholic Spain. Enriched by New World gold and silver, Spain was the Catholic "super-power" of the previous century. By Louis's time, however, Spain is in decline; the Holy Roman Empire, seated in Vienna, has been ravaged by thirty years of Protestant-Catholic warfare and France, under Louis, is set to become Europe's leading Catholic power. Protestant Holland and England, however, are *not* declining; they are ascending in power, thanks largely to their newfound prowess in usury and banking...

France, then, differs from the other great powers of the time. Not only is she not weakened, like Spain or "the Germanies" (to use Belloc's term in this book) but she *never succumbed to Protestantism*. For unlike in England and the Netherlands, the French Protestants (the Huguenots) *lost* the wars of religion. They never took power—this point is key. France *held in check* the new Protestant-Capitalist forces. Thereby, the French Monarchy was retained, indeed, strengthened.

Here again, the modern reader may stumble: "Are not Holland and Britain kingdoms even today, while most of Europe, including France, remains solidly Republican? Does not the English monarch descend from William the Conqueror, who established the British crown in 1066?"

Here we must be very clear about one thing. For Belloc, these monarchies are nothing but a sham. For him, they entail puppet figures for the real power. This power is not simply the obvious Parliamentarians, but something less obvious, more elusive behind them. It is, of course, the Money-Power calling the shots in Amsterdam and London. And what Belloc means by this Money-Power is the forerunner of what many today would call our Globalist elites...

Indeed, this is central to this book: the sharp contrast between the French Monarchy of Louis XIV and the English Monarchy of that time. This latter was the weakened Protestant Monarchy of the Stuarts—entailing Charles I, II and James II—which Monarchy was steadily reduced to a shadow of its former self by the rising power of an emerging Plutocracy. So much so, that by 1688, the Plutocrats usurped the throne. For James II had done the *unthinkable*: he had converted to Catholicism. Not only that, he also produced an heir to the throne who would be raised Catholic! England faced the "threat" of a new line of Catholic kings! Unacceptable.

Thus the last Catholic king of England was overthrown to be replaced by an acceptable Protestant from Holland: William III or William of Orange (later inspiration for the Orange order in Ireland).

Now, as we shall see, 1688 is a date that changed all of European history. It is the *key date in the entire book*. For now, though, we simply note it as the date that, as Belloc tells us bluntly:

> The first of the puppet kings called in by the Money-power was . . . William.[8]

Belloc argues then that the British Monarchy became a mere ghost, controlled by the Capitalists, while the French Monarchy remained the *genuine article*. Louis XIV remained *a king*—a king who meant to *govern* the Protestant Capitalist factions in his land. Not the other way around. By contrast, the Protestant cultures of the Netherlands and Britain worked against Kingship. They readily fostered control by the banks, thus creating the seedbed of today's Globalist Capitalist empire.

BELLOC AND THE MODERN MIND

Needless to say, this is highly controversial stuff for the modern mind. But Belloc meant to challenge the modern mind! He was convinced modernity was diseased by the Protestant-Capitalist spirit that initially triumphed

8   P. 203 in this book.

in Holland and England. The modern mind, of course, regards him a "reactionary," Catholic dupe. Yet it never stops to ask whether *it* might have been duped by relentless non-stop propaganda—a propaganda funded, ultimately, by... the banks.

No, the modern mind rarely consider the enormous opportunity here for *plain bribery*. Something else it does not consider—that this Belloc "dupe" started out with considerable agreement with the modern mind. His early works are *not* defences of Monarchy, but apologies for the French Revolution! Later, Belloc was elected in the 1905 and 1910 British Parliamentary elections—as a radical Liberal. This is to say: *on the left of the Left*. For the Liberals were the major party of the British Left at that time. (They descended from the Whigs, whom Belloc later criticised intensely.) But things changed for Belloc. He emerged from the British Parliament thoroughly disgusted: convinced both parties *represented the same thing*: a uni-party, if you will, secretly controlled by cliques beholden to the banks. (Today, we mean much the same thing with talk about the "Deep State.")

Unlike the modern mind that endlessly regurgitates propaganda, Belloc could *think*. He began to question his youthful sureties. Moreover, his quest for truth was motivated by something else that rarely troubles the modern mind: horror, visceral horror at the injustice of Economic Liberalism—or Capitalism. One feels real pain throughout his works expressed in lines like this:

> Capitalism has in its present phase, other grave evils attached to it, besides the loss of freedom, for the twin evils of Insecurity and Insufficiency are attached to it.[9]

---

9   Hilaire Belloc, *An Essay on the Restoration of Property* (Norfolk, VA: IHS Press, 2009), p. 5.

Let us note how he emphasises "Insecurity and Insufficiency" with capitals and continues:

> The main body of citizens...are not sufficiently clothed, housed and fed and even their insufficient supply is unstable. They live in *perpetual anxiety*.[10]

Belloc's heart, like the heart of His Lord, bled.

Now, no fallen, tiny, broken human heart will ever register the world agony like the Heart of Our Lord. Nevertheless, this, I say, is core to this book: *a heart which bleeds*. Belloc's compassion becomes especially evident when one not only studies the book closely, but reads it in tandem with his Distributist works and parallel histories of the British monarchs Charles I, II and James II. These kings essayed the same task, at the same time, as Louis XIV of taming Capitalism. They failed—miserably. Yes, *Monarchy* is best read in conjunction with all these works. And those who read them carefully may see what I mean: Belloc was a *bleeding heart conservative*. Had Catholic tradition been conserved, how much less suffering there would be today! Here is why I say Belloc felt visceral horror at how easily the modern mind *tolerated* Capitalism, manifesting in *tolerated* monstrosities like Wall Street's grip on the global economy and even global politics. Were the man alive today, he would recoil just as viscerally at things like the IMF, the World Bank, the World Economic Forum, and all the rest. This bleeding heart informs everything about *Monarchy*.

A Partial Success by a Fallible King

But let us return to the Sun King. Louis XIV, it should be stressed, only partially succeeded in taming Capitalism. As we heard earlier:

---

10   Ibid., 5, emphasis added.

> We shall see how Louis wrestled with the Money-
> power, *however incomplete was his victory over it*, and
> how, from first to last, over more than fifty years,
> it fills all the business of the reign.[11]

This took tremendous dedication to his duty as king—
something Belloc can only praise:

> It is to Louis's extreme honour that he never allowed
> caprice to interfere with his function of guide, mas-
> ter, and controller of the realm. He worked every
> day for hours at his function. He fulfilled it till the
> very last days of his life.[12]

Yet today's traditionalist reader should be put on guard
that King Louis XIV was hardly an ideal, devout Catholic
monarch! Now, in later life, Belloc says, Louis did penance
for the sins of his youth, growing at least somewhat closer
to a Catholic ideal. But many will be rightly disturbed by
Louis' sexual immorality in the private life of his younger
days. As to his non-private life, others may be disturbed
by the man's ruthlessness at times. Still others will object
Louis's reign was *too* centralised, *too* absolute. Tied in with
this is the grievous matter of Louis' attitude to Gallicanism, which Belloc laments, but fails to condemn as much
as many might wish.[13] Perhaps, at times, Belloc forgives
too much, though he argues Louis' assiduous dedication
to his duty went with the *realpolitik* of a strong, centralised
reign and that nothing else could have saved the Catholic
culture of France from the forces seeking to invade and
destroy her.

At any rate, this book is hardly meant as a study of the
Sun King's sins! (Although Belloc *does* address these in

---

11   P. l in this book, emphasis added.
12   P. 9 in this book.
13   See final section of the book for Belloc's arguments regarding
Gallicanism.

terms of disgust.[14]) No, we have heard already how Belloc means to explore both the advantages and disadvantages of Monarchy. And here the main theme is how even an imperfect monarch, who *sacrifices himself for the good of his people*, may yet offer real resistance to the Protestant capitulation to Capitalism sketched in this book, a capitulation that has led to today's Plutocratic Globalism.

Real resistance does not mean complete success! Belloc considers the Sun-King's many failures, but argues that he nevertheless preserved the Catholic spirit and culture in France, with far reaching results. For Belloc saw, as I do myself, that even secularised France remained distinctly different from the Anglosphere. Even today, the country still exhibits considerable resistance to Liberalism—social and economic—that may startle Anglophones who truly discover her culture. Again, I say this as someone who has lived in France, speaks her language (however grotesquely!) and has tried to observe her carefully—all of which has helped me see what Belloc saw so well. Even in our highly globalised world, France still remains *a place apart* from the Anglosphere. And Belloc would say that Louis XIV was a significant part of the reason why. As Belloc writes, Louis XIV had an:

> ultimate partial but *sufficient* victory. *He stopped the landslide.* He restored France.[15]

Belloc sets out to show how and why Louis stopped the landslide. Much of this, we will see, comes down to this king's courage, strength, determination and judgment. Indeed, Belloc goes to considerable length to point out the man's sheer *assiduity:* his self-sacrificing dedication to his *duty* as God's appointed ruler of the French Kingdom.

---

14 E.g. "abomination"—see p. 136 of this book.
15 P. 263 in this book, emphasis added.

Religion: the vital force of every culture

However, *Monarchy* turns on more than just this. *Deeper, more mysterious factors* are working here. But these numinosities remain controversial for secular Anglosphere intelligentsia and Belloc's Anglosphere critics have long dismissed them as nothing but the "pet theories" of a crank. Were they simply eccentricities? Or might they ultimately point to *mysteries*—mysteries Belloc understood better than his critics, due to his intense Faith, his intense immersion in French Catholic culture and, thus, his capacity to see beyond the Anglo-American mainstream? The reader must decide for himself. Whatever the case, they can never be satisfactorily approached with the empirical methods of materialistic academia.

Now, before we approach these mysterious matters— which entail this *cri de coeur* for Sacred Monarchy in the face of Plutocracy—one central thing must be ever borne in mind. It therefore bears repeating. For Belloc, Louis's (partial) victory was owed to something else, something far more important than his dedication to his duty as king. That something is critical to the whole book! It is the fact that France, unlike Britain and Holland, *never succumbed to Protestantism*. This meant everything to Belloc. It dominates all his thinking—the notion that Catholicism possesses a *powerful, vital energy that creates and sustains culture* (as indeed do other religions, including Protestantism, Islam and so forth). Truly, in grappling with Belloc's oeuvre, one can hardly emphasise enough how much the man believed:

> Cultures spring from religions; ultimately *the vital force which maintains any culture* is its philosophy, its attitude toward the universe.[16]

Alas, many folk fail to appreciate this properly:

16   Hilaire Belloc, *The Great Heresies* (Rockford, IL: Tan Books, 1992), p 76.

Everyone knows that religion, whatever its form, even in the form of negation, exercises a strong effect upon the character and action of individuals. Everyone will, upon reflection or observation, though not usually at first sight, appreciate that *the corporate effect of religion upon groups of human beings is a notable factor in the formation of society*; but what is not widely appreciated, even today [is] the truth that difference of religion is at the root of difference in social culture. The difference between this nation and that, this district and that, this society and that, may largely be explained by difference of race, of climate, of instruction, of opportunity, and the rest. But *there remains one permanent and profound cause of difference*, which is superior to all others, though it acts in a fashion remote and concealed; and that is, difference in philosophy, in the attitude towards the universe, and consequently in the direction of human action; in the moulding of human motive.

This is true long after the original beliefs, the doctrines of this or that religious system, have ceased to be observed universally. It remains true when they have ceased to be held by the great bulk of men who were once affected by them. The ethics, the social habits of a group, survive the doctrinal influence which brought them into being. *Something remains, something very strong*, of that atmosphere and condition under which a society has grown and been moulded.

Hence it is true that in Europe, while you have contrasts of races and of climate, often general and vague but universally perceived, while you have more immediate and obvious contrasts of political organisations and aims, you have at the very foundation of things a still more permanent and effective contrast of cultures. There is the northern, which may be called a Protestant culture, fixed now for two hundred years. There is a Catholic culture, *the chief place in which has been held successively by Spain*

xxiv

and by France . . . there is the Greek church or orthodox culture of the East.[17]

Here are subtle factors, indeed *forces*, that unsubtle, materialistic historians scarcely heed. But Belloc was not materialistic. He was awake to vital matters secular historians
remain fast asleep to. This led him to conclusions they do
not countenance, conclusions that inform every aspect of
this book. Conclusions they call crank theories . . .

FRANCE AND THE ANGLOSPHERE BIAS

Most pertinent in all this is the matter of France. For
Belloc, France is bound up with the Catholic spirit, something modern Anglo-American historians scarcely understand. As we noted earlier, the Mass was never more than
temporarily interrupted in France. Thus the sanctifying
effects of the Mass have hardly ever stopped spreading out
through the whole of France, in contrast to Britain, where
they were more or less terminated for centuries. A Catholic traveller who is sensitive can feel such things, as he
voyages back and forth between Catholic and Protestant
cultures. Certainly, I have felt them acutely going back
and forth between France and England. I trust that Belloc,
in his less globalised age, felt them more deeply than I
do in mine.

Moreover, France, following a century of Spanish domi-
nance, became the most powerful country of Catholic culture in Europe. As Belloc tells us:

> France, after the storm of the Reformation, had
> settled down on the traditional side. *It preserved
> the continuity of Europe.* Louis XIV's crown was the
> chief power—the chief ostensible, temporal, obvi-
> ous power—in the Catholic culture of Europe. It

17   Hilaire Belloc, *Napoleon* (London: Cassell and Co. Ltd, 1932),
62–63, emphasis added.

was as the head of the Catholic culture that he was hated in his own time by that culture's opponents, and is maligned by them today. [There is a] line of cleavage...between the Catholic and the anti-Catholic culture of the West.[18]

By contrast, Western modernity has been dominated by two great Capitalist superpowers, first the British Empire (on which, famously or infamously, the sun never set) and now today's American Empire. Certainly, the culturally Protestant values of Britain and America stamp the modern mind more than French or Spanish ones do! What is more, the English and American mentality, *even when it is Catholic*, take on these values more than is generally realised. Subtle bias is thereby fostered. Let us pause to consider this bias, as Belloc saw it. For it *is* subtle, easily missed. Only Belloc's constant contact with Catholic Europe made him aware how much the English mind was trapped in itself:

> With the exception of Ireland, the area covered by English speech—that is, Great Britain, the white Dominions, and the United States—have *a character of their own* so far as the Catholic Church is concerned.
>
> The English-speaking world, though now morally broken up, had *a common root*. Its institutions, at their origin, sprang from the *English Protestant Seventeenth Century*.
>
> The American social groups arose for the most part as emigrant colonies with a definitely religious origin, and nearly all of them with an origin strongly anti-Catholic. In England, Scotland and Wales, the Catholic Church had been defeated by 1605...
>
> It dwindled after 1688 to a tiny fragment—about one percent...[19]

18   P. 277 in this book.
19   Hilaire Belloc, *Survivals and New Arrivals* (Rockford, IL: TAN, 1992), p. 17, emphasis added.

Here it is again—that *key date*, wherein the rightful King James II—that unexpected convert to Catholicism!—was driven from his throne by the British and Dutch Money-Power with, as we shall see, enormous consequence for all of Europe. However, what concerns us now, is the equally enormous effect for the nascent Anglo-American world. For it fostered subtle bias:

> That pitiful atom [of Catholicism in Britain] was of no account in the national life nor of any effect on national institutions. From such a source flowed . . . the colonial system of America. . .
>
> The stuff of all this culture was one from which Catholicism had been driven out, and till the mid-Nineteenth Century the United States, Great Britain and her Colonies had little need to reckon with the Faith within their own boundaries.
>
> In our own time all that has largely changed. The chief agent of the change has been the Irish people dispersed by the famine. They brought a large Catholic body into England, Australasia, Canada and America. . . . Catholic minorities and Catholic influences have appeared in the English-speaking world, but have appeared in societies of an historical foundation different from that upon which other parts of the Protestant culture repose.[20]

"Different from . . . other parts": Here Belloc means other Protestant nations such as Germany and Holland. And he explains why the situation of the *Anglophone* Catholic diverges from that of Catholic minorities in such countries. That is, why he is more likely to fall victim to bias:

> Where a very large Catholic population is part of the State . . . where the character of Catholicism is familiar to all, holding an ancient historic position, and where large Catholic societies of the same blood and speech lie just over the frontiers, *Catholic literature, ideas, history are known.*

20   Ibid., p. 18.

But in the English-speaking world it is otherwise. There Catholicism reentered late as an alien phenomenon after the character of society had become "set" in an anti-Catholic mould. There all national literature, traditions, law and especially history were (and are) fundamentally anti-Catholic.

All the Philosophy of Society was long settled in the anti- Catholic mood before the first recrudescence of Catholicism appeared.

Therefore it is inevitable that the Catholic body within this English-speaking world should breathe an air which is not its own and should be more affected by a non-Catholic or anti- Catholic spirit than . . . in other Protestant nations wherein an ancient Catholic culture exists with unbroken traditions . . .

Similarly the great body of [continental] literature in the Catholic culture is closed to these minorities of Catholics in the English-speaking world. They have no powerful daily press. They get nearly all their news and more than half their ideas from papers anti-Catholic in direction. The books which make the mind of the nation help to make the mind of its Catholic minority—and that literature is, in bulk, vividly anti-Catholic.[21]

OLIGARCHY VS MONARCHY

Anti-Catholic prejudice, then, has been subtly, gradually, insidiously fostered in the Anglosphere. In Belloc's view, this blinded us to certain important connections he makes in this book. Here I do *not* mean Belloc's linkage between Protestantism and Capitalism. No, many people have grasped this link, including renowned atheist sociologists like Weber who wrote *The Protestant Ethic and the Spirit of Capitalism.* (Alas, many American Catholics do not grasp it and try to champion *laissez-faire* Capitalism—spawned by the Calvinist, Puritan origins of their own culture—and

---

21   Ibid., p. 19, emphasis added.

Catholicism at the same time. For Belloc, of course, this remains a bootless task, entailing a contradiction in terms.)

Instead, I mean more unusual notions than Weber's famous thesis. Belloc goes much further! For example, he *almost seems* to say that Protestantism possesses a *vital force* that not only spawns Capitalism, but government by Oligarchy—an Oligarchy that too easily degenerates into Plutocracy. He is *almost* saying that Protestantism, Capitalism, Oligarchy, Plutocracy belong, pretty much, to the same impulse, really. And he is *almost* saying that, by contrast, Catholicism, Distributism and Monarchy likewise belong, pretty much, to the same impulse, really. I stress the word "almost", because careful reading reveals Belloc more cautious and nuanced than this. Still, this captures—however inadequately—a certain *gist* to the book. Belloc sees that Catholicism, Monarchy and a more just distribution of property *went hand in hand* in the old world. But our brave new world, rooted in the Reformation, tends naturally to the opposite: wage slavery, Proletarianism, and Plutocracy.

As provocative as all this is, even more is tendentious. For Belloc points out that not only does Protestantism foster Plutocratic evil, but that the great Protestant countries—including the Netherlands, Britain and America—have long touted something called *Parliamentary Democracy*. That which we all take for granted today owes considerably to Protestant innovation! This innovation sounds good in theory, as the Parliamentarians, Congressmen, Deputies (whatever names we call them) are theoretically the people's representatives. Yet what if *theory* is all it is? What if we see, as Belloc saw, that this theory seldom, if ever, works out in practice? For again and again, vested interests replace the people's will. *In practice,* Parliamentary Democracy often looks like rule by a *rich, Oligarchical elite*—or Aristocracy.

We have already mentioned Belloc's bitter experience as a Member of Parliament, where he felt powerless to represent his constituents. The show was run by secretive elites, not elected representatives like himself. Elites which represented banks and business more than the people. It mattered not whether Britain's Conservative or Liberal Parties swapped power. For the same, broad policy of the British Empire persisted—which was, at heart, *a banking policy.* The same stooges did the same old stuff, whichever party they belonged to. The real government was not for the people, by the people, but an immensely wealthy, concealed cabal, playing musical chairs. In a word: Plutocrats.

This, at least, is how Belloc experienced his time in Parliament. And how many of us possess his experience? And how many possess his vast knowledge of history? Be that as it may, these things led the man to a controversial verdict:

> Parliaments are the negation of democracy.[22]

History and his own personal experience then, convinced Belloc that representative democracy, except in very small countries, had invariably failed. Thus he contentiously asserts:

> Men can only live in community: but communities must be governed or they crumble from within. The instinct and experience of man has discovered *two ways* in which *large* communities can be governed. They may be governed by one man, or by a group of men. The first form we call Monarchy, the second Aristocracy—class government.[23]

For Belloc, then, only two main typologies of government for large-scale societies were viable: rule by the few or rule by the one.

> Of these two main forms, Monarchy and Aristocracy, Monarchy is the commoner by far. Men

---

22   Quoted in Robert Speaight, *The Life of Hilaire Belloc* (London: Hollis & Carter, 1957), p 172.
23   P. 4 in this book, emphasis added.

XXX

perpetually associate themselves under individual Rulers: they only here and there, and exceptionally, form permanent states ordered by a ruling class.[24]

ABSURDITY OR REALITY?

Here is a major key to the entire book. And yet it may strike the modern Anglophone as peculiar, even absurd. For today, Monarchy seems rare indeed. Yet the ruling elites Belloc terms "Aristocratic" are everywhere. Look at the bureaucracy ruling Brussels, for example, or the Washington apparatus.

How different everything still seemed in 1938! For example, today we are long accustomed to the Federal *Republic* of Germany. But when Belloc was writing, German society had hardly ever been republican. No, apart from the very brief Weimar Republic (1919-1933) what we call Germany today *was always ruled by monarchs*—mainly the King of Prussia in recent centuries and before that the Emperor at Vienna. Then came World War One. Then came a very brief—American inspired—experiment at democracy. Then came Hitler.

And so it goes throughout European history. Anglo-American Parliamentary democracy—if democracy it truly is—came late to the Continent. The brief Weimar Republic owed its existence to Woodrow Wilson's post-1918 efforts "to make the world safe for democracy"—*American style*. Even France had only abandoned its kings and emperors relatively recently (in 1870) for a Parliamentary democracy (so-called). Yet Belloc considered this new-fangled French Republic disastrous. Thus, in this book, he speaks of:

> that moribund diseased effort at parliamentarianism which is ruining the French today.[25]

---

24   P. 4 in this book.
25   P. 100 in this book.

We might add that, arguably, this post-1870 Republic did more than anything else to destroy French Catholicism, closing Catholic schools and forcing children into materialistic, nationalistic schools where love for the Revolution was drilled into their tender minds.[26]

Here are long forgotten aspects of European history. While we cannot tarry long with them, I must point something out: that which we easily forget today, *Belloc never forgot*. His arguments in this book, regarding Democracy, Aristocracy and Monarchy, drew on an astonishing historical memory that not only takes in the vast sweep of French history, but stretches further back in time to such ancient pre-Christian governments as the Oligarchy of Carthage and the Monarchy of Alexander the Great.

Belloc then remains alert to multiple factors that most of us hardly think of! His histories of France and England were written by a man who knew France and England from inside and out. Most historians only know their own country from the inside. Being secular and materialistic, they also miss the vertical dimension. In other words, they lack Belloc's depth *and* breadth. Such folk should be more careful, accusing Belloc of "crank theories". For their own theories may be more narrow, parochial, and culture-bound than they suppose...

None of this means Belloc is necessarily right in all he utters in *Monarchy*. Speaking personally, I do not think he is. But I do say *Monarchy* is a great book worth listening to, *carefully*. Belloc was 68 years old when it appeared in 1938. It represented a lifetime's *work*, contemplating the afflicted, even schizoid soul of Europe—at a time prior to its far-reaching Americanisation in the wake of World War II, Bretton Woods, the Marshall Plan and all the rest.

---

26   I have explored this, too, elsewhere. See Buck, *Cor Jesu Sacratissimum: From Secularism and the New Age to Christendom Renewed*, p. 360–379.

Now, by 1945, Belloc had suffered a stroke. He could no longer write. We cannot know for sure what he thought of the brave new post-war world. Still, it is not hard to imagine! For he would have witnessed a world transformed by American or largely American innovations like the atomic bomb, NATO, the United Nations, the IMF (headquartered in Washington) and massive investment in Europe, which rendered European economics and politics ever more like the American system. And certainly he would lament the destruction of his 1938 hopes for Monarchy renewed that now seem so strange in our post-1945 Americanised world. I think, too, he would naturally link 1945 to the earlier Americanisation of 1918—the year Woodrow Wilson worked to redraw Europe's borders in a manner more pleasing to Americans.

Now, we *do* know what Belloc made of that. He deplored Wilson's savage treatment of Catholic Europe, which dismembered the Austrian-Hungarian Empire, among other things. Moreover, he warned, ominously and accurately, that 1918 would not bring true peace. Something like a "Deep State" existed—which had something else in mind. As he predicted in 1929, *before* Hitler's rise to power, the banks of the Protestant countries had agendas inimical to lasting peace:

> We celebrate the Armistice, not the Peace. We do well. No peace was concluded when the Great War came to an end; and the reason no peace was concluded was that the powers which, in a sort of alliance, *did not at all desire a complete victory*: *quite half of those powers*, national and financial, desired to frustrate the end for which the young men had died... The [victors] had diverse objects. The *chief financial powers* amongst them ... were determined to save the Reich. *The common religious feeling which creates a natural bond between London, New York and Berlin* added to the division [from those in the Catholic culture].[27]

---

27   Hilaire Belloc, "The Truce," *G. K.'s Weekly*, 9 November 1929, emphasis added.

Here it is again: Belloc's belief that religious feeling remains a much more potent force in modern history than most suppose. Now, we cannot tarry with this tangled web. But even a fleeting reference to Belloc's ominous premonitions may illumine why he considered Capitalism the natural enemy of Catholicism and, therefore, *why he wrote this book*. For he understood the complex, centuries-long history of banking far better than most of us do. And he would have sadly concurred, I think, with John C. Rao that Wilson's famous 1918 appeal might have less to do with genuine democracy than efforts:

> to destroy man, nature and culture—in order, ultimately, to make the world safe for shopping.[28]

At any rate, Rao's suggestion is one that might make Belloc laugh bitterly today—if it did not make him weep.

My main point, however, is that the modern mind, conditioned by the great American projects of 1918 and 1945, cannot easily grasp Belloc's profound 1938 nonpareil. For many, what he writes will sound as irrelevant as the dodo. But if the sympathetic reader pays careful, close attention to the book, parking his modern biases firmly at the door, he will see a work studded with jewels. Wide-ranging aperçus regarding historical personalities and human nature, faith, culture, politics, economics are strewn throughout. We cannot reference them all. More needs saying, though, about the year 1688, about France, and about Sacred Monarchy, and in that order.

1688: THE TIPPING OF THE SCALES

We have already pointed out that 1688 is the key date to this tale: *the year that changed everything*. In this year, James II—that unexpected Catholic convert—was deposed from

---

28   John C. Rao, *A Centenary Meditation on a Quest for "Purification" Gone Mad* (Waterloo, ON: Arouca Press, 2019), p. viii.

his Throne and exiled from England. For Belloc, this was the Sun King's great fatal mistake: he did not do enough to support James II. Had he used his mighty forces to protect him, *the entire history of Europe would be different.* I beg the reader to pay careful attention to this passage, which is among the *most important* in the book:

> It has often been remarked that the change in the fortunes of Louis came with *the final victory in England of the Money-power over the national Monarchy,* with the triumph of that wealthy oligarchy of great landowners, great merchants, and the new banking system behind them; with the failure of James II and with his exile.
>
> The cause of this is not obscure. All that side of European culture of which Louis was the chief figure was opposed to the newer culture produced by the Reformation. Louis stood, in the main, for the peasant, the traditional bonds of society inherited from times before the great religious revolution. Opposed and rapidly increasing in power was that other spiritual force which was to make Capitalism. *Now London, rapidly expanding in numbers, wealth and consequence was, with Amsterdam, the pole or focus of that new force.* When the English Government was captured by that rich class which became the leaders of the nation, when the English yeoman began to disappear and the townsman to replace him, above all when the ruined English Monarchy at last collapsed, in 1688, *the balance of Europe was changed: the scales were tipped against what Louis represented and towards Plutocratic oligarchy.*[29]

From now on, Belloc claims, rule by the few triumphed over rule by the one. Protestant Europe (which tends to Capitalist Oligarchy) ascended, while Catholic Europe (which tends to traditional Monarchy) went ever more on the defensive. An originally Dutch and English

---

29 P. 1 in this book, emphasis added.

Protestant-banking culture increasingly dominated the West, as Britain established the most powerful Empire the world had ever known. Britannia ruled the waves and a quarter of the world's land. Its Capitalist model, imported to the world via the British colonies, was embraced by liberals everywhere as progressive and free. Alas, the model was hardly all it was cracked up to be:

> Government by the rich in England destroyed the independent farmers of which the English State had formerly consisted. Whether we call them peasants (the Continental name) or yeomanry (the specifically English name), such a body of free men was at the basis of all English society until the rich destroyed the English Monarchy ...
>
> The English ... were generally transformed from a comparatively small nation of independent agricultural men, shopkeepers, individual traders and sea captains owning or part-owning their ships, into *a vast mass of proletarian men existing upon a wage*, their livelihood more and more dependent upon a few masters who controlled all the activities of the State. Today the life of England has fallen almost wholly into the hands of monopolists, *especially the monopolists of credit under the banking system.*[30]

Elsewhere Belloc argues:

> Britain, during the Middle Ages, had been what every other Christian society of the West had been: one governed by a strong Monarchy, but ... its citizens had, for the most part, possession in the instruments of their toil and in the land which they tilled ...
>
> With the [Reformation seizure of the monasteries and] confiscation of the Church lands the gentry were enormously enriched; from possessing a large minority of the acres in England they

---

30   Hilaire Belloc, *Charles II the Last Rally* (Norfolk, VA: Gates of Vienna Books, 2003) p. 18-19.

passed within a generation to the possession of some two-thirds. They then entered upon the career of further monopoly which has been completed in our own day—until at last one may say that the land of England as a whole is in the hands of one small class.[31] The public rights over minerals, forests, wastes and even the shores of the sea were gradually extinguished. The very roads of the country became, by legal decision, no more than rights of use over the land of the great owners.

The same religious movement destroyed the cooperative associations [the guilds] which were the defence of the small man because it destroyed the instinct for corporate action and turned the mass of the State into a dust of individuals...

The new religion of the English led to most vigorous action in commerce and in all economic affairs. It produced the great bulk of mechanical discovery and the application of that discovery to the production of wealth. But this mill... condemned the mass of men, in larger and larger numbers, to a lower and lower economic position until it ground out at last the propertyless millions of today.

Everything the Reformation did converged to the establishment of Capitalism in that England which had adopted Protestant principles.[32]

Needless to say, similar arrangements were extended to the American colonies—which in time yielded amazing results in terms of economic and mechanical productivity—but with arguably even greater disregard for the poor! To descend into the current vernacular, American Capitalism has been like England's—*on steroids*.

---

31   Belloc wrote this in 1915 before British Socialist governments started heavily taxing the rich, leading to a somewhat different situation, at least for a time.

32   Hilaire Belloc, *The History of England from the First Invasion by the Romans to the Accession of King George the Fifth. Vol. XI., 1689-1910* (Sands & Co.: London, 1915), p xxi-xxii.

To all this, 1688 remains key. For Belloc, it is the year the scales of the West tipped. From that point on, a new rationalist spirit of rule by rich elites steadily replaced the old royalist spirit in Europe. People, increasingly, no longer found protection from the Monarch, tradition and the Holy Church.

FRANCE

In all this, England blazed the trail. But Belloc, knowing France intimately, beheld its different spirit. Something *survived* there, something profoundly at odds with English Liberalism (economic and otherwise). France had never completely surrendered to the new spirit of the world. Even post-revolutionary 1789 France was *poles apart* from the Anglo-American culture. The peasantry was not destroyed there. Wage slavery was much less rampant. A great Capitalist class never quite gained the same levers of power and expropriation as they did in the Protestant world. This is why young Belloc did not smell the same "stench" in France.

Yes, Belloc saw difference—vital, important difference—as he repeatedly criss-crossed the English Channel from childhood on, carefully comparing the two cultures. At least, this is what emerges for me as I contemplate his life and works. And again, it also emerges from my own personal experience of having lived in France and England (also America), comparing and contrasting Protestant and Catholic culture. For this reason, I hope some personal digressions from my own life might shed light on this book—a book all about juxtaposing French and British culture.

At any rate, living in France seventy years after *Monarchy* was written, I saw the same juxtaposition Belloc did. Even today, France remains *startlingly different* from the England and America that raised me! The poor are treated better. Modern chain stores are not yet omnipresent. The economy is regulated in ways highly unpleasant for the New York and London financial institutions. Credit has not been dispensed with quite the same abandon. Old family businesses are still plentiful. There is a certain distaste for the vulgarity of "bling-bling" *luxe.* There is more economic and cultural protectionism than in the Anglosphere. There is, alas, also more appetite for Socialism, even Communism. At the same time, the Traditional Right (including the so-called "Far Right") is much more prominent in France. (Although it can be anti-Capitalist in ways that may astonish Americans!) Moreover, the French demand *educational and cultural excellence,* not simply economic prowess. The overall ambience feels less utilitarian and the arts are more cherished (while we in the Anglosphere tend to denounce French "snobbery"). Beautiful buildings are lovingly preserved—not pulled down to put up a parking lot. Even recent architecture remains less hideous. Even now, there is less room for "ultra-liberals" like Thatcher or Reagan to wreck the culture, to wreck the poor. And as mentioned earlier, there are mighty demonstrations against same-sex "marriage" and the Latin Mass flourishes like nowhere else on earth. . .

Here we might profitably invoke Charles de Gaulle. Like Belloc, de Gaulle was thoroughly disgusted with France's so-called Parliamentary Democracy and the Money-Power. After coming to power in 1958, de Gaulle could not restore the Monarchy—too much revolutionary thinking had been inculcated in France for long generations. Instead, the man re-made the French presidency into something like an "elective Monarchy," with seven year terms, transferring power from so-called representatives in Parliament to an executive elected by direct suffrage. He also challenged growing American power—whether cultural, commercial or military—in Europe. For instance, he pulled France out of NATO's integrated command, amidst many other actions that have been widely interpreted as petulant fits of anti-American pique. (At least, interpreted by Americans that way, if not necessarily by the French!)

Had Belloc lived to see this, I imagine he would have profoundly sympathised with de Gaulle. For the two men thought much alike and both were troubled by the capitalist and cultural values America exported to Europe. Indeed, I have personally found many French share the same anxieties even now. Such concerns inform their culture more than ours. And de Gaulle, along with many Gaullists today as well as other members of the French Right would concur with Belloc that at least *some kind* of:

> Monarchy is the sole effective protection, in a large state, of the common citizen against the mastery of wealth. Napoleon summarised that truth in lapidary fashion. Monarchy, he said, is the one device discovered by man for the curbing of the money-power.[33]

Now, since the 1960s, France's "elective Monarchy" has been whittled down by Atlanticist successors de Gaulle would deplore. Even now, though, it is still sometimes called a "hyper-presidency." Even now, *France remains a place apart from Anglo-America.* As mentioned, France remained monarchical as late as 1870 (despite two brief interruptions after 1789). And many would argue that, even today, it still retains something of that monarchical spirit—in the sense of being more ordered, centralised and anti-Capitalist than America's *corporate libertarianism.* This is why corporate libertarians tend to scream and shout about French bureaucracy, "red tape" and any other attempt to limit their power for the sake of justice and culture.

None of this, I stress, is to idealise the French. Far from it! Like every nation, they are distinctly fallen and have drunk deeply of the revolutionary elixir. No, I only mean to make

---

33   p. 6 in this book.

Belloc's point clear: that *even cultural Catholicism remains different from cultural Protestantism.* Or as we heard him say earlier:

> The corporate effect of religion on groups of human beings is a notable factor in the formation of society... this is true long after the original beliefs... have ceased to be observed universally... *Something remains, something very strong,* of that atmosphere and condition under which a society has grown and been moulded.

To which I add: the Sacraments still pervade Catholic countries like France, far more than they do England and America. Living in France, I felt that explained something at least of her remarkable resistance to Liberalism (whether that be Economic Liberalism or the Liberalism of same-sex "marriage.")

I trust, then, my digressions into France are relevant. Belloc's thinking has been often misunderstood by Anglosphere critics, who cannot easily get into the French "skin" as it were. But Belloc had French skin, *literally* (or at least DNA) and *Monarchy* remains a very French book—despite being written in English! It is not easily appreciated by a purely Anglocentric mentality. May my French excursus foster at least a little understanding in an Anglosphere prone to misunderstanding the French!

SACRED MONARCHY

At last, we come to the numinous theme of Monarchy. For Belloc, it needs saying, Monarchy need not exclusively refer to hereditary bloodlines, but simply *visible, accountable personal rulership by one man.* This is why even an "elected monarch" like de Gaulle with strong powers over the country would be preferable, for Belloc, to Britain's oligarchic rule.[34]

---

34 It also accounts for something else that may baffle certain readers: that in 1938, Belloc saw America's Presidential system

All this may seem strange, inasmuch as Western Monarchy has normally involved the *Blood Royal*. But this was not always the case. For example, the Pope was the elected monarch of the medieval Papal States and remains so today of their vastly reduced tiny remnant: the Vatican City statelet. Here is why we can be confident Belloc would salute de Gaulle's stand-off against Plutocracy, even if it is also true that Belloc maintains:

> Monarchy should be hereditary to become a principle sacredly interwoven with the people.[35]

Still, the need for one accountable man, powerfully, visibly standing and working for his people is the central idea of *Monarchy*. Here Belloc means *all* of the people: rich and poor. Whilst "democratic" oligarchies represent the vested interests of a certain class of society, Monarchy ideally represents the *whole* of society, not pitting one level against another. Here lies its numinous appeal to something transcendent, beyond what Belloc calls "mere wealth" or materialism:

> Filled with an obscure resentment against the power of mere wealth, or even caste, men will applaud and follow One who shall be master of *their* masters. The Monarch incarnates the common man, in his multitude, as well as the whole society over which he himself presides.[36]

Indeed, as the reader will see, Belloc actually contends Monarchy is more egalitarian and democratic *in spirit* than the wealthy oligarchies that rose up in places like England.

---

moving towards Monarchy. Here Belloc may not have understood American politics sufficiently to adequately judge. Still, the puzzled reader should keep in mind this was the era of Roosevelt's New Deal, when this powerful president significantly strengthened the Executive in America.

35   P. 382 in this book.
36   P. 5 in this book.

For instance, Belloc argues that oligarchical Britain *depended on its intense class system*. By contrast, he suggests, monarchical France did not need the same sharp differentiation of class and thereby possessed by a more egalitarian spirit.[37]

Now, Belloc was certainly aware how monarchies also frequently betrayed the people! Indeed, *he points out their failures repeatedly in this book*—a book which endeavours to weigh up the "pros and cons" of Monarchy. This is no simplistic, one-sided polemic! Historically speaking, Monarchy has been a "hit and miss" affair—but with more hits than misses. Such is Belloc's argument. Here is why he constantly appeals to history, rather than simply theory: how things *worked out in actual practice*. We recall how Belloc, youthful partisan of all things revolutionary and republican, lost his faith in representative democracy. For he concluded it had never really worked. Invariably, parliaments (outside very small countries) represented plutocrats more than the people. And so, for all its innumerable failures, Belloc believes Monarchy has the better "track record" than Parliamentarianism.

In terms of history—*how things worked in practice, not theory*—personal, visible, accountable Monarchy protected all levels of society better than impersonal, invisible, unaccountable rulership by slippery, financial entities who mainly protect the rich.

Here is Belloc's thinking, which, however controversial, drew on vast knowledge of the past. Moreover, his immense erudition was not limited to the English language. The man read French historians in their own tongue, as well as Latin and Greek. All this, of course, led him to very different convictions from what we are all taught at

---

37 This fascinating aspect of the book may only make sense to people truly familiar with England and how the upper classes are distinguished by their accents, elite education, etc. To examine it properly would make this introduction overlong and perhaps opaque to many who do not know the British class system. It deserves noting, however, as yet another important argument in this complex work.

school. But our schools and universities are bankrolled by those same slippery, financial entities. And history, as the old maxim has it, remains written by the victors.

Writing these words, I think to the Vendée in France: birthplace of the French Counter-Revolution. In the Vendée, the French *peasants* rose up to defend their Catholic king. They rightly sensed, I think, that the 1789 French Revolution was instigated by the bourgeoisie, who did not represent their interests. These bourgeois-instigated revolutionaries then subjected them to genocide. Things like this are not much taught in our brave new universities of Political Correctness.

At any rate, Belloc neither mentions the Vendée in the book, nor does he need to. He draws other examples of the monarch-people bond from his vast historical knowledge. For instance, we have heard already of England's land grabs as its Monarchy weakened. In other ways, too, Belloc showed how post-1688 English Liberalism—social and economic—treated the poor worse than less liberal, more monarchical France (and indeed other European monarchies). Here is what emerged from his historical work that was not pay-rolled by modern academia, funded by the victors. In others words, he was not beholden to systems invested in interpreting history according to their own political agendas. As George Orwell chillingly said in *1984*:

> Who controls the past controls the future: who controls the present controls the past.

INTO THE NUMINOUS

Belloc, then, offers a different history to that offered by our present masters—one drawn from Faith, immense erudition and *intimate* understanding of non-Protestant Europe. And yet Belloc's arguments are not only historical. For instance, passages like this point to more subtle, even mysterious, matters:

Men perpetually associate themselves under individual Rulers... This prevalence of Monarchy through the ages is due to two forces: first that men think of themselves, at heart, as equals in right; next, that men armed for battle or organised for civil action can best achieve their objects under... a hierarchy of command *leading up to one Commander*: nearly all great common enterprises must be ordered so, and in the supreme test of war armies are led and battles won by a single will and brain. "Two good generals are no match for one mediocre general." Men demand a name to lead them, and in victory they worship one successful captain...

But Monarchy has, besides the two roots of Human Equality and Military Action, *a third root penetrating deeper* into the nature of man and therefore more sustained and flourishing. This root is Religion: man's instinct for worship... .

Men subject to a Monarch see in him a present deity. *He incarnates the state and themselves.* Their loyalty to him is one with the service they owe to the nation, and hence it is that after the wealthy have destroyed the powers of Monarchy and supplanted it, the name and title of "King" are still sometimes retained in order to dignify a ritual figure who personifies the state. All real power may have been taken away from the Crown and given over to a ruling class... Yet such a class is confirmed in power by acting in the name of that very crown which it has ousted.[38]

Once again, Belloc indicates England. The English, he suggests, see how Monarchy meets deep needs in human nature—and use it to camouflage their rule by oligarchy. Modern England's Monarchy was no longer the real thing for Belloc; it was only a (useful) idol. But with the Sun King, in France of old, it was different:

---

38 P. 4-6 in this book.

> The Crown and France were one—that *ideal figure of the nation* . . . was under Louis XIV *alive and present in him*. France was indistinguishable from the actual human being who was crowned and anointed, the incarnation of his people.[39]

Here we enter realms more ineffable, more numinous, dare one say mystical . . . ? Now, I do not think Belloc felt comfortable making mystical arguments. His arguments are usually more pragmatic: how things played out in history. Nonetheless, the careful reader of *Monarchy* will find repeated indications of more elusive layers to Belloc's thinking. To take just one example, there is an enigmatic chapter, "The Annealing of the King"[40]. Here Belloc suggests Louis made a terrible self-sacrifice, precisely because he was not simply an individual responsible for his own destiny, but indeed something greater and more mysterious:

> Louis was not a living soul answerable to itself and its Vision. *He was France* and therefore he himself must be broken and lost in Kingship. Now indeed did he know the meaning of that word "Monarchy." It weighed more than all the world. Its reality and mass crushed all on which it lay, and first of all the man in whom it was.[41]

Louis was France . . . he must be broken and forged . . . to incarnate his people. Here lie numinosities we cannot dwell on. I only indicate there is more, *far more*, to this extraordinary meditation on Monarchy than immediately meets the eye. I enjoin the reader to search for it, paying close attention to the text.

---

39   P. 105 in this book, emphasis added.
40   P. 63 in this book.
41   P. 66 in this book, emphasis added.

In Conclusion

Much in Belloc merits close attention! At least, I have personally found incalculable gifts in listening carefully—really carefully—to this Anglo-French giant of the Faith. Still, even giants are not infallible. Yes, Belloc possessed penetrating, immense, and original insight amounting, I believe, to genius. That genius is still insufficiently recognised. But even genius remains conditioned by a man's time, place, and particular nature—which nature is, of course, always decidedly fallen. Speaking personally, I have already said that I do not assent to all Belloc's conclusions here. In some cases, history has proved the man wrong. In other instances, Belloc—pierced in his heart by Plutocratic tyranny—may have sometimes turned too easily to other sorts of tyrants as saviours.

What can I say? Sometimes a milestone along the way is more important than a terminus. No book is a final be-all and end-all destination. *Monarchy* remains laden with riches, even if one cannot accept all its conclusions. Perhaps its greatest treasure is *a heart on fire*. For Belloc's heart was awake, as few hearts are, to the sheer tyranny of modern Capitalism, ruining not only the poor, but ruining culture, ruining souls. For me, it is deeply moving to see how much his heart bled for all those crushed by the "Beast", the "Deep State", the camouflaged "uni-party", *corporate libertarianism*—call it what you will. His profound Catholicity likewise moves me to the core of my being. His history, unlike others', grapples with the Catholic Mystery in all its aspects—including the numinous call of Christendom and Monarchy. In Belloc, we see an aching Catholic heart, fuelling a puissant Catholic mind, in search of Catholic truth. The fruit of his lifelong quest is profound. And so it *feeds* me, just as it fed so many before me. Like manna in an arid land, it nourishes the Catholic soul famished for mystery and meaning.

At any rate, dear reader, here is an opportunity for a French-English genius to take you to a different time, a different place, *a different mind* to the liberal mind that dominates the Anglo-American world today. If you read it carefully, you may find this French Catholic world of Sacred Monarchy more rich, real and relevant than anything your pro-1517, pro-1688, pro-1776 and pro-1789 education ever told you. I encourage you, then, to let Hilaire Belloc take you to another universe. You need not embrace every one of his ideas as final, definitive, pre-digested answers. But perhaps you may take them as *pointers* to a luminous world beyond the "definitive" pre-digested answers the secular leviathan has so long sought to instil in your mind.

PREFACE

THE PRELIMINARIES TO ANY BOOK are tedious if they grow numerous or are prolonged. They interfere with its reading and thus defeat the purpose of its writer.

I hesitate, therefore, to add even a brief preface of the sort I am about to set down here; yet I think it necessary to do so for the explanation of what I have written.

The book which the reader has before him makes no pretence to be a life of Louis XIV. It is of a quite different sort from biography. It is a *study* of certain matters whereon those who have written about this great formative period in European history have widely differed; and that Study is directed to exploring the old and half-forgotten, the now rapidly reviving, principle of *Monarchy*.

My book is no more than an attempt to give examples of how all the soul of this long life and its action, illustrate the character of monarchy. It is written because, as I have explained in the text, monarchy is certainly returning after a long eclipse; its strength is already present among us, sometimes in most violent forms, and the tendency to it is working everywhere before our eyes. I have written in order to discuss and illustrate both the strength and the weakness of that institution as it appears in the capital example of Louis XIV's very great reign. I attempt to discover how monarchy deals with the threat or the actual existence of civil war (the Fronde), how it deals with foreign enemies (the three great wars of 1672-78, 1687-97, 1702-1712), how it depends upon the human character of the monarch, and how it is affected by the vigour and decline of that one mortal man far more than aristocracy can be affected by any personal condition. With that alternative form of government, Class Government or Aristocracy, I contrast Monarchy throughout these pages.

The matter which I think is central to this study and which I have particularly emphasised is the natural conflict between Monarchy and the Money-power. That is the political core of the whole story, from Fouquet to the struggle with the Dutch merchants (that is, with the bank of Amsterdam), and on to the struggle with the City of London, its newly-established banking system, its brethren and allies, the big English landowners.

This essential, this inevitable duel to the death between Monarchy and Money-power, must run through any appreciation of the time. Those who omit it, not only in the case of Louis XIV but in the case of Charles Stuart (Charles II of England), in the case of the United Provinces, in the case of the Spanish decline—in everything of the period— omit the one thing salient, the one thing omission of which renders their judgment worthless. We shall see how Louis wrestled with the Money-power, however incomplete was his victory over it, and how, from first to last, over more than fifty years, it fills all the business of the reign.

And that reign is but one chapter in the endless struggle between Monarchy representing and defending the mass of men, their needs, their freedom, and Money-power working for the exploitation of mankind.

The subject is of practical and vital interest today, now that Plutocracy is everywhere challenged by that extreme form of popular Monarchy which is properly called Despotism or Dictatorship.

But I also discuss, as the reader will discover, the way in which Monarchy affects religion. Its direct effect here is the effort which Monarchy always makes to obtain unity by Authority. Class-government conducts a more effective effort, aiming at religious unity not by an imposed scheme

1

but by the gradual elimination of all serious dissent. The complete moral unity of the English people today, which is but an example of their religious unity, was achieved in this fashion by a governing class. Louis's attempt at the more mechanical method failed to produce a similar unity among the French. On the other hand, in that part of the English effort which escaped from English class government, the control of Ireland, an alien religion survived to harass England from without, just as the Huguenot survived, not in a special district but throughout the body of France itself, to harass that nation from within. Here, in the central test of efficiency, moral unity, neither Monarchy nor its rival Aristocracy succeeded.

There is a last effect of Monarchy with which I have dealt, and which is surely of the highest interest: I mean the effect of Monarchy upon the monarch himself: upon the soul of the King.

To examine this I have added to the sections which deal with the main external action of the reign in its first period, the time of the king's youth and maturity—his life "without"—brief but close appreciations of his life "within." Of this the test is the king's relations with women. Three women successively mark this personal and inward life. Louise de La Vallière, in his youth; Athenaïs de Montespan in the full vigour of his manhood and of the central years; Frances d'Aubigné, Marquise de Maintenon, the guardian and the good mate of half his life, of his conversion, of his moral re-establishment—she who averted the moral degradation that threatened his decline.

This last long phase when Madame de Maintenon was his permanent companion and led him through his own old age and hers to the dignity of death I have not divided into two contrasting aspects—that which was without, the man's external action, his wars, his policy, etc., that which was within, the business of his soul. I have treated both combined, though indeed from the moment of his marriage, in 1684, to his death nearly thirty-two years later, the inward change in him, the strength of religion, the repose of the spirit, coloured all the outward action and saved the reign.

H. Belloc.
KINGS LAND,
June, 1938.

Monarchy:

SOME PRELIMINARY CONSIDERATIONS

I N THE CHAOS THAT FOLLOWED ON the Great War a man wrote these words: "The world is hungry for Monarchy."

The phrase seemed foolish and was passed by, almost without comment. For the ancient thrones of Europe had fallen in ruins; the chief dynasties, Hohenzollern, Romanoff, Hapsburg-Lorraine had vanished, and the empty word "democracy" filled the air. No active kingly power remained. Newly arisen states called themselves Republican, and Anarchy menaced or invaded half the towns of our civilisation.

Within a few years it was successively apparent in one country after another that authority vested in one man could alone stem the rising flood of dissolution. Italy was the first to save herself: the German Reich belatedly followed. Poland joined the system. In the United States where National Unity had long depended upon an Elective Monarchy of increasing authority (the Presidency), that principle was reinforced. Greece, Portugal saved themselves under the orders of a single will. France sank lower and lower in the absence thereof, and Spain fell into dissolution for this same reason. Only England, the unique modern example of Aristocratic Government, formed an exception, and, under its strongly organised governing class, remained

I

plutocratic and an oligarchy, stable without recourse to personal power.

Monarchy has returned—often in the extreme form of despotism, often disguised under other names, but returned. Monarchy as the principle of government is now fully established in all eyes that are open to reality.

These things being so, Monarchy having come back throughout our culture, it behoves us to examine the nature of the thing, since for the future we must live with it and under it more and more.

What is written for readers of English tongue must especially dwell on this: for in countries of English speech the re-arrival and new presence of Monarchy is masked. America has it indeed, manifest more and more in all political action but dressed in Republican terms. The United States are monarchical in the government of their great businesses, of their great cities, of their component districts, and especially at the centre of Federal power where, in the President, all the factors of enduring Monarchy are combined; the personal choice and action of one will, its support and restraint by impersonal institutions and by tradition, above all the popular character of the office: its stand for all the people as against sections or privileged groups. In England things are just the other way. Active Monarchy has so completely disappeared that its very nature is forgotten. But the name and its ritual function, are enthusiastically preserved and make part of the national unity and strength. Because it is thus veiled in exactly contradictory fashion by two mighty modern states the more reason is there for each to appreciate the meaning of Monarchy.

Literature, instructed opinion, fashion, have opposed and obscured Monarchy for two long lifetimes. It has been caricatured, insulted, ignored. It has been rendered ridiculous by puppets taking its name (so-called kings and queens shorn of all real power), while all around it, save in aristocracies,

2

things went from bad to worse. Even where Monarchy was at work it was masked by false names and subjected in theory to assemblies which made a mystical pretence of being "The People." The coming generations must learn, all over again, the meaning of that permanent human figure, A Ruler.

In order to bring out ancient institutions long forgotten or hidden or overlaid, recourse must be had to history wherein the lively examples of the thing in its fullness may be found. Here, in Christendom, Monarchy has stood throughout our centuries in many forms, but especially in one typical form: the king who is king by Hereditary right of primogeniture which guarantees continuity. The prime example of such monarchy is that of Louis XIV.

Louis XIV of France, and his reign, give the main picture of an effective Monarchy in modern civilisation. His court, his victories, his defeats, policies, failures and permanent effects are all so many tests of Monarchy alive and in action. We see in that story what Monarchy is; its value to mankind; its abuses; its temptations; its reactions upon the character of the man called to a real throne. This individual King Louis is of the more value as an example in that he was built on the general model of men, excelling in nothing save the spirit of his function. We are not distracted by special personal gifts in him from contemplating that function. Exercising that function through an exceptional length of years, absorbed in it as in a trade or craft, Louis XIV discovers for us what Monarchy can—and what it cannot—do.

This is the interest of what I present in the pages that follow; for now that Monarchy has reappeared among us throughout Christendom and cannot but strike new and deeper roots it is our business to understand that which will overshadow coming time.

❊　❊　❊

3

Men can only live in community: but communities must be governed or they crumble from within.

The instinct and experience of man has discovered two ways in which large communities can be governed. They may be governed by one man, or by a group of men. The first form we call Monarchy, the second Aristocracy—class government. Under either of these the unity of the State, its internal order, its power to resist attack may be permanently maintained.

There is indeed a third and nobler way than submission to the rule of One or of A Few, and this third way is that where all families in the State combine to frame the decrees which they shall collectively obey, and choose by lot, or by open selection among themselves, the officers who shall enforce the laws. Such government "by the people"—the ideal of all free men—is called Democracy. Alas! It is possible only in small states, and even these must enjoy exceptional defences, moral or material, if they are to survive. So defended, whether by natural obstacles, or by an agreement among their neighbours, democracies very limited in scale have endured: Andorra after at least a thousand years in her mountain valleys is still here. But, for the most part, the lesser communities are absorbed in the greater, and not till these break up can democracy (in the smaller fragments) reappear. The human story, as a whole, tells of Kingship on the one hand, on the other of Republics under accepted authority of the rich; of enduring democracy hardly anything.

Of these two main forms, Monarchy and Aristocracy, Monarchy is the commoner by far. Men perpetually associate themselves under individual Rulers: they only here and there, and exceptionally, form permanent states ordered by a ruling class.

This prevalence of Monarchy through the ages is due to two forces: first that men think of themselves, at heart, as equals in right; next, that men armed for battle or organised for civil action can best achieve their objects under a leader. Filled with an obscure resentment against the power of mere wealth, or even caste, men will applaud and follow One who shall be master of *their* masters. The Monarch incarnates the common man, in his multitude, as well as the whole society over which he himself presides. Also, men can only act if they are embrigaded under a hier-archy of command leading up to one Commander: nearly all great common enterprises must be ordered so, and in the supreme test of war armies are led and battles won by a single will and brain. "Two good generals are no match for one mediocre general." Men demand a name to lead them, and in victory they worship one successful captain.

Therefore it is that when, after prolonged civil wars, the fighting forces emerge as the masters of the State, no lon-ger its servants, they crown their Commanders-in-Chief. Armies are of their nature monarchic, and victory over foreigners, too, is only to be achieved under a leader. In both ways, by civil war as by foreign expeditions, even by mere resistance to an invader, the old saying is proved, "War makes the King."[1]

Thus it is that monarchic states excel in war, that states steeped in war tend to monarchy even when they began in other forms, and that the rare but powerful and most enduring oligarchies of history have been not military but mercantile, based on commerce and usually insular, depen-dent on a fleet. They are chary of engaging a foe by land, and, when they do, they rely on mercenary armies and allies.

But Monarchy has, besides the two roots of Human Equality and Military Action, a third root penetrating deeper

---

[1] Mark how the great American Civil War in the last century increased—and how the present social and economic disturbance continues to increase—the Monarchic element in the United States, the power of the President.

into the nature of man and therefore more sustained and flourishing. This root is Religion: man's instinct for worship.

Men subject to a wealthy ruling class will, indeed, worship that class after a fashion; but as a rule with awe rather than affection, and also as symbols of what they themselves would wish to be or as leading lives which they themselves might by good fortune enjoy. But men subject to a Monarch see in him a present deity. He incarnates the state and themselves. Their loyalty to him is one with the service they owe to the nation, and hence it is that after the wealthy have destroyed the powers of Monarchy and supplanted it, the name and title of "King" are still sometimes retained in order to dignify a ritual figure who personifies the state. All real power may have been taken away from the Crown and given over to a ruling class; all policy may in fact proceed from that class; it may have taken over the making of laws and exercise of policy, order, and justice, by officers drawn from its own body. Yet such a class is confirmed in power by acting in the name of that very crown which it has ousted.

Such is the sway of Monarchy over men's minds. But there is one practical quality about it which, in social effect, outweighs all others and is connected with all its qualities. Monarchy is the sole effective protection, in a large state, of the common citizen against the mastery of wealth. Napoleon summarised that truth in lapidary fashion. Monarchy, he said, is the one device discovered by man for the curbing of the money-power.

Age after age has proved this truth not only by reason but by experiment. Seeing what wealth can do, nothing can check its control of society save the presence of a master too rich to be bribed and too strong to be beaten down. Alternatively, in the absence of such a head, society may from force of habit accept as inevitable and (in time) as even natural, the direction of itself by the rich. When that state of things has grown mature and is established, what

6

we have called "Aristocracy" is present—the most stable and permanent of human arrangements. States so governed last on for centuries in splendour, and even during their decay they are monuments of their own past greatness. Such was Carthage, such was Venice, such has England been for now nearly three hundred years and perhaps may so remain indefinitely so long as she is ruled by gentlemen.

The aristocratic state is menaced by two things only: the moral menace of falling into mere plutocracy, a cancer which rapidly kills,[2] and the material menace of invasion by a large army. For in aristocracies the masses will never accept permanent military service.

Order is the main mark of aristocratic states and a unity not to be matched in any other kind of society. Their internal cohesion is at once firm and elastic; their foreign policy unbrokenly successful so long as they maintain a sufficient standard of intelligence and instruction in their gentry. There is also necessary a certain standard of personal honour; not a very high one but a minimum, failure to maintain which is mortal.

A Government by class, perpetually recruited, never lapses. It is never imperilled by the minority of a King. Class Government suffers no intervals of error due to personal caprice, or to youth, or to old age. It automatically gathers information from every source through its many members as they experience life by travel, commerce, adventure and comradeship. Its discipline is instinctive and therefore never rigid; its form of authority is suited organically to its structure; and that authority, being impersonal, elusive and manifold, is never challenged.

But these aristocratic states demand for their continuance the desire of the citizens to be so administered, and demand therefore an absence of egalitarian feeling. The

---

2 Here is the test of this disease appearing: it is present when a very rich anybody is treated as the superior of a very poor gentleman.

Equality of Men, the all-importance of the human substance compared with the individual accidents of fortune
and capacity, must be forgotten or unfelt if Class Government is to flourish. Hence it is that, to the mass of
mankind, there is something base and infamous about the
inward spirit of class Government in spite of its magnificence in outward show. Hence it is that societies of this
aristocratic sort are so rare in time and in space—because
only an exceptional temper will tolerate them. Hence it
is that this exceptional temper of theirs produces against
them a general antagonism. Hence it is that they must hold
well-defended positions lest they be absorbed or destroyed
by the very different ideal of civic dignity which is held by
the great and lasting majority of men.

To that great and lasting egalitarian majority, oligarchy,
even when it becomes aristocratic by use and acceptance,
is odious; its social air is resented and men will not pay
the price of what is, to them, spiritual degradation even
for the manifest advantages which class Government displays. They may, when they are few, express the feeling
of equality through democracy. Even when they are few
they will often, when they are numerous they will always,
express it by Monarchy.

Thus are states *great in numbers* divided into two kinds,
those Aristocratic and those Monarchical.

The latter may be of various characters, looking to the
Authority of an elected or of an hereditary ruler. They will
admit differences of rank and delegation of power, and
variety of influence and command; but they all have this in
common: that they look to one man to restrain and repel
the arbitrary action of wealth, knowing well in their hearts
that, lacking such a man, they must accept wealth for master.

By all this we see the meaning and advantage of Monarchy to the state, to organised mankind, for which it secures
representation and a personal voice, protection, direction

8

and order under authority. Monarchy is also the political guarantee of the governed and Charles Stuart spoke that truth on the scaffold when he said that he died for the People of England.

But there is another truth to be told of Monarchy. It imperils the soul of the Monarch. A King is a necessary man, if citizens are to escape the baseness of class-rule: but necessary men are victims. The Monarch is sacrificed to the state. His individual being, the man himself, ceases to be, and that in two ways. First, that he loses his choice of private action—since he must not act for himself but for the state; second, that he is in peril of losing that moral sanity which is the fruit of companionship. He is alone—and he must, he cannot but be, worshipped. Now a man worshipped becomes to himself a god unless he watch every moment of his life and ride himself continually on the curb. The essentials of his own spiritual life have been sacrificed to his office and he sacrifices others to his desires. Things intolerable in other men are tolerated in him and his conscience atrophies.

Of such things the life of Louis is a prime example. His high early exaltation of supreme affection, his Beloved, was denied him because he was not a young lover but the Incarnate State. That frustration seared him and left him numb to such glories for all his life. The best of manhood was lost to him.

It is to his extreme honour that he never allowed caprice to interfere with his function of guide, master, and con-troller of the realm. He worked every day for hours at his function. He fulfilled it till the very last days of his life. This assiduity in duty does put him among the greatest of mankind. But the Monarch in Louis half consumed his private virtue. It rendered him during all the earlier half of his active life careless or unheeding of that domestic unity by which a man should live and lacking which the soul starves into imperfection and sterility.

True, Louis did penance. He was granted the opportunity for recovery. He grasped that opportunity and was grateful for it. All the last half of his life—thirty years and more—he gradually made his soul: remade it. But Monarchy had wounded it very deeply. Did the wound wholly heal?

Louis is a picture of Monarchy there also, in such a fate both of good and evil *within*.

And indeed he was in all ways a very image of kingship, for he came at the last, and was the most powerful, of that line wherein kingship in our civilisation, in Christendom, has been most fully manifest: the central throne whereon the other thrones of Europe were modelled.

Of kingship in Europe, in our race and tradition, this central example and model—the French Monarchy, was hereditary for centuries in the Capetian House.

Never despotic, based on institutions coeval with itself, creating and created by the Nation, it was the fullest type of kingship.

The Root was Roman.[3] That which inspired the age-long development of the French crown was the succession of the Roman Emperors, commanders-in-chief of the armies. It was a Roman general of Federated troops, Clovis, Belgic by birth, the son of a father of similar position in the Imperial forces, who took over the government of Gaul when the central taxing system broke down and with it direct administration of all the West by the central city. In his family, rule over France as a separate monarchical unit

---

3   It was thus in the High Destiny of that Rome (whence we all proceed) that the City, in spite of a Republican form, never fell into the baseness of mere aristocracy. Though inheriting a Patriciat, and therefore Republican, she kept alive the sense of equality because her citizens were always soldiers. The sense of equality is at work, perpetually and increasingly as her story develops. Rome could not prevent the rise of vastly wealthy men and their predominance, but she never *worshipped* the wealthy man: rather did she worship the soldier. She avoided the moral fate of Corinth and of Carthage, and when at last she grasped the world she established full Monarchy, open and adored.

began. Generations later the lieutenant of his last descendant took over the task and founded a family illustrious in Charlemagne, to whom fell the fruits of Gallic and Christian expansion beyond the Rhine. When the Carolingian house decayed, the western and larger part of Gaul, grown feudal in the welter of the Dark Ages, agreed to the vague supremacy, hardly exercised, of that one local magnate who had direct rule over Paris and its neighbourhood.

In these the title "King of France" remained. From a suzerainty of shadowy sort but of high moral prestige the power of this central family grew by inheritance and war for five hundred years until at last the French king, really ruling from the Mediterranean to the Channel, became the type of all the new national kingships of Christendom. Finally by the late sixteenth century, the last of feudalism was dying and the Crown was fully supreme. The violent French civil wars of religion, proceeding from the creative mind of Calvin, just failed to destroy the mighty structure of French Monarchy. It was repaired, it was further strengthened and rose to new and unquestioned power as the Germans through a similar commotion of religious wars, disintegrated and declined.

The Architect of that great revival, Richelieu, died just before his master the King, Louis XIII. They left on the throne a little child who, after the strain of yet another lesser civil tumult, was to reign with unchallenged right and complete personal power from his twenty-third year as Louis XIV.

This man, who was to present the most perfect example of Monarchy in all its advantages and disadvantages, had a life exactly suitable for our examination of kingship.

He was king all his days, from the day when he succeeded as a little child hardly able to understand the words around him, till the day when he died, in full possession of himself, at the very limits of old age. It was a life wholly filled with the business of Monarchy. He fulfilled that function actively and in person, ruling by his own decision and will, working unceasingly at his appointed task for more than fifty-five years. He lacked six months of twenty-three when—to the astonishment of his Council!—he declared his single power on the very morrow of Mazarin's death. He lacked but a few days of seventy-seven when he accomplished his last act of sovereignty and fell into the brief coma that was his end; an astonishing sequence!

That life falls markedly into the four phases which make up our mortality: adolescence, young glorious manhood, maturity and age. Each phase is well defined, each has its own set of happenings, and, of the last three, each has its separate group of public and of private experience: of state action and of personal things: of the life Without and the life Within.

He remained a boy till very late; growing to full stature, dark and strong, receptive and silent; giving little expression to opinion and none to command. He seemed but a subject to his mother and but a pupil to the subtle Italian Mazarin whose vast experience of men formed the lad daily, first by example, later actively, in the maxims and practice of government. So Louis continued until that first profound desire seized him on his very entry into manhood, during his twentieth year. The woman who was the object, the necessity, of this intense exalted mood was denied him. That denial left him incapable of other passion for ever. He lived fully, but he never loved again.

Thenceforward for six years he rules in the strength of youth. It is the second chapter of his story and the first of his mastery over the state. For sixteen years more he conquers beyond the frontiers and administers all in the fullness of maturity. It is the third chapter. The fourth chapter is his resistance to counter-attack. He maintains himself against increasing peril for more than thirty years of ageing and ends his reign as he had begun it, to the noise of decisive victory. The cavalry charge of Rocroi opened that story; the bayonet charge of Denain closed it.

These four divisions are the separate volumes of his life. The first covers his formation; the second a sheaf of creative action achieved before he is thirty; the third a climax of assurance, the march of armies and their triumphs, extension everywhere of the realm, and primacy in Europe, all to the accompaniment of high verse and prose, high rhetoric, and the minds of men at their strongest; the fourth is the gathering of enemies, the hostile siege of what he had established; a strain, growing desperate, which all but overwhelmed him and his people. He emerges from it in extreme old age still erect, exhausted but undefeated, with a final decisive battle in his favour at the end. Thereon he dies.

The same four divisions distinguish the life within. The first is his boyhood and adolescence. It concludes with that flame of passion which determined all that was to come. The second is the insufficient nourishment which is furnished by chance attractions and by one strong affection from another: received by him, not bestowed on that other by himself. The third is maturity: the well-founded and sufficient but limited relations with mere beauty, mere vitality. This also weakens from lack of spiritual substance and is killed by a shock. The fourth is that consolation of ageing, a strong and permanent friendship, even a marriage. This companionship extends through all the second half of his life, supports him and saves him: but has not about it even the echo of love.

To each of the last three I would give, not indeed an equal length and detail of statement, but an equal weight in justly estimating the whole outward work of the man and his whole inward experience.

How should that be, seeing that the first of these three is but six years in extent, the second more than double that, and the third nearly twice the second? I will explain.

The opening of Louis's active kingship dates from that day following on Mazarin's death when the chief spokesman for the first estate of the Realm, had asked "To whom was it the king's pleasure that they should turn for their orders"—meaning "To what minister whom your majesty has been pleased to appoint." He got the immediate, novel and astounding reply: "To me." It was March, 1661. The next epoch opens with the invasion of the Spanish Netherlands in the spring of 1667. This first part of the active reign of Louis is one of six years.

The various wars of the Netherlands and their sequels, the highest military moment of the reign, may be closed anywhere from the year of Nijmegen eleven years after the first invasion of Holland, to the surrender of Strasburg three years later—say from eleven to fourteen years: 1667 to 1678-81. It continues in an air of triumph two more years—all 1682 and 1683.

After 1681 there follow one after the other the things that make up the third part, the decline of the reign from its summit: the hostility of Rome, the League of Augsburg, the fall of the Stuarts, the increasing coalition, and at last the mortal peril of the realm in the final war, that of the Spanish Succession. The king rallied his people at their last gasp, and Villars in a sudden victory won the peace. But not till March, 1714, was the final treaty signed—thirty-one years of anxiety turning from danger to dread, from dread to a losing battle for life and from this to the very brink of disaster: the full half of one long active life, the last half and the worst. In the next year the great king was dead.

How shall the brief and early splendour, the longer but still limited sixteen years that follow, the long-drawn struggle and desperate defence at the end, stand on a parity?

Thus: that the scale of any section in human life is not measured by its years but by the intensity of its action and feeling. Louis in that early blaze was under thirty still. In the splendour of his maturity he remained till over forty—to forty-three—some would say to forty-five. But in the forties comes the turn of human life and after that change the thoughts and acts of a man rest rather on memory than on deed; and time grows less and less: it hurries to be off: after forty-five the years put on pace. Another decade and they go racing by.

Let any man who has lived long look back. What shows up in the landscape? The morning hours. What has on it a full light? The noon and the first following time—fruition. But the shadows lengthen, the air chills: dusk, and a long passage into night.

So Louis saw it at the end. It is in those same divisions, then, that I shall order the survey of his mortality.

hours not ruly until 1661 ∴ for shorter than £ig7.

I
Formation

I

The Birth

LOUIS XIV WAS THE SON OF SO
strange a father and came into this world under
such strange conditions that his legitimacy has
been doubted. But the dates are well known, and they
belie all doubts on paternity.

Louis XIII King of France, Henry of Navarre's strange
son, had for many years refused his wife. He had married
her, daughter of Spain (and born in the Escorial), as a
matter of State. She was a child entering her fifteenth year:
he but a year older. From the moment of the wedding he
neglected her for his old pastimes. Nevertheless not too
long after the wedding—at least when the girl was old
enough—he proposed to have children by her. It was the
purpose and necessity of the match that the new Bourbon
dynasty should be strengthened; and in due time the young
woman was with child. But she was still a romp, and one
day, as she with her companions were sliding down the
long gallery of the Louvre, she fell and miscarried. The
king, already sufficiently averse to her, could not forgive
her his disappointment. He would have no more to do
with her, and for *eighteen years* the woman was not a wife.

There is no such enigma in history as the nature of that
man. He was courageous, he loved arms, yet he was without initiative, his power of command was reduced to inflict-
ing annoyances. He loved to test his domestic authority
not by action but by such vagaries as keeping his courtiers
frozen on winter days while he ferreted, and sneering at
their sufferings. He delighted in giving offence—yet he

was not petty. He had no statesmanship yet discerned the
greatest genius in statesmanship that his time produced—
the chief architect of Modern Europe, Richelieu; and, after
some vacillation, steadfastly maintained that genius in an
absolute power, exercised till the very day of his death in
the name of the crown.

Louis XIII understood war yet never designed it. He
had genuine piety yet without warmth; was a resolute rider
yet never led. But by far the most inexplicable thing in
that incomprehensible mind and body was his relations
with women.

He had no vices, yet absurdly intimate male friendships.
He had no mistresses, and, it would seem, needed none.
Yet, after so long a lapse of time without intercourse—
nearly all that period during which a woman can bear children—during which he had lived apart from his queen, he,
by an accident, not only suddenly continued his line but
became the father of two children at the very last.

He had arranged on a winter's day in December, 1637,
to hunt, and was leaving Paris for Fontainebleau, when
a violent storm detained him on the approach of night.
The King of France in those days, like many another great
man, travelled not only with his retinue but with all his
furniture. Thus detained in Paris, his bed gone forward
ahead of him, he had no choice but to ask hospitality of
the Queen. In the due time, to a day, his first son was
born and was given the ancestral name, Louis. It was the
5th of September, 1638.

The event was not isolated. A second son followed. Then
Louis XIII died on the 14th of May, 1643, only a few
months after his great Minister who had re-established the
Royal Power. Even at that moment, with a child of four
succeeding to a vacant throne surrounded by a mass of
violent intrigue, all the central power in disarray, certain
attack by the Spanish armies in Belgium impending, a

great victory was to decide the future and mark the opening of the Reign: Rocroi.

It happened thus:

ROCROI

The King, as he felt death approaching, had nominated to the command of his armies his second cousin once removed, the young Duke of Enghien, a man not yet twenty-two, but even at such an age the man was remarkable enough to have merited the attention given him. He was of the blood royal, of course, son and heir to Condé, the second cousin of the King. He was to inherit his father's title not long after and is known in history, through his continued military triumphs, as "the great" Condé.

Side by side with him Louis had nominated the elderly Hopital, a man thirty-three years older. The plan was to balance the immaturity and violent temperament of Enghien by the experience and moderation of his elder, but it soon proved that the young man was so great a master of war that the older was of less and less weight in military councils and the capital business of Rocroi made Condé's later superiority incontestable.

The situation a month before Rocroi was this:

Louis XIII was certainly dying. The Spaniards were masters of the north-eastern frontier, that is of Flanders. The Spanish war machinery with its unconquered and most famous infantry—its Tercios—was commanded by Melos, a man of courage and decision and not without ability for his task.

Melos made a double calculation. Each limb of it was apparently sound. In the first place he counted upon the violent quarrels which would arise and the violent rivalries for power, division in command and all the rest of it, when the King of France should at last be dead. The

King of France was certainly dying and the news of his end might come at any moment. In the second place he counted upon a recent tide of successes for the Spanish side which might carry him on to complete victory against the French crown, to the invasion of the heart of France and the dictation of terms such as Spain had never been able to impose during the now age-long struggle against her rival, the crown and government of the French people.

There were indeed, within the Spanish Netherlands, certain French garrisons still holding particular points. Arras was held, the most important fortress on the frontier flanking the main roads into France, and at intervals sundry other strongholds retained bodies of French troops; but they were isolated and could be reduced. Melos proposed to give up the siege of Arras (which had been the first idea), to turn aside eastwards, and take Rocroi right in the central line of advance on Paris which lay before him hardly a hundred miles away.

Rocroi, though fortified, was ill fortified. It was a small place with a small garrison and that garrison ill found. It should be an easy matter to carry Rocroi, if not by assault at any rate after a few days' siege; and with Rocroi taken the way lay open into Champagne, the home districts of the enemy and the Capital itself.

Enghien's concentration was taking place in Amiens, where Gassion already stood with a part of the army. Espenan had another group at Laon. Enghien proceeded to call in the detachments till the whole army should be unified for the advance to the north-east against the invasion.

In the first days of May, 1643, Enghien had news that Melos had concentrated at Douai with his considerable force and a specially strong body of artillery. He further heard that Melos was facing towards Landrecies, but he could not yet know how much further Melos would advance in that easterly way before trying anything. As a fact, Melos had, as we know, chosen Rocroi, beyond Landrecies, as the determining point, the best base for a victorious march on Champagne and so to Paris.

Enghien was in Joigni when he heard that Melos had not only arrived before Rocroi with his army but had actually opened the first trench for the capture of the place. It was the 10th of May. Melos had with him 8,000 horse under Albuquerque and 18,000 foot. By his calculations, he was superior in numbers to anything the French could bring against him in time to save Rocroi and was certainly superior in personnel as well as in numbers; for remember again that the core of the Spanish forces in the Netherlands was that incomparable and still undefeated Spanish infantry, men of long training, professional, filled with the certitude of victory, bound together by a body of officers who were the pride of their men.

There was nothing to compare with this force round which the Spanish army was grouped. We may appreciate what it meant to the men of that day by drawing a parallel with the British fleet of our own. Suppose a naval action to be threatening in which one party could count upon the presence of the British fleet with its unbroken tradition, its professional excellence and its confidence in victory, while the other party could only gather an inferior number of units of less power and with no tradition of complete, continuous success. On such a parallel we can judge how the two antagonists looked at one another in that moment when, apparently, the fate of the French future was to be decided.

It was, I say, on the 10th of May, 1643, that the first trench was opened in front of Rocroi by Melos. News of this had reached Enghien within twenty-four hours. Treading on the heels of that news came the news of the King's death. Enghien heard on the 15th of May that Louis XIII had died the day before.

He alone, in the high command of the army, had had that news. He kept it secret and he did well to do so. Perhaps he was tempted to forego action and return to Paris at such a moment, when the fortunes of his own house were at stake and when the confused but violent struggle for power was about to open. If so, he decided for the right course, making up his mind at once with that firm decision which was a mark of his character. We may guess why he so decided. Two motives combined to move him. First that he was avid of glory and believed himself to stand some chance of a new and sudden victory; second he preferred the general good of his country and of the royal family whereof he was a member to every personal gain.

Whatever his motives were, he acted. He kept his face firmly fixed to the frontier and turned away from Paris. He would relieve Rocroi and perhaps (who knows?) might (but that he kept to himself) obtain a decision in the field.

He could not see how mighty would be the results of that decision but he undoubtedly thought it possible that a victory in a general action was before him.

Melos did not think this possible. He underestimated both the numbers of his opponent and the abundant promise, hitherto not fully revealed, of this very young man who was marching against him. As a fact Enghien had with him some 22,000 men—15,000 foot and 7,000 horse—wherewith to attack 26,000. Even so the odds against Enghien were not so heavy as Melos had imagined, for that governor of the Spanish Netherlands had been insufficiently informed. He did not appreciate the rapidity of French marching, the pace and promptitude with which Enghien had called in his detachments from all sides, and the swift growth of the army. He seems to have estimated Enghien's total force at not much more than half its real strength. The consequence was that element of surprise which is always of the first importance in war.

Rocroi is a very small country town. It stands rather higher than the surrounding country, the centre of a desolate clearing in the midst of great woods which in those days almost surrounded it. In those days also the woodland was even deeper than it is now—for some part of it has since been cleared—and the approaches to the town were rendered difficult by the character of the soil as well as by the density of the forests. That soil is still marshy and was marshier then. The approach to Rocroi through the woods from the south and west, the direction in which Enghien lay, was not only impeded by the body of trees and undergrowth reaching, with a few clearings, for miles, but also by the pools and meres, and treacherous boggy soil through which comparatively narrow ways alone were available. These were the "defiles" by which alone a French approach to the coming action could be made.

Gassion—learned, and a pupil of Gustavus Adolphus—had gone forward with his advance body of French troops, reaching the neighbourhood of Rocroi just after Melos had taken up his position. Gassion saw that if a general action were intended everything would depend upon getting the French army through the defiles and deploying in the big open clearing in the midst of which Rocroi itself stood. Enghien's command would have to debouch from woods and marshes at the far north-eastern end of these defiles too near the enemy and would have to form a line at great risk, but the risk was taken.

The French were favoured by the decision Melos himself took not to defend these defiles but to await contact beyond them on the Rocroi side.

The thesis of either general was this: Melos said to himself, "If I defend the defiles I can certainly prevent the mass of the French forces getting through, though perhaps I cannot prevent their getting a certain number through, sufficient to reinforce the garrison at Rocroi and keep up its resistance for a few days. I shall by thus defending the defiles make certain of reducing Rocroi within a short time, though perhaps after a longer delay than I had anticipated. If, on the other hand, I permit the passage of the defiles by the enemy and wait for him in the open ground between the woods and marshes and Rocroi itself I shall be luring him on to certain destruction. His numbers are inferior, and the best of his personnel far inferior to my incomparable Spanish infantry which inspires all the forces grouped round it. A general action would be decisive of the war and of the whole policy of Spain. The French are certainly about to quarrel among themselves, for their king is dying, if not already dead. He leaves a little child upon the throne and warring factions all round it. If I tempt the advancing French to a general action its decision must be certainly in my favour and will decide the whole war at a blow. The way to Paris will lie open, and Spain, after a short further advance, can dictate her own terms."

The thesis on the other side was this: Enghien said to himself, "I am only twenty-two to his twenty-six, and the certain reputation of his incomparable Spanish infantry is superior to anything that I can muster. On the other hand, although the odds are against me, *if* I get a decision everything will be changed. The crown will suddenly acquire a new prestige which the death of the king and the minority of his heir mortally need. The country will be free from invasion for an indefinite time to come. The shaken throne will be securely founded. Even if I do not obtain a decision, I shall, by passing through the defiles, delay the enemy and then I shall be able to gather further support from more distant garrisons and carry on the war. If I lose I lose everything, and so does the crown and the nation; but then the enemy will stake all on victory anyhow, so the risk must be taken, and though weaker than they, I am stronger than they think for."

To this thesis, special and military, which was Enghien's, fate might have added another clause: "Yes! And also you are young. And also, though you do not yet know it, you are a genius."

There is a village called Romigni standing on what is now a country road and was then the main way of approach to Rocroi from the south and west. Thither, when Gassion had rejoined him, did Enghien call the body of his officers for consultation and orders. It is half a day's march—rather more than five miles—from the entry into the defiles, the paths which thread their way through the marshes and woods that make a screen round Rocroi. It is a full day's march—some twelve and a half miles—from what was to prove the battlefield. It was a long day's march—fourteen to fifteen miles—from the steeple of Rocroi itself where it stands conspicuous on slightly higher and drier land in the midst of the clearing beyond the forest.

To the officers so gathered round him, that very young, dark, long-nosed, low-fronted, somewhat fierce commander revealed for the first time the news of the King's death. On what followed (he said), the fate of the nation would depend. "We must maintain at this issue the repute of French arms." Thence he moved to the village of Bossus close at hand, more central to the various units of his command, and there drew out the orders of the march and of what deployment should take place in the clearing beyond the woods, should the defiles be successfully passed.

It was the 17th of May. The dead king still lay in state, unburied, a hundred miles away in St. Denis.

The deployment, should the passage of the defiles succeed, was to be drawn out in two bodies. Over on the left he planned to leave the elderly and too cautious Hopital, who was now belatedly given news of his sovereign's death. The command of the right Enghien would keep in his own hands, having with him as second in command Gassion.

This right-hand wing was to be first of cavalry intermixed with units of musketeers, and next, towards the centre, his infantry. This centre was continued by the infantry of Hopital and beyond that again, further to the left, was to be placed Hopital's cavalry.

Gassion had first "taken soundings" of the defiles, and though he had found but a few of Melos's men in front of him, Hopital again objected to the rashness of the attempt, but Enghien mastered him, insisting upon the superior command which had been placed in his hands.

On the 18th of May the advance through the defiles began and met with no appreciable resistance, for none had been planned. The long processions of armed men took their way through the scrub and the woodland and the meres. By evening the heads of the columns were in the open country beyond and the steeple of little Rocroi stood out on the higher land against the sky.

Nor were the French troops disturbed during the business of deployment. Enghien had so skilfully screened his movements that Melos and his commanders could not fully discern how far the debouching of their enemies had gone by the time it was dusk, for the young French commander occupied with his staff and the open order of his cavalry a very slight rise in ground which hid what lay between it and the trees. Melos may, however, have guessed that the force approaching him was larger than he had imagined, for he sent to Beck, who lay some miles beyond, to come up and join him.

While the light still lingered a roll of Spanish drums was heard as though for an attack; for Laferté, on the French left, facing the Spanish right, had made a false move, pressing on too far, so that he left the protection of a mere on his flank and exposed it: but Enghien recalled him in time. No Spanish attack took place: had it been launched we should have had played out in the last hour of this May evening just the same situation as arose the next year at Marston Moor when, at the end of daylight, the issue was decided.

The night of the 18th of May fell. Far off in Paris all was being prepared by torch-light for the funeral of the King. Here on the frontier it was pitch dark.[*] There was no movement. Melos had missed his first opportunity. Had he taken the risk and attacked at the moment when Enghien's force was debouching from the woods he would have destroyed it. But he pondered upon the situation and he went on pondering till it was too late.

The hostile lines lay all through the night so close that the lights of their bivouac fires were confounded into one glare.

As the dawn of the 19th of May broke faced the one the other, each drawn up on the crest of its slight swell of land with a shallow depression in between. The army of Melos—Walloons, Germans, Italians (with the Spanish infantry in the centre as the main strength of the whole)—looked south-westward towards the forest line, that of Enghien north-eastward towards the roofs and single steeple of little Rocroi close at hand behind their enemies.

When it was fully day Enghien engaged upon the right and Hopital followed suit upon the left. Enghien on the French right was checked by a wood wherein most of the timber had been recently felled, a place through which it was impossible to move a large body. He used to his own advantage that very obstacle. Though the Spanish artillery, more numerous and better served than his own, harassed the manœuvre, he sent Gassion round by the extreme right, beyond the wood and so held the enemy. When they should be thoroughly engaged it would be Gassion's task to wheel round further beyond the wood and catch the Spanish cavalry in flank.

---

[*]   The moon was twenty-two days old.

Gassion accomplished his mission; and just as Enghien's force were at their work of "hooking on to" the Walloons and Germans opposed to them, Gassion came thundering round the wood on their left open flank and charged. There was a clumsy attempt to change front but it was too late, and the mass of Melos's horsemen were driven back pell-mell beyond the main line. Then it was that Enghien played that classic tactical manœuvre which the French boast to be his invention but which I think may be traced to the earlier story of the German religious wars and particularly to Gustavus Adolphus. At any rate, whether it were his creation or not, Enghien used the "interrupted charge" which a few months later Cromwell was to use at Naseby. But in truth no one can tell the origin of these things. The thing appears in all these seventeenth century battles at that same moment and perhaps research or greater knowledge than mine could trace it to the great Gustavus himself, who had fallen eleven years before. Enghien refused to pursue the flying enemy cavalry. He left it to Gassion to drive them off, himself reined up his men and wheeled to the left.

It was high time, for at the other end of the line the elderly Hopital had been badly mauled. The French left had charged the Spanish right at a gallop, taking off too far from its objective, and bringing up blown and exhausted horses only to be shot down, and in the counter-offensive the enemy horse had driven the French before it. Hopital himself was wounded; and, seeing the French had thus lost the support of their left wing which was in rout, the magnificent Spanish infantry of the centre pressed forward against the French foot. That Spanish phalanx which had long been as famous as the Macedonian, passed imperturbable over all before it, and there was some considerable space of time, therefore, in which it seemed that the day was lost to Enghien. He himself indeed had with his cavalry now ridden round the Spanish centre and was pursuing the Spanish horse beyond while they themselves were pursuing the flying Hopital. But the Spanish infantry, unmoved by the presence of the horse first behind them and now on their further flank, went forward unbroken and still assured of victory.

Then it was, the day already well advanced, that Enghien charged again, this time on the far flank of that Spanish phalanx which had hitherto despised his approach. His appearance encouraged the French foot to rally and stand for a time against the enemy. The Spanish phalanx halted, its ranks opened, eighteen guns which had hitherto been hidden by the mass of the Spanish foot were revealed and crashed grapeshot into Enghien's horse, but did not break his charge. Immediately that charge was in the midst of them and for the first time within men's memory the Spanish infantry fell into disarray.

It did not break; its will to fight on remained; but its cohesion was gone. That seemingly immortal force was coming to its end.

It was now surrounded on every side, sabred by the horse, mown down by the fire of the enemy foot. A massacre began. But even as that butchery opened a tragic error marred the close of so famous a day. It was believed on the one hand that quarter had been asked for and granted, on the other that there had been a treacherous attack after the demand for quarter had been made. Enghien in the very heat of the roaring turmoil grasped the truth. He moved through the line shouting that quarter should be given and saved not a few of the enemy officers with his own hands, but in the din all was confused and though some were heard and saved themselves, the great mass were killed or wounded and the remainder captured.

The day was ending. It was not yet dark when the last poor hundreds of Melos's broken force fled eastward and found refuge at last amid the troops of Beck that had come up too late to be of effect. These few Beck's command gathered in and drew off. They had already left the field.

Of 18,000 foot which had mustered in that morning, 8,000 lay dead and of the remainder and the remnants of the cavalry, 7,000 were wounded or unwounded prisoners. As for the officers, all, or nearly all, were killed or taken. The eighteen Spanish guns that had done such work in the midst of the fury were captured, of course, as was the battery of six heavier pieces in the midst—and the great battle was done. It had taken up the whole day.

On that same day they buried the king with due solemnity at St. Denis. But in these hours also was buried for ever the invincible infantry of old Spain.

The little child, now king, had been established on Rocroi field.

THE FRONDE

That child grew up, like all children, surrounded by adult men and women whom he did not understand nor care to understand. All those grown-ups are a world apart to little boys and girls, especially to boys not yet even in their teens. The confused important military drama that was being played out on the Eastern Marches of France in the debatable border land between the Gallic and the Germanic traditions made a noise that reached the child but told him little. It came nowhere near his immediate interests and educated him in no fashion. His cousin Condé went on from victory to victory, of which little Louis heard the names, and at which no doubt he now and then rejoiced. But that was all. The "breach in the wall," the flats of the north and east, had been defended and carried against the Hapsburg powers and Condé's name had become more famous than ever. But of the jealousy against his cousin the boy could know nothing, of why Condé was sent to waste himself on the Catalonian front and of his failure before Lerida. All the boy could have retained concerning himself during those first years is that they were passed to the distant sound of arms.

Louis was within a month of his tenth birthday when, on the 10th of August, 1648, Condé triumphed once more in the great victory of Lens. The poor remnants of Spanish infantry surviving from Rocroi were then finally destroyed and the Spaniards lost what was, for those days, the large number of thirty-eight guns. Five thousand unwounded prisoners, three thousand dead, marked that famous action. It was a sequel to, and a consecration of, Rocroi.

But in the same days of August came news much nearer to that little king and remembered the whole of his life.

He was brought up against the noise of combat, against the sound of musketry and the roar of charging men in his very halls.

Just as the news of Lens was coming into Paris, only ten days after Condé had stood on that field triumphant, even as they were singing the Te Deum for the victory in Notre Dame and as the Household Guards were bringing in the captured standards, there broke out the beginnings of a civil war. It was not a vital conflict. It was but an inevitable incident of regency, and regency by a woman and her foregoer of genius, The Mazarin. The confused fighting that follows is petty for us; to him it was terrifying and immediate, clamouring at the doors of what was still for him not much more than a nursery. The streets of the city had been more and more filled with the clamour of angry men; with the fall of the late evening the narrow streets were aglow with musket shots, the noise of the heavy chains lifted to cut the traffic and interrupt the soldiery who stood on each main corner, and the barricades had begun to rise. It was the night of the barricades.

What had happened? What had happened was that, as usual, a side issue which was not the decisive issue had provoked a catastrophe. The main issue was this: Who should have the control of the little king during his minority, who should handle the revenue (to his or their own advantage), who should set the new reign on lines that would preserve such advantages to those who had controlled the king's youth? On this main issue grievous quarrels were arising when the lawyers of the highest legal bodies in France butted in and supported the irregular claims of others against the queen regent.

By the long established rule of the French constitution—one might almost call it now a fundamental law— the widowed mother of the new king was regent during that child's minority. That is what had happened in the generation before, when Henry IV was stabbed and Marie de Medicis became regent; she was promptly blackmailed by the great ones, the companions of her husband whom, while he lived, he had kept in order—old Sully, for instance, added all he could to his wealth during that first Bourbon minority, the childhood of Louis XIII, as did many others. Now there was a second minority, that of Louis XIII's little son, and once more a queen dowager was regent, by the strength of a custom there was no over-riding. It was a custom founded upon the family instinct of the French; a deep sense that the widowed mother was the natural head of the family until the heir should be of age, and that to her, above all others, the heir owed respect and obedience.

That was all very well in a private family where the widow would be of the same sort as those around her, but with royalty in the seventeenth century the arrangement had one grave weakness. The widowed mother was certain to be a foreigner, the close relative and perhaps the inheritor of a foreign dynasty. Therefore, those who desired to share with the queen regent the advantages of government could appeal to the popular prejudice against foreigners and make her path difficult.

This happened now with Anne of Austria, daughter of the King of Spain, who was put in constitutional control of the French state.

Since the whole virtue of monarchy is that it makes government personal, its defect is that the life of the throne follows the life of a man and the vicissitudes thereof. A monarchy is weak when the monarch is weak. It is at its weakest during a minority.

Here and now in 1643 and the following five years the French state was faced with a prolonged minority. The king was a little child not five years old; it would be long indeed before he could act and during the interval all would be in question. There could not but be turmoil; every menace gathered and at last broke out in violence and armed rivalries; that confused civil war which French history calls "the Fronde."* The Fronde broke out in that day of the barricades just mentioned, and the day of the barricades was provoked by the lawyers.

But before we consider the business of the Fronde an interruption and digression is necessary. We must appreciate the position of this new Dynasty, the Bourbons, in order to see how here also monarchy is all-important. The Fronde

---

* "Fronde" means a "sling," and "Frondeur" one who casts stones from a sling. It is by no means certain how the term got applied to the rebels of Louis XIV's minority. One plausible—and easy—guess at the derivation is that of the contemporary Cardinal de Retz in his memoirs. He had a right to speak as a witness for he did much (and pretended he did more) to animate this imperfect civil war. *He* says the term came in as a slang metaphor taken from the lads who used to play at slinging stones in the empty and dry moat outside the walls of Paris. This dangerous pastime was forbidden and the boys would hide their slings when a patrol appeared, and then take to them again when the patrol passed and they felt safe. Hence in derision the nobles and lawyers who lashed sporadic attacks on the legislative government of the Regency were called "Frondeurs." It may be so. But the truth is that no one knows the origin or even the first appearance of these slang political terms. They crop up suddenly in all countries (as did "Whig" and "Tory" in England) and take root.

itself, though apparently an abortive revolution against the monarchy, was rather against the constitutional guardian of the monarchy, and was essentially monarchic. The rivalries which produced it were rivalries of the blood royal, rivalries within the sacred family. It was marked by the secession of Condé, the king's cousin. It was helped in Paris by another cousin, the "Grande Demoiselle," suggested in part by the illegitimate cousins, the Vendômes. The lawyers played their part in the welter, trying, like others, to usurp powers, but they could have done nothing without the princes and princesses around them: Bourbon blood royal.

2

The Bourbons

WHAT WAS THAT FAMILY, THE Bourbons? What was the new dynasty?

In a real monarchy everything turns upon the dynasty, that is, upon the family the head of which is for the moment king.

Of course in the larger sense of the word "dynasty" there had only been one dynasty upon the throne of France for over six hundred years. It descended from that military leader of the Dark Ages whose origin is uncertain and who was called in his day "Robert the Strong." He and his descendants became the hereditary rulers of the district round Paris known as the "Duchy of France," and it was his grandson, Hugh Capet, whom we have seen founding what is called the "Capetian House." After a sort of false start in crowning his uncle, Hugh Capet was made King in order to distinguish the separation of the western regions, the Gallic regions depending on Paris, from the rest of Christendom. For the rest of Christendom there was acknowledged, however vaguely, the authority of the Emperor. The title of King had become the means of virtual independence from the Emperor's authority and the symbol of a groping, tentative national unit.

The French Crown had descended from father to son unbrokenly for three hundred years. Perhaps it would not have done so save for the accident that each reign was furnished with a fully grown and competent heir crowned before his father died. But this age-long tradition confirmed the King of Paris until he had become by marriage and inheritance and conquest the real ruler of North-Western Gaul.

This unbroken chain of succession from father to son came to a sudden halt with the great grandson of St. Louis in the early fourteenth century. The king of that day died, leaving only a daughter to succeed him; the throne was claimed and seized by his nearest male cousin, and to excuse the act he got his lawyers to affirm that, by an ancient law of the Salian Franks (with whom the Capetians had nothing to do but whose monarchic rights they claimed), *land could never pass to a woman or (perhaps) be inherited through a woman.* The Crown was compared to a Salian estate and succession denied to a woman.

Thenceforward whenever the direct succession in the male line failed a relative was sought out, no matter how distant a cousin, upon whom the kingship should devolve because, although there might be any number of people descended through women and possessing a prior claim, he was the latest male representative of the Capetian House.

This had happened somewhat before the end of the religious wars in France when Henry III, the last of the Valois branch, was assassinated in 1589. He had no children, nor had his two brothers left any children. The man with the sole right, by the now long accepted rule of the Salic Law, to follow Henry III was his cousin Henry, the son of the King of Navarre. To go back to a common male ancestor one had to leap more than three hundred years. Henry the Prince of Navarre was through his *mother* the second cousin of the last Valois king, but in male descent there was no common ancestor until one got back to St. Louis, eight generations away.

This distant male cousinship could not weaken the claim of Henry of Navarre to succeed to the French Throne and unite it with his own petty kingdom in the Pyrenees. What really did weaken his claim was that he had been, though a man personally indifferent to religion, the military leader on the Calvinist side during the religious wars. On that account Paris refused to accept him. His deficient uncle the Cardinal de Bourbon was proposed and even called "King Charles X." Paris stood a terrible siege rather than admit a heretic king. But Henry compromised, was reconciled with the Church (1593), his title admitted by the Pope, and at last ruled universally as Henry IV, the first king of what is known as the Bourbon Dynasty, because that younger son of St. Louis, the common ancestor from whom through many generations Henry IV descended, had married the heiress of the Bourbon lordship in Central France, and henceforward that younger branch was known as "The Bourbons."

Henry IV's father, Anthony of Bourbon, King of Navarre by right of his marriage with the heiress of that military mountain realm, had had a brother bearing the title of Condé, from whom descended the Princes of Condé, whose eldest sons bore the title Enghien during their father's lifetime.

Henry IV himself had, by his marriage with the foolish but dynamic Marie de Medicis, two sons, Louis and Gaston. Louis succeeded his father, under the title of Louis XIII. Gaston, the younger brother, had the title "Duke of Orleans," and throughout all the first twenty-two years of his brother's reign, during which the King had no child born to him, Gaston Duke of Orleans was the heir apparent and it was taken for granted that he would succeed after Louis XIII should die. Gaston Duke of Orleans had one child, a daughter, known in history as "La Grande Demoiselle." To Louis XIII, after those long childless years, his wife Anne of Austria unexpectedly bore a son, as has been written. That son was Louis XIV.

Henry IV had also had, by his famous mistress Gabrielle d'Estrées, a bastard who bore the title Duke of Vendôme, one of the titles already inherited by Henry's father;

THE BOURBONS

Beginning with Charles Bourbon of Vendôme

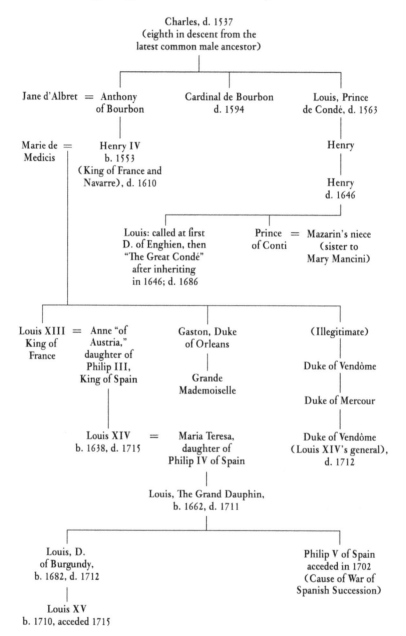

Charles, d. 1537
(eighth in descent from the
latest common male ancestor)

Jane d'Albret = Anthony
of Bourbon

Cardinal de Bourbon
d. 1594

Louis, Prince
de Condé, d. 1563

Marie de = Henry IV
Medicis   b. 1553
(King of France and
Navarre), d. 1610

Henry

Henry
d. 1646

Louis: called at first
D. of Enghien, then
"The Great Condé"
after inheriting
in 1646; d. 1686

Prince = Mazarin's niece
of Conti   (sister to
Mary Mancini)

Louis XIII = Anne "of
King of   Austria,"
France   daughter of
Philip III,
King of Spain

Gaston, Duke
of Orleans

(Illegitimate)

Duke of Vendôme

Grande
Mademoiselle

Duke of Mercour

Louis XIV   =   Maria Teresa,
b. 1638, d. 1715   daughter of
Philip IV of Spain

Duke of Vendôme
(Louis XIV's general),
d. 1712

Louis, The Grand Dauphin,
b. 1662, d. 1711

Louis, D.
of Burgundy,
b. 1682, d. 1712

Philip V of Spain
acceded in 1702
(Cause of War of
Spanish Succession)

Louis XV
b. 1710, acceded 1715

40

and this Vendôme branch, though they were illegitimate, counted almost as much as the more distant but legitimate relatives of the king.

Since as far back as 1310 a son of St. Louis (Louis IX, King of France) had married the heiress to the Bourbon land and title, the son of that marriage was the first Duke of Bourbon—called "Duke" because, though the name Bourbon came from his mother, he was of royal blood and in the Middle Ages the title "Duke" connoted a royal connection. This royal duke's descendants continued to a certain Charles, the eldest of three brothers, who died in 1537. When, thirty-five years after this, in 1572, the religious wars broke out in France, the last kings of the older Valois branch succeeded, one after the other, without children.

The last of these childless Valois kings was Henry III; and since he had no heir it was obvious that on his death the Bourbon heirs would be heirs to the throne in the order of their birth. Anthony, the eldest, who had married the queen of Navarre, queen in her own right to that little independent kingdom in the Pyrenees, was dead, leaving this son Henry of Navarre. The third brother, who had the title of Prince of Condé, was also dead. The second brother, a churchman, known in history as the Cardinal de Bourbon, was still alive when Henry III, the last Valois, was stabbed to death in 1589. By that time Anthony Bourbon being long dead, his son Henry became in that year 1589 the rightful king of France under the title of Henry IV, as he was also, through his mother, king of Navarre.

But there was that complication just spoken of, that Henry of Navarre had been brought up a Protestant; for his mother, the queen of Navarre, had been strongly anti-Catholic in the height of the Reformation. She had been the female champion of the reformers.[*]

[*] She boasted that the Mass would never again be said in her lands, which, by the way, included Lourdes.

Henry of Navarre had found himself, therefore, in 1589, the undoubted king of France, and yet on that side of the religious quarrel which was hateful to the French people as a whole and especially to the people of Paris the capital. He had been the official Protestant champion all through the religious wars, though he himself cared very little about the theological quarrel. Paris, and the mass of the nation, would not accept Henry IV until he himself should promise to accept the old religion. This he did in 1593, and so reigned as the first king of the Bourbon dynasty.*

After so long a digression we can return to the day of the barricades, its occasion and consequences.

The French constitution included bodies known as "*Parlements*." The similarity of the name with that of the English Parliaments is confusing—for both ultimately sprang from the same source, the "Parlement" or "Palaver" of the early French-speaking mediæval kings of both France and England, when they met their nobles and chief legal advisers and talked over matters on which they wanted advice or on which they needed general consent.

These early rough unorganised bodies, "the King's Courts," became systematised, as all things become systematised with time. They differentiated into various branches— those who were expert in the laws, those who stood for the great feudal fortunes, those who were sent by large towns and districts to discuss exceptional grants in aid of the king, and so forth.

---

* It would delay us to go into the complicated relationships produced by this rule of only allowing descent through males, but the facts are worth stating. By the accession of Henry of Navarre the throne jumped more than six generations; counting the common ancestor and this claimant, eight generations. Henry of Navarre was eighth cousin of Francis I, the grandfather of the last Valois king who had been stabbed. Of course there had been any amount of intermarriages during those 300 years and the relationship, if we count by ordinary family rules, was much closer. Henry of Navarre's mother had been the niece of Francis I, and the aunt of the last Valois kings.

In England the term "Parliament," after going through a dozen twists and turns, as is the fashion of words in the course of years, became attached to the particular function of the king in consultation with his principal nobles and bishops and abbots, leaving out the legal bodies. Later the notables who came up from the districts and towns to talk about exceptional grants of money to help the king in difficult times, attended on grand occasions. At last these grand occasions were the only ones in which the term "Parliament" was used.

Meanwhile in France it was just the other way. The peers and the bishops and the representatives of the clergy and the delegates of those who were summoned to discuss grants came to be called the States General, because gatherings of this sort in the provinces were called "The States of such and such a Province." So, on the rare occasions when the whole nation was consulted the special term "States General" was used, while the specific term "Parliament" was confined to the lawyers. There was not only the main lawyers' body in the capital, "The Parliament of Paris," but other less important provincial ones.

The Parliament of Paris had considerable powers. It sat in seven chambers, one of which was pre-eminent and called "La Grand' Chambre." Care had been taken by the monarchy to prevent these various departments of the lawyers acting together lest they should be too great and overshadow the Crown. Most of them were concerned with the details of administration and justice, but the "Grand' Chambre" came in also for many major decisions. It had the right to register laws and decrees, including what was the most important of the real needs of the populace, and that was decrees of taxation. It could therefore put up a formidable opposition to the royal rights. This body of lawyers, the Parlement of Paris, was in no way representative of national opinion, but it could repose on that opinion in moments of popular opposition to the government, and thereby increase its power and position. It also had, of course, that invaluable asset (which attached throughout Christendom to all lawyers, from the market-town solicitor to the highest judge) of *knowing the law*, or, at any rate, being the official exponent of the law. Such a body may not have the technical right of making laws, but it can in practice mould them and has in this fashion great scope in managing men's lives, unless it is checked and curbed by a strong central power.

It was the very object of the French monarchy, the cause of its being, to curb and check every separate function which should allocate to itself sovereign powers. It was the business of the king to defend the common man and the nation against not only the money-power—though that was its principal function—but also against the lawyers. Therefore the lawyers were, in times when they dared to be so, natural opponents of the crown, just as the money-power was the natural opponent of the crown.

A minority such as that of this child Louis provided was a golden opportunity for the lawyers and for their Parliament of Paris. When popular irritation had risen to a certain height the lawyers could use their opportunity to the full.

Underneath the whole trouble lay what underlies nearly every civic commotion, especially among the French, the disturbance and disarray of public finance. The chief minister of the queen regent, Mazarin, had completed the work of his dead master, Richelieu. He had extended the boundaries of the realm and, what is more important, he had begun to fix them. He had introduced the people to a new era wherein France was to be increasingly powerful and, in spite of heavy burdens, increasingly proud of itself. He had opened the doors on "the great epoch." But of regular revenue on a fixed economic basis the French State had far too little. The throne which Mazarin served and continued to restore lived from hand to mouth by every expedient, getting what was urgent by borrowing money at eight, and sometimes ten, and sometimes even twelve, per cent. It was in debt to sharks of every kind, from those more noble great ones who only preyed grandly upon the public weal and were by this time almost bankers, to a swarm of smaller moneylenders. How much went in current interest will never be fully known, so complicated is the story. The larger estimates sound fantastic, but they may be true. It may be that one-third of all that was raised by desperate artifice and heavy new burdens went to the money dealers and their touts, and to those who took commission of them. It was certainly one-fifth. In such a ditch did the State wallow even while its foreign policy was triumphant, through the genius of Mazarin, in the Peace of Westphalia—of which more in a moment. Chaotic finance means uncertain employment for the wage-earners, wildly fluctuating prices for the housewife in her marketing, written contracts becoming unjust, bargains not observed. There spread throughout society the miserable mood of the embarrassed man. All France was angry; as it is for the same reason today.

The scapegoat of the popular anger was this foreigner, the Italian Mazarin, the queen's right-hand and, by the judgment of all, the queen's lover. The queen herself was also a foreigner. The lawyers opposing this government in the hands of foreigners became at once immensely popular.

They were the stronger from the misunderstood example of what was going on across the Channel. In England the Squires (the class which is called in France "la noblesse") and the town-merchants with whom the smaller landed gentry were inextricably mingled, had already won their battle against the Crown and put the King in prison prior to killing him. The lawyers had been their strongest allies. It was they who had invented the myth of Magna Charta, round which the opposition to the traditional and constitutional government of Charles I had arisen.

The lawyers in Paris took to copying a number of the catch-words used in that struggle. One of the most comic examples of this absurd parallel between two utterly different things was a demand of the Parliament of Paris that no one should be imprisoned save by the lawyers themselves, or, as they called themselves, "the natural judges of the King's subjects." In England this demand corresponded to a social reality; the lawyers were already far more powerful than the King and were about to contest the royal function of punishing evil-doers, especially conspirators against the poor remnant of the royal power. Hence the fuss about "Habeas Corpus." But in France the Monarchy was universally revered; it was only the accident of a minority (with a little child on the throne) that made even partial rebellion possible, and that partial rebellion had not, as in England, a large minority of the people behind it. It only worked through the actual royal family itself: the discontent of the Princes and Princesses of the Blood Royal with the anomalous power of Mazarin.

They were the heroes, not only of the mob in Paris who were to raise the barricades, but the middle class which were now behind the mob, of pretty well anyone who had a grievance as a taxpayer or who was a ruined man or who had ambitions as an adventurer during such a social welter. The great Mazarin who served the queen regent Anne of Austria had continuously extended and strengthened the French power against its chief rivals, the Hapsburgs, Spanish and German. But neither the populace nor even the professional classes appreciated that. They appreciated the financial trouble much more clearly and the anomaly of an Italian man governing France under a Spanish woman.

The day of the barricades had been provoked by the arrest, at Mazarin's orders, of one of the more popular, more venerable, and (to be fair to him) least avaricious of the principal lawyers. The stroke was a bold one, but

Mazarin, for all his genius, was not lucky as his predecessor Richelieu had been lucky in bold strokes. He was made for the rapier rather than for the broadsword. He yielded.

In her distress the queen mother appealed to the soldier of the moment, whose prestige with the people was also high. She called on Condé, and Condé, in spite of his temptation to take advantage of the distress of his little cousin the king, and his detestation of Mazarin as a foreign intruder of low birth, and his dislike of the queen dowager, did consent to defend that little cousin on the throne. Anne of Austria had prayed bitterly in her chapel for help in such perils, putting her boy down on his knees beside her to offer the same plea. In the temporary support of Condé her prayer was answered; but the confusion was not resolved at all, even by that rallying of the best of the French generals to the royal side for the moment. At last he also left her.

For five years the turmoil of civil war continued. Twice the pressure was such that Mazarin had to fly. But in the end that necessary man, that only brain worthy of the task, came back to govern as fully, as unchecked, as his maker and master Richelieu had governed.

At first, in the tumult he took the queen and the royal boy off to Rueil outside Paris to the west preparatory to reducing Paris, its mob and its lawyers. But as yet there was no fighting. By the autumn (in October, '48) a settlement was arranged.

The queen and the young king had again left Paris for the Palace of St. Germain, twelve miles away to the west, in the beginning of the trouble. They went in such haste that they found the Palace unfurnished, and camped out that night as best they could on mattresses upon the floor.

The whole affair turned on the name and person of Mazarin. By February, 1651, the storm was so violent that Mazarin had to fly for refuge to Bruhl in the Electorate of Cologne. Thence he still counselled the queen in her terror, surrounded by her enemies. He could not be present himself. It was as much as his life was worth.

There arose a recurrent anarchy. Condé went off to the south. The queen dowager led her little son against him and when Condé, now at last in open rebellion, was thrust back into his government of Guyenne, beyond the Garonne, Mazarin returned, in December, 1651. His return only made the anger against him flame up more violently than ever. By the next August—1652—he fled again, this time to Bouillon, closer at hand. But he was not exiled long; before the end of the next February he was back again in Paris. Why? *The young King had recalled him.* That public summons had gone out in the name of Louis. It was obeyed and the mass of the nation was prepared for such obedience.

Now, why was this? *It was because the King was growing up and something of substance and reality was being given to that spirit of monarchy by which the French people lived.* Already Louis had been declared of age—that is, major and free to function as King—the year before. The day after his thirteenth birthday, that is, on the 6th of September, 1651, the formality had been solemnised. Of such magic was the royal name that even distinction whereby a boy of schoolroom age was deemed to have attained manhood transformed everything. Therefore it is that you find Mazarin back again at the queen's side in February, 1653. The Fronde was dying. The lawyers collapsed, and the more readily because a golden bridge was built for their retreat. Mazarin had always used public money too liberally for his private purposes as well as for his public and he enriched the parliamentarians out of those very taxes which they had made it their business to protest. You may take it as the very last date in the struggle, long after all action was over, when upon the 13th of April, 1655, Louis, now in his seventeenth year, booted and spurred, strode in and stopped short the palavers in the parliament which had half-heartedly begun.

The legends that surround that day are legends only. Louis never said on being told that the lawyers had the right to decide affairs of state, "I am the State," nor was his entry made in a brutal or domineering fashion. He was always courteous and, in these early years, retiring. But the mere fact that the King thus appeared with no great ceremony, to stand as constitutional master in their midst, was the end of all that long sedition. The Fronde was thoroughly dead.

It is remarkable, and to be borne in mind for the understanding of future things, that during the whole of the troubles the Huguenots lay quiescent. They did not budge during the whole of the Fronde. The Edict of Nantes was re-issued just before the end of the civil fighting, and Mazarin himself congratulated the Protestants on their loyalty. The reason of this Huguenot support lay in the nature of the Fronde itself. The Fronde was a by-product of the very thing it was attacking: the monarchy. The Huguenots had no standing in the monarchical tradition. It was not of their nature to be either monarchist supporters from the courtiers' point of view or to be helping any claimants for the guardianship of the young king. They had obtained, as a result of the religious wars, a great deal more than their numbers or even their wealth could have led them to expect. To enjoy what they had and to maintain it was their obvious policy.

Those years of civil war, though the fighting was desultory, were years of great misery. With public finance gone to pieces and private trade so largely interrupted, there were whole districts where life stood still, population declined and even where famine appeared. The exhaustion consequent on this gave Mazarin an addition, if that were possible, to his now unquestioned power, and he and the queen dowager settled down to complete mastery over the country, or rather, Mazarin settled down into such mastery, exercised in the name of Louis, who stood obedient to his mother.

She was, at this moment, a woman of great presence, strong featured as to face, which gave an effect of command more than her voice or decision warranted. She was an excellent figurehead for the real power of government, and the good fortune of the state had given her for companion, and lover, and servant, this singular Italian genius of her own age (they were both now just over fifty) and a political devotion at least, probably a personal devotion, worthy of her own profound attachment for him. She had known during all the early years nothing but isolation and bitterness, humiliated by her husband, still more by her husband's great minister Richelieu. Now at last she was free. And though there lay but few years between her and a painful, lingering death, those years were royal.

Was she married to Mazarin (he was bound by no vow of celibacy)? Probably—it is a question that has never been answered. Whether they were married or not, it was equivalent to a marriage, and the young king already revered the great statesman as a father.

Mazarin undertook henceforward the political education of Louis. At first there was no more than example, it gradually became watching and at last tuition. It was a task constantly and carefully pursued. The Cardinal's fine brown eyes, his delicate Italian face, his quiet speech, his every manner, were the atmosphere of the king's adolescence. There was inspired into the hitherto taciturn, reticent but secretly vigorous character of the very young man the atmosphere of the older one. He learnt from such a guide that very soul of ruling, "Continuous Action": never to know fatigue: never to lose contact: always to make one's task of governing the main function of life.

It has often been said that the Fronde with its violence, noise and goings to and fro, its perils, its occasional fierce discomforts, principally determined the king's later appetite for order and for rule.

But it is not so. He was too young. It is not the vivid troubles of childhood that determine character, still less is it the obscure memories of that time. It is example, presence and especially precept received from puberty to full stature. What made Louis were the lessons of Mazarin growing more precise and vigorous as Louis passed from adolescence to early manhood and culminating in a last intensive preparation for the Throne.

The circumstance was exactly suitable to the task. The boy was just at that age when he was beginning to watch and listen to older men. He was fifteen and the older man who was there to instruct him had not only the prestige of his fifty years and more, nor only the reputation for high political wisdom which all men repeated all around the young king. Mazarin had just won a great and permanent victory: the standing proof of his genius; he had overcome the Fronde.

For all those years in which the boy grows into a man, the last of our modern school years and the University years that follow, for eight years (1653-1660) Louis was to receive at the very moment in life when the seeds of wisdom are sown all the wisdom that the wisest of statesmen had to give in the business of statesmanship.

Moreover, the growing pupil of such a tutor was exactly consonant to the part of learner: to the reception of experience. He was silent, knowing himself to be hitherto slow of thought, even exaggerating his own backwardness in this; therefore he listened without that dangerous loss by doubt and inward contradiction which is the peril of the too brilliant young. Had he been dull as men still thought him and as he at first thought himself to be, he would have but half learnt. Had he been undetermined, he would have lost the most part; but he had already within him developed the aptitude for a task and every word Mazarin spoke in private, every example given by Mazarin at the Council table, sank in and was retained.

Here at the outset you have what is continued throughout the life of Louis, the necessity for reading into his deeds the nature of his thoughts, motives, and spiritual habit.

It was a chance in a thousand that such a king should have had at such a juncture the inheritance of two such lifetimes of experience: the combined, political legacy of Richelieu and his successor.

Mazarin's later method in the training of the lad was twofold. He would have Louis sit by him in the Council, listening to all that passed and noting how the greatest of politicians did his political work. That in itself was a full training. But to this he added much counsel in private, the nature of which we can surmise, but no particular points of which have been handed down to us. The result is the proof of his thoroughness.

On the other side very little could have been said, for Louis was by nature silent, and some so misjudged him as to think him effaced, but every word through all those hours seeped in, and there went with such wisdom, one permanent note which informed the whole—"*Govern.*" In one, simple, major rule, Mazarin framed what was to be the whole greatness of the greatest phase of the French monarchy, "Take no Prime Minister!" In other words, "Let the politician be a servant: never a master." What a man has to do can only be done by himself.

Portions of a true king's task may be delegated, but the task as a whole must be under one command.

This might have seemed a risky doctrine to inculcate in one who had as yet exercised no command, one whose own father had been overshadowed by the greater powers of a minister; but the risk was well taken, for we owe to it all the impress of the lifetime after Mazarin's death: all the story of the great reign for fifty-four years.

What Mazarin had done was enormous. We shall count the harvest when we look at the years after his passing. He had broken up the German menace on the east; for more than two hundred years to come the Germans did not combine, even for one of those brief episodes of crude unity which they attempt at long intervals in their tribal story. True neither Richelieu nor Mazarin after him could have achieved what they did had not the Germans bled themselves white in civil wars. But the folly of an adversary is not enough: it must be supplemented by wisdom on our own side.

Now in statecraft Mazarin was wise indeed. One erroneous idea, however, haunted him, and he handed it on as a bad legacy which Louis followed; the idea of absorbing the Netherlands. We shall see later how that quite feasible plan would have been fatal to France and why by the good fortune of the Nation it failed. But in all else Mazarin saw very far ahead and saw justly.

He finished off that interminable drain on French power, the old Spanish War. He was victorious against Spain on his northern frontiers * by the excellent stroke of alliance with Cromwell. He erred, as did all the men of his time, in thinking the Protectorate in England to be permanent. He looked upon Cromwell's usurpation as the beginning of a new dynasty. Statesmen are thus always short-sighted on some one point, for they are necessarily preoccupied with detail and with the situation of the moment, but Mazarin was not short-sighted; in his general aim he continued and he completed Richelieu. He left to his adopted country a secure frontier on the south, a less uncertain frontier on the north and to the east the frontier of the Rhine. For it is to Mazarin that France owed the possession of Alsace.

---

* It will be remarked that what we call Belgium today was then ruled from Spain.

The Cromwell Alliance

The rivalry between France and Spain for the support of Cromwell must be understood.

England had at this moment (1657-58) one of the best armies in Europe and an excellent navy to support it. The English navy is, of course, the creation of Charles I with his moderate and honest use of a special small tax called "Ship Money," but what had given it particular value was the long training which the sailors had received through the many years during which the Civil War lasted and the unending rivalry with the Dutch. That the English navy should be of such a character was natural enough; it had long been the best force of such a kind in Europe; but the then powerful English army requires some explanation.

The military strength of Cromwell by land lay in three things, numbers, long training and professional Cadres. The long training and professional Cadres were due to the years of Civil War followed by the conquest of Ireland and to the system which Cromwell instituted of keeping a very strong armed force, whereby the large and well endowed Puritan minority of which Cromwell was the chief could keep the rest of England in subjection. Cromwell was able to keep this large and highly trained army in being because he was able to tax on a higher scale than had ever been thought possible under the old regular governments and on a higher scale than was possible to the free governments which succeeded him. Not only were Catholic properties confiscated wholesale (and Catholics still formed a much larger proportion of England than is generally understood), but every opportunity was taken of confiscating the goods of those who had supported the constitutional government of the country against the rebellion. Very many loyalists were sold up, the rest were ransomed. Even those who enjoyed a certain favour, like Milton's brother (who had property in the City of London) had to pay a very large fine before they could redeem it. Then there were the regular subsidies, arbitrarily imposed on a very high scale, and every year the large and rising revenue from duties levied at the ports, especially the Port of London.

It was a close thing which of the two rivals, Spain or France, would secure the invaluable support of Cromwell's army. Each bid against the other and Cromwell himself was naturally flattered to see himself holding the balance in such a fashion. The Spaniards had no one to pit against the talents of Mazarin, who knew far better than any man in Europe when to bribe, whom to bribe, and how to bribe. He only won Cromwell at the last moment; but he won that prize hands down, and with such support he was able to undertake the reduction of the frontier strongholds on the Flanders border and turn out Spanish garrisons and substitute French.

The main part of the price paid for Cromwell's support was the town and port of Dunkirk, east of Calais. It was agreed that when it was reduced it should be handed over to the English Government. The Spaniards marched to relieve it: there was present in their army Condé, who, as we know, had since the Fronde been serving the Spanish Crown against his cousin, the French king. There was also serving on the Spanish side that younger Stuart who had been exiled from France together with his royal brother by Mazarin's policy; he was called the Duke of York and was later to make the last effort at retaining kingship in England, and was to fail.

Upon him I must digress, leaving for a moment the story of Dunkirk and of the Cromwell alliance, in order to consider at his first appearance in these pages, the man whose fate was so profoundly to affect all the difficult close of Louis's own life.

JAMES II IN YOUTH

This reserved, dark, determined boy, the French king's own first cousin, was to play, though indirectly at first, directly at the end, a great part in the life and reign of Louis. It is worth considering what he was even in those early years. His character has been misunderstood and, still more, ignored. Yet to understand it is to understand much of what happened to France and to England in the next half century.

James Stuart, Duke of York, grew up under certain impressions which strongly moulded his isolated, limited, but solid character. In the first place he felt himself, much more than did most lads in high position at that time, especially those cosmopolitans who were of royal birth, to be national. He was English and foreign surroundings repelled him. His recently murdered father had been the same, especially in youth. The Spaniards had seemed to Charles too alien to be dealt with when he visited them as a young man during James I's proposal of a Spanish marriage for him. Later, when the marriage had been concluded with Henrietta Maria, princess of France, daughter of Henry IV, sister of Louis XIII and aunt of Louis XIV, it had worked very ill during the first years. Frenchmen exasperated Charles. These monsieurs—"mousers" he called them—who had come over to the Court with his young wife, Charles drove out—"like wild beasts," to use his own expression. Therefore the French mother of this boy, James, had no effect upon him save an effect of reaction. She was strongly attached to the general Catholicism of Europe. She and those about her did everything to make the growing lad understand that philosophy, appreciate it and at last embrace it. Such pressure bred in him a reaction of the strongest kind. Never would he have any truck with the Church of Rome; he was an Englishman!

This new world into which he had been pitched was odious to him in that aspect as in every other. His elder brother, Charles, inheriting the royal crown of England at his father's death, was more absorbent though also unyielding to the pressure brought upon him. But in Charles's case the pressure was less, for a king is a king, and he was born to be king by right of a nation now in the main Protestant. That nation had more claim on him than his mother, and when it came years afterwards to the saving of the crown whereto he was so unexpectedly restored, Charles knew very well that the acceptation of Catholicism would be fatal. He must follow the religion of those who counted most among his subjects, those who were much the more numerous, those who disposed of most wealth. With James, there was no such cause for his elders to relax their efforts. He was only a younger son; his conversion could more easily be urged. But he stood out rigorously, the strength of his conviction increasing with the years. Protestant he was born, Protestant he would live. This Romish religion was that of the magnificent court in dependence upon which he found himself now in exile.* It *was* dependence, and that alone, apart from his internal conviction, would have turned his face away resolutely from the Court Faith: not only resolutely but defiantly; not only defiantly but with an increasing will not to be entrapped, not to be coerced, not to be other than he was, a strongly Protestant young Englishman. Such was James II at twenty-four.

---

*   He had escaped at the age of fifteen from England and from Cromwell, who would probably have murdered James as he did, just after, James's father. For had he not escaped he would have been a leader of plots against the Protector. He took a commission under Turenne in the French forces, but when Mazarin turned him out, to please Cromwell, he went over to the Spanish side of the war under Condé. That is why we now find him here before Dunkirk at the age of twenty-four in 1658.

That idealisation of home things, in the sense of English things, remained with James all his life. Very famous is the cry which escaped from him at the end of his long lifetime, standing on the cliffs and watching English seamen board a French man-of-war below: he exulted in their courage. He was not born to the throne of England, he was not to know for many years that this throne must at last be his, but he was English as none of that younger generation were English; he was if anything too national for a royalty of his day. Young boys often make a national idol of this kind in their hearts especially when they are in exile, still more if they are thrown into an international air; it becomes part of their persons which they guard as a man guards the things most intimate to his soul. It was consonant to such a character that James should take now, on the restoration of his family, when his brother Charles II was on the English throne, that which was becoming essential to England, the growth of her power by sea. A false legend pretends that this determination of the English political life by the fleet was Elizabethan. It was nothing of the kind. There was no fleet in Elizabeth's day. The Cecils never made one, and the England of that older generation was too profoundly divided between its fiercely persecuted ancestral religion and the interests of its new millionaires, the enthusiasm of its small but growing Puritan minority, to be greatly preoccupied with so special an interest, so peculiar a preoccupation, as the making of a fleet. But this young boy, James Stuart, was to be the maker of the fleet of England. It was prepared in his childhood by the Commonwealth, the first epoch in which there grew up the long service of a professional body of sailors, long inheriting, as it were, the men-of-war which were the permanent property of the government.

Charles, his father, having begun the thing and seeing the necessity of it, had wisely determined upon a special fund for the making of the fleet. All his reward was revolt of the wealthy against such a tax, moderate though it was, and for generations the Whig historians made of the phrase "Ship Money" a sort of offensive tag. To this day the last of them still quote these two words as they do the two words "Star Chamber" to brand the monstrous wickedness of royal authority and to proclaim the power of the rich under the title of "the people." This fleet which Charles had made against such opposition, which the wealthy Hampden and the rest had done their best to ruin before it was yet in full being, and which the Commonwealth had perfected through the accident of a long service such as its wars involved and its necessity of defence against a Restoration, devolved upon young James Stuart when he became Lord High Admiral of England. His brother Charles, the king, was wrapped up also in the making and increase of the English force upon the narrow seas, but it was James who, with untiring industry, supported by able men whom he had in part chosen, completed the new arm and made it what it was to be ever since. James II, as Duke of York, is the Founder of English sea power in organised and permanent form. He created, and he was the first to create, a corps of professional naval officers serving entirely without a break, their training as lads secured by his institution of Midshipmen. *

His courage inspired that fleet in its great actions, notably in Sole Bay. He risked his life very finely during the longest and most hotly contested of the naval actions against the Dutch, standing on his deck he was spattered with the blood of his companions at his side and remained undisturbed. He also developed quite early in life a talent for command by sea, inventing the new system of

---

* The name was at first a sort of joke, the original term "midshipman" applied to non-commissioned officers. The young gentlemen nominated to the fleet were put under these and assimilated to them.

signalling and the new tactic of fighting in line with which he replaced the old ship-to-ship action. His name should be remembered not only as foundational but as one of the greatest of the sea captains of England. The hatred and opposition of that oligarchy which was gradually mastering all the English public life and which ended by supplanting the Crown altogether, broke his career mid-way, but in later years he once more could organise for a while that naval arm which he had principally made and to which he was so devoted. When he died in exile his last instructions to his son insisted on the prime function of English policy: "Look to your Fleet."

That vivid picture of England and English power which inhabited the closed mind of James, and the corresponding mistrust and even disgust for the foreigner—which meant for him the Frenchman—never left him. Though when he came to defeat and to exile, his cousin, the great King of France, had received him warmly and defended his cause with chivalric energy, he still resented. We shall see it accountable in large measure for that fatal error whereby he estranged his great cousin in the very crisis of his own fate. Louis XIV would have saved him from the danger of William of Orange; James refused that necessary aid and so lost his throne. Later when he was attempting to recover the Crown with insufficient untrained troops and still more insufficient artillery in Ireland, he felt most bitterly even the small help which Louis chose to send. With him we shall deal again later, but he must here be introduced as he was in those bitter days of his adolescence which formed him.

In manhood he was to be converted to Catholicism by the strong influence of that very remarkable woman, his wife, Anne Hyde; once converted his tenacious character remained anchored to the new conviction. But never must it be forgotten that during the years when the mind is formed, James was not only intensely national in spirit but thought that patriotism of his indivisible from the religion of those who were to be his subjects and from the Anglican Church for which his father had laid down his life.

When he had tardily accepted his wife's religion he still held himself the natural head of the Establishment. The man is lied about and caricatured in our official history. James had very bad judgment and obstinate misunderstanding of human motives. But he had the qualities which accompany such defects: sincerity and an iron devotion to duty.

THE FALL OF DUNKIRK

To return to Dunkirk:

Cromwell then lent his fine six regiments, backed by ample shipping and transport, for the reduction of Dunkirk.

It was said by men of the next generation who had knowledge of past political affairs from state papers and the rest, that Cromwell had intended, after getting Dunkirk as a reward for helping the French, to turn round and get Calais as a reward for helping the Spaniards. The story is not improbable, for it fits in well with his character and with his well-known hesitation as to which of the two rivals he should support, and with his natural desire to confirm his power: for Calais was a word deeply rooted in the English imagination and tradition. It must always be remembered that Calais was not a French town in the sense that Boulogne was a French town; it was Flemish speaking, just as Dunkirk was. Not that people cared much in those days about the popular language, but there would have seemed nothing outrageous in making Calais the sequel to Dunkirk. As it was, Cromwell died and the project, if there was such a project, died with him.

The resistance of the Spaniards was determined and prolonged, but failed, largely because their commander had not
allowed for the fall of the tide. His right, stretching to the
east coast, lay open, and the French cavalry could act at will
upon the hard sand. While the main forces, especially the
English, were engaged in the sandhills above high water
mark and filling the belt between the coast and the big
parallel draining ditch inland, a mounted detachment coming up along the shore charged the Spanish line in flank,
and this determined the fate of the fortress. Soon after it
surrendered and was duly handed over to Cromwell's forces.

The whole thing was a triumph for Mazarin's policy. He
had caused the young king to give Cromwell the royal title
of "Cousin," he had sent the exiled Stuarts out of France,
and the general manoeuvre had so shaken the Spanish hold
upon the frontier that the line began to crumble. Oudenarde was taken, and Ypres, and Furnes. It was like a fore-
taste of the big wave of invasion which was to come later
when the young king should be fully in the saddle and pro-
posing to claim his wife's inheritance of the Netherlands.

Meanwhile this episode of warfare led to something
which determined the character of Louis's life. It led
to something on the inner spiritual side which was all-
important to his character and fate. It led to that intense,
exalted, flaming experience whereon his fate turned in this
his twentieth year.

Mary Mancini was to bend over him with devotion in
the very article of death.

The few weeks that follow are of such capital moment
in the story of the King's soul that they deserve a volume
apart. All the man's self was molten, cast and formed in
that furnace. Yet I must put them briefly as they themselves
were brief: but they were ever at his side from this very
early youth till the hour of death—and perhaps beyond.

3
The Annealing of the King

IT HAPPENED THUS:

The graves of the dead in the sandy soil surrounding Dunkirk, where the action of the siege had been laid, were exposed by the sea waves: after the fall of the city they spread a pestilence; Louis in the full eagerness of his youth was struck down.

It was a sudden business; not long before, he had ridden forward to within a musket shot of Bergues when that fortress was under siege. He had shown a fine contempt for death—which he was to repeat in sickness as on the field. The fever was excessive: he was despaired of. Anjou, his younger brother, was already receiving the visits of the courtiers against the approaching day when the death of Louis should put him upon the throne. But Anjou did not desire that day. His effeminate nature was still affectionate and perhaps still untainted. He sincerely suffered, as did the Queen, as also did Mazarin, whose anxiety it is unjust to put down only to the threatened disturbance of his rule.

The young man looked death fairly in the face, a confrontation the memory of which sunk into him forever. His mind remained clear; there was no delirium; he expected the end. He was in fact saved by the intervention of a local doctor from Abbeville, but before the fever left him one face had been before him and one presence he knew to have haunted the place where he lay in Calais to which they had removed him. The face and the presence, the tenderness and now the anguish, of Mary Mancini.

There falls upon some very few human lives an experience transcending every other. They that have received it stand separate from all their fellows. It has no name.

To call it exalted love or love inspired means nothing. The word "love" is used in every tongue and by all mankind to mean things so different, so varying in degree and quality, that to use it here is meaningless. It has no name.

The thing has no name. For names attach only to things generally known and *this* thing, a revelation, is known to very few and is incommunicable. The only parallel to it is the experience of the mystics, their momentary union with the Divine. This, those who have been so transfigured can never later describe.

But—though what Mary Mancini awoke in him has no name—we can call it a flame of fire. It seized his whole being as from without and from above. It is not of mortality; and in one great English line it has been justly saluted "the ultimate outpost of Eternity." Such a Visitor met Louis in his twentieth year.

Mary Mancini was two years younger. At Fontainebleau an exceptional affection had arisen between them, so marked that it bred anxiety in those who watched them and were responsible for the State. That affection had grown in repeated visits to the house of her invalid mother, the sister of Mazarin, whom the Cardinal had brought to France from Italy. Her household was that in which the young king had come to be most at home, for he was not so with his own blood. Mary's sister Olympia, lively, more openly vital, touched with wit, had attracted him; but Mary meant more to him and again more. Yet it was but affection growing familiar. At last, during this encounter of his with death at Calais, the shaft struck home and all was transformed. On his recovery they two breathed the air of Paradise.

Here the imperfect and presumptuous will say: "It is the story of millions: all first love is so." Not at all; no more than dreams are Visions. Not millions, but one in many millions, and then, in millions more one other, in millions more again one other are thus elect of the gods.

It will be asked: "How can you affirm so mighty a truth of one silent lad dead these two centuries ago? Louis was limited and of the common sort, one who only became great through industrious aptitude for a great function. Moreover he left no hint of all this—indeed, less record than do most men leave of what has pierced their souls. How then do you know?" By one unfailing test: the immortal passage left him immune to Passion henceforward forever.

He was amative. He was vigorous, sane, normal, of especial inclination to women, and not so much as considering restraint in those affairs. Such men—especially if they have all that fortune can give—become the possession as well as the possessors. Passion takes them, sometimes for good and all, and in one bond or, more often, in successive episodes, they give of themselves and are absorbed in another. They are subjected and enthralled, even if only for a time. With those who have known the one much greater thing it cannot be so. It was not so with Louis. For fifty-eight years he lived on as what is called a lover and what was in all the last half of his life and time wedlock. In all that complete tale of a human life from its early beginnings to its very distant end he never gave himself again. He was never again absorbed in another. The women, even that last one to whom he was faithful so long, on into old age, were external to his very heart and had it not.

For this major, this compelling desire consumes the sensibility of man. If it be satisfied it consecrates. If it be frustrated it sears and therefore anneals.

❋   ❋   ❋

There followed a blazing insistence of demand by Louis for Mary Mancini. In nothing had he yet ordered though

65

he had been crowned and anointed King some years—for the Kings of France were thus solemnly enthroned on their legal majority. Nor did he now act as King but as himself—as a human soul free to make a supreme choice, lacking which he might as well not live. He demanded in vain. The union was forbidden him.

Anne of Austria imperiously forbade it: Mazarin firmly. It is not true to say (as some contemporaries believed) that Mazarin had hoped to see one of his blood upon the throne—to the ruin of the throne. His life, his whole self, is a contradiction of that. To marry a subject, that subject not even of rank—a steward's family—to ask the court to accept Mary Mancini would have dealt the Monarchy a blow of incalculable severity—perhaps mortal. The thing was dismissed as fantastic and impossible.

One voice spoke otherwise. Christina of Sweden, herself in voluntary exile and abdication, said openly that the marriage ought to be, and the rest thrown overboard, as she herself had thrown overboard the business of ruling. She herself had been of the Caste and of the quasi-divine office, a queen, and therefore she spoke with authority. But she was not heard. Louis was not a living soul answerable to itself and its Vision. He was France and therefore he himself must be broken and lost in Kingship.

Now indeed did he know the meaning of that word "Monarchy." It weighed more than all the world. Its reality and mass crushed all on which it lay, and first of all the man in whom it *was*.

The two held close to one another as do lovers on the approach of death. He with his forward young face full-lipped and eager, she with the large good eyes, intelligent, slightly smiling—to him—black, and brilliant as jet in the fine pallor of her face.

All day he would be at her side. In the last long voyage—not five months after Calais—he rode hour by hour at the door of her coach, till the court reached Lyons—during the Savoyard farce: for Mazarin, even while designing the Spanish marriage for his King, had pretended to consider a marriage with the House of Savoy.

Then, when it was plain that he was lost to her, she struggled for a while: would rouse him by jealousy. Then—even on the eve of his espousal to Spain—she called him back to her. Then all was over. When the court had returned after the Spanish marriage to Paris she still shone—but her own marriage and departure was arranged: with a Colonna, great enough. She was off to Italy, and that was the end. But those who have written "she was soon forgotten" know nothing of mankind.

THE SPANISH MARRIAGE

The young King went off southward to the Spanish marriage, to his cousin, King Philip's daughter, and there he found at the frontier a good-natured, submissive, fair little dwarf, with hardly anything to say for herself. And that was the Spanish marriage.

The public ceremony was in the church of St. Jean de Luz, a fine big barrel of a church, on the 15th of June, 1660; the solemn entry into Paris on the 26th of August, and, from one window, two women looked out at the state coach passing by; one was Mary Mancini, by her side was another, who knew nothing as yet of what she would mean in the future: the wife of Scarron.

II
The Founding of All
(*Without*)

1661–1667

4
Louis Emerges

IMMEDIATELY UPON MAZARIN'S death (March, 1661) there happened something with which history is so familiar that it has become worn smooth by usage and has lost its emphasis, although it is a major landmark in the story of European institutions.

There is also about that "something" a quality so individual that it stands quite apart from other transitions of the kind. One who was, in years, little more than a boy, a young man twenty-two and a half years old, one who had been effaced both deliberately by his seniors (they had kept him in the background) and also by what we now see to be his own rigid hitherto concealed *Will*, emerged in a single moment as Master of the State.

Mazarin had been everything and had done everything. He had been to the France of his day what the English Prime Minister was to the English State during the highest moment of English parliamentary government under Victoria in the nineteenth century—and much more. For the Prime Ministers of the English were but class leaders in an oligarchy: Mazarin was an individual chief at whose quiet orders defeated rebels and even the lawyers stood attentive. Mazarin had governed precariously but really from Louis XIII's death in 1643 till the end of the Fronde ten years later: thence onward for the last eight years of his life he had governed supremely. All the public plan and every detail had depended upon him.

Now that he was dead the spokesman of the Estates of the Realm, approaching the very young king, asked him to whom they should refer in future for orders, expecting the answer always hitherto given on a change of authority, that this man or that would take the place of the dead all-powerful minister. Louis, formed by Mazarin, answered "To Me." Henceforward everything whatsoever was to depend upon him. No point could be finally fixed save by his direct authority. Henceforward a King *ruled*: full Monarchy had suddenly appeared.

It had come in the person of one head, and that head of such an age! Henceforward to the end Louis was to be not only Master, but in great part Maker, of the State, and when we say "henceforward to the end" it means from this first unexpected grasp of power in the middle of his twenty-third year to his death at seventy-seven. Is it not true that nothing of the sort had been known before since the last effective Emperor of the West?

Men are great through a great function: are made great by that function if the function be great, and make the function greater by their own greatness. So it is with every craftsman and so it was with this man in the chief craft of kingship. He dedicated himself, so young, to indefatigable daily labour, to the weighing of issues, to the comprehension of advice and to the framing and the carrying out of plans. Had there been in him what is called creative genius he could not have thus acted. He had the good fortune to lack the fire and the vagary of genius. That good fortune of his was a good fortune for his country also.

How should the task be undertaken by one so very young, and acting, apparently, single-handed?

It could not have been undertaken at all had he indeed been single-handed. Louis inherited, and carried on for the earlier part of his reign triumphantly with, the aid of singularly able men attached to his fortunes and working at his side. They had been in office before he came out into the open for they were older than himself and had been trained, every one of them, by the man who had also trained himself. Many of these pass through the story of the reign in their order. Among the most effective we shall find one who did not come into great play until after the first years were over, Vauban; but at the beginning you have names which are a bridge, as it were, between the Cardinal under whom Louis's own youth had been formed and the high development of his own active reign.

It is part of fate that great rulers find to their hand exceptional servants. The thing is not a coincidence, it is cause and effect. He that desires to govern, that has the appetite and the instinct for government and the energy to conceive and bring into being, will discover his own instruments. But also those instruments which he inherits will he use to right purpose.

And there is more than this: the attraction is mutual. For an exceptional rule raises of itself as exceptional a staff by an instinctive action. And there is yet more: latent powers are brought to life; insufficient development matures; the mere light of glory is permeated by the warmth of achievement. Therefore have you the Pleiad of poets as a testimony to the greatness of Ronsard; his marshals as a testimony to Napoleon.

Such groups of acting men go with monarchy, not with aristocracy. For Aristocratic states are Oligarchies and in Oligarchies the individual is merged in his social class. As for Democracies, those brief and brilliant little things— brief in their glory, brilliant in their high names—individuals do stand out, isolated, among them, but these names form no coherent body of talent. Consider the men who served Louis XIV and remember that each is a function of the reign, that it was he and the monarchy for which he stood which gave them their cohesion, that it was, he, and the Monarchy, which nourished their careers by Authority and gave to the whole of their business a continuity unbroken through long years.

The first name in that galaxy is Colbert, not because he had a higher standard but because the duties he performed were of the highest effect, for it was he who saved the finances and erected the principles of order; it was he also who created a Navy.

The second is Louvois, who levied and organised the new Armies wherewith that foreign policy was carried out.

The third is Lionne, who conducted (but conducted under orders) the foreign policy of the opening reign.

But before these three could come into action under the Monarchy the prime obstacle to such action must be removed. That obstacle was the Money-power, incarnate in Fouquet, nominally the Minister of Finance, but really representative and chief of all the credit-mongers large and small who at once battened on society and held by a hundred handles the machinery of the State.

In commercial societies—which are always aristocratic—credit-mongering is admitted. It is a prime political function working in the open and interwoven with all the life of government. The Money-power and the State are one. But in societies based on the peasant and the craftsman it is otherwise. Such societies when small and simple may flourish as democracies; but when they grow old, complicated, of large population, they must be Monarchic, directed from one exalted post, or they fall into an impotent chaos. To such central authority the Money-power is hostile: a rival, who will destroy the King unless the King masters it. Therefore the first task of the New Reign was the breaking of the Money-power. Swiftly and most thoroughly did Louis perform that task.

5

Fouquet and the Breaking of the Money-Power

I N THE FIRST WEEKS OF THE REIGN
Fouquet was one of the small intimate group of
administrators, who sat in private with the young
King, determining public affairs. Louis had inherited him
from Mazarin, for under Mazarin Fouquet had risen to be
superintendent of the finances. It was he who controlled
the gathering and spending of a National Revenue. Colbert, whose name was to be identified with the French
Treasury for half a lifetime, was as yet but a subordinate
watching his chance to rise.

The Cardinal had never attempted to master the money-
power. His failure to do so was in part due to necessity, but also in part due to long habit, confirmed by the
immobility of old age. Moreover, after the long chaos of
the Huguenot rebellion—1560-1590—and the consequent
eclipse of French international power, the looting of the
State by its higher servants had become traditional. Sully,
the great Huguenot companion and survivor of Henry IV,
is an example. How shamefully he had blackmailed the
government of Henry's widow after Henry's death!

Mazarin may not have fully appreciated how very bad
and corrupt Fouquet's administration of the public revenue was. He certainly had a general knowledge of it but
not a detailed one. He had been hampered at the very
beginning of his ministry by utter lack of funds. We know
how this ridiculous and shameful condition of public affairs

had afflicted every Government in Christendom after the catastrophic economic changes of the preceding century. The precious metals of the American mines, a flood of silver, had, on the completion of the Spanish conquest of Central and Southern America, swamped the old currency of Europe. Prices rose everywhere, continuously and enormously. What a man could buy for one pound when Henry VIII of England died,* he could hardly have bought for three pounds a long lifetime after, when James I came to the throne. And prices continued to rise on through the seventeenth century. They had multiplied by something like eight before its close.

Now we all know from unhappy modern experience, how much society is disturbed by changes in the real value of currency, and what made it worse in the seventeenth century was that the Government of every country, the "Crown," got most of its revenue in customary, not competitive, form. Thus the lands of the crown paid rents: but the rents were not the full value obtainable: they were fixed. Their nominal value in currency remained the same, while their real value was perpetually rising. The crown of England, like the crown of France, would get so much a year from such and such a source—say, royal dues payable on a set of fishing rights—inherited from feudal times; and the money value of these dues remained unchanged. But the cost of everything which the crown had to *buy*—labour, materials, food, etc.—was rising by three, four, five times the old amount. The crown had to pay out larger and larger sums for all that the state needed, yet it got no more from its fixed, ancient sources of revenue.

At the same time, all the change, social and economic, which was creating the modern State, made things necessary

---

* "One pound" that is, at full value. The nominal pound at Henry's death was worth far less, for it had been deliberately depreciated and falsified by government, as money is today.

to the government more expensive continually. For instance, the armed ships were growing larger and their armament heavier, their provision of powder greater and their crews more numerous. Moreover, national navies were becoming permanent, instead of being, as they had been under Elizabeth in England and the Valois kings in France, temporary.

The equipment of infantry even was growing more complicated, and the administrations and the people occupied on them were increasing continually.

From all this and much else a seventeenth-century government, when it was a Monarchy based on agriculture and not an Oligarchy based on trade, grew more and more indebted and at its wits' end for funds. That state of affairs was paradise for the dealers in credit—the moneylenders. The Kings and their Ministers lived from hand to mouth, borrowing, at high interest, short loans which had to be perpetually renewed. They never paid less than eight per cent.—often twelve. They mortgaged future revenue, and were driven to every shift to procure the wherewithal for immediate necessities. That strain broke the English Monarchy at last. It came very near to breaking the French Monarchy.

Fouquet, running the financial machine of France independently of any real control, was not only amassing an enormous fortune for himself (from which he made advances to the Queen Regent and to Mazarin) but also acting as Patron and example to the herd of lesser and similar men down to the little local moneylender of the country town, to whom the municipality came, cap in hand, and the unfortunate taxpayers as well.

It is not just to Fouquet, the man, to make him out a mere villain. He had the base greed and the lack of proportion which we find repeatedly in public men occupying lucrative positions, but, morally, it is something to his credit that he was so obvious and simple in his greed, in his passion for display and in his grasping at every perquisite, commission, rake-off, profit, or even bribe that fell in his way.

He met with no obstacles. He was already well on in the forties when Mazarin died and had been rising in the treasury service for years. Since he was a lad Fouquet had been in the heart of state affairs. He shared with another the command of the whole treasury machine before he was forty. By the time the active reign of Louis began he was master of the state on its financial side.

On the death of Mazarin he was, to the young King, what a man would be in modern England who should be permanent under-Secretary to the Treasury and head of the Bank of England combined. He stood thus almost without any serious check upon him, for the eight years before Louis took over active power. We have seen how he lent money personally to those who were identical with the State and even to the State itself. Perhaps he called himself patriotic and generous in so doing, but he repaid himself handsomely. He took profits off public contracts in every conceivable way. Our moderns, as they read of him, will read of him with mixed feelings for he lived in a time when, on the one hand, the opportunities for private enrichment by a public man were boundless, but, on the other hand he lived in a time when a large private fortune could challenge the State itself because the income of the State compared with large private incomes was so much smaller than it is now. Today the largest amount amassed by an individual is insignificant compared with the general revenue. A private fortune of ten million pounds is but one per cent. of the total government and municipal revenue. In Fouquet's time it was greater than the whole revenue. Therefore the evil done by such men was greater and more likely to call down vengeance.

One favourite method of his was to give, in payment for a contract, a paper promise, not cash; to negotiate that paper at a heavy discount; then to present the full bill for payment by the Treasury and to keep the difference.

He also bribed. He bribed everybody, he bribed Soissons, he bribed Lionne, he bribed the Queen's almoner and he even *tried* to bribe the King's confessor! He was, in principle, no worse in all this than the average public man of his own or any other time. But he was quite out of proportion. It was this that ruined him. A politician today may sell peerages at large and take his commission as is the practice of commerce; no one thinks the worse of him. But if, instead of taking his commission like anyone else, he asks exorbitant sums and forces the pace as well, he will be blown upon and lose his chance of carrying on, even in a country governed by politicians. In a country governed by a king he runs a greater risk than that. But against such a man the government could have done nothing if he and Fouquet and the rest had been individuals jumbled up together in a common oligarchy. There being a young master of the state, a king, Fouquet's extravagant ostentation cried out against the proper headship of Louis.

Fouquet took it for granted that a very young king, surrounded by new pleasures, and greatly drawn towards them, could be fobbed off with any accounts presented to him. He would not have the leisure, let alone the capacity, to find his way through a maze of figures.

Fouquet, then, had depended upon the courtesy and indolence of an inexperienced, very young, royal master. He bowed profoundly as he presented cooked accounts, trusting to the muddlement of an untrained brain presented with page upon page of figures. As for Colbert, who helped to look over those figures, Fouquet did not take him seriously, wherein he badly bungled. There came suddenly that order for Fouquet's arrest, and his splendour was cut off in a night.

Such a fall was the most striking example Europe could have been given of what monarchy was about to mean.

Here, at the very entry into his sovereignty, the new and greatest monarch had tried a fall with the money-power, and the money-power lay bleeding.

It is possible that Fouquet's plan of hoodwinking Louis would have succeeded, but for the rivalry of Colbert, who was watching his opportunity to replace Fouquet. To that we will return in a moment, but the Will that acted, and the Hand that struck, were the Will and the Hand of Louis.

It was during that summer of '61, the bright sunrise of his reign, when the festivities of Fontainebleau were at their height, that the plan was secretly drawn up for the ruin of Fouquet. In September (that is, before the first six months were over), just at the moment when Louis was completing his twenty-third year, Fouquet was arrested at Nantes.

He might have fled oversea, had not the King's action been as sudden as it was. His trial was prepared by officers of the Crown, and the incriminating documents and reports submitted to the High Court which was to judge him. The delays were prolonged over the better part of three years. It was not until 1664 that sentence was delivered, and when it came it was a sentence far too mild. Had not the Executive, that is the King, overridden the Lawyers, nothing that followed could have cured the nation of its mortal disease, a disease from which modern France is now in danger of death.

It was amply evident that the Superintendent had abominably abused his position, but dog does not eat dog, class interest coincides with individual interest where the great are concerned. It is to check, tame and dominate such conspiracies that Monarchy was invented.

We may neglect as subsidiary or even unimportant all the gossip that gathers round the arrest and the supposed motives of every personal sort directing the young King. There may or may not have been some correspondence between Fouquet and La Vallière, as there certainly was a mass of correspondence between him and the ladies about the Court, particularly those attached to Henrietta of England and the Queen Mother. There was of course the personal rivalry of Colbert. There was the jealousy aroused by his extravagant display, and a general story goes that Louis had been particularly offended by the magnificence of a special feast at Vaux, the splendid palace of the financier.*

The upshot of this long trial, then, was a sentence unexpectedly mild and insufficient to the policy of the state. This amiable, vain, most able, debauched, corrupt and vigorous man was condemned to exile and to the confiscation of his goods. The first part of this sentence meant no very severe penalty—troublesome rather than poignant. Such men can live anywhere. The second part must not be taken literally. It would mean, of course, a very heavy loss of immediate wealth, but certainly not a total loss of such wealth and perhaps no ultimate loss at all. A great deal of his possessions in one way or another would be present for his use as always happens in cases of this kind, and he could have built up another fortune quickly by his old connections. Such men are said to be ruined by such accidents, but the term is relative.

The causes of so imperfect a conclusion are various. He had friends on all sides, bound up with the whole life of the time, many of them among the highest felt a genuine affection for him, some were even touched by that quality, rare among the rich, of gratitude—and certainly he had been prodigal of his wealth in gifts of every kind to them as to all the smart world. Then there was the point of honour specially felt by those among his judges who were known to be particularly hostile, for lawyers pique themselves upon the outward forms of impartiality.

---

* All that story is confused. Even the details do not correspond. There were contributory factors of every kind, but the only one that counts, the one determining the whole affair, was the struggle between public kingship and private gold.

But the major cause of the leniency shown by the judges was without a doubt the still vigorous quarrel between the lawyers and the Crown. Of all those whom true Monarchy threatens, the lawyers come next after the money-power, which indeed they commonly serve. In the past years it had been the Parlement, that is the highest expression of the Lawyers' Guild in France, which had, as we have seen, been half of the resistance to the throne during the minority. Even by 1664, let alone three years earlier when the trial began and the tone of the proceedings was started, the lawyers had not yet realised what the restored kingship was to be: its majesty and supreme power.

Upon this sentence there followed something which vividly shows the temper of the new reign and the practical value of the young King in action.

Louis commuted Fouquet's sentence by right of his prerogative. Such a right in modern times has nearly always been interpreted to mean pardon or mitigation of the penalty pronounced, in this case the very opposite was done. Louis ordered this man, the Money-power in person, to be not exiled but imprisoned: to be imprisoned in a fortress and that the most distant and inaccessible of his fortresses: not only to be imprisoned but to be cut off from all communication. Thus only could a man who had relations with a whole web of secret espionage and intrigue within and without the kingdom be reduced to impotence.

The seclusion ordered was absolute. Fouquet might indeed read such books as were sparingly afforded him, but he might not write a line, he might not speak upon any but petty personal matters to St. Mars, the Governor of Pignerolo, that stronghold properly Italian, naturally dependent on Savoy, on the further side of the Alps, which was the outpost or bastion of French power there. In an isolation of such a kind Fouquet was held for years. It was an isolation only slightly relaxed in the last years before his death, which fell (though we are not quite certain of the date) presumably when he was sixty-six, after he had thus been cut off from men for nineteen years; for just at the end his wife and his family were allowed to be with him inside the walls, his wife even sharing his room and his daughter close at hand in the same building.

So ended Fouquet. His fate was not an example of cruelty, cruel though it was, still less was it an example of vindictiveness, though Colbert, who was behind the King in the whole affair, was vindictive enough; it was an example of true policy, of political sense. The money-power—centralised, backed by experience and supported by a whole network of interests and understandings woven through a course of years, become a habit of mind with a whole world of people in touch with each other at home and abroad, permanent, lucid, more elusive than any other kind of strength and ubiquitous as is no other kind of strength—the money-power thus developed is almost invincible. The hydra can be destroyed only by one vigorous, throttling grasp at the common root of its manifold neck.

There was a parallel here between what Louis did in 1664 and what his ancestor, King Philip, had done in 1307, when he crushed the Templars who had a banker's grip upon all Europe. Nothing short of what the King did would have served himself or the State. The threads were torn and the paralysing conspiracy was at an end.

Of all the acts which Monarchy decided and effected in that long reign, this one coming at its outset was the most effective and was the foundation for all the rest.

6

Colbert

SO MUCH FOR FOUQUET: NOW FOR
the three men who took over the main departments
of State work under the unwearied and close super-
vision of Louis: Colbert, Le Tellier (to be followed by his
son Louvois) and Hugh de Lionne. The first, Colbert, took
over the economic side, including the building of the new
Navy. The second, Le Tellier, built up the new Army. The
third, Lionne, continued, enhanced and solidified that Foreign Policy on which the fame of the period is based. For
twenty years—the first half of which was Lionne's administration—the French Crown and people increased steadily
and largely in external Power.

Of those men, inherited from the older generation but
without a doubt sustained and developed by Louis himself,
of those men who were making the great reign before the
reign began, but who would not have made the great reign
but for their king, Colbert is not the greatest nor even the
most remarkable, but the most typical and, in his effects,
the most enduring.

His special mark was, like that of Le Tellier and of Le
Tellier's son Louvois after him, a combination of exactitude and hard work. These three men, Le Tellier, his
son Louvois, and Colbert, put at the service of the state
the most valuable of French virtues: precision combined
with industry. But Colbert had neither the defects nor the
inspiration of his colleagues. He could pursue an opponent
tenaciously but not privately. In other words, he did not
waste effort on the side issue of his personal feelings. When

he did fight as an ally and prompter to the King in one great action with one opponent, Fouquet, he worked after a fashion of which the animus has been exaggerated. Perhaps his own ambition to obtain Fouquet's office came into his motives, but more than his own ambition his disgust with corruption and still more his exasperation at waste came into them as also that which so often urges able men, the craving for opportunity. His drive against Fouquet had been a struggle by a State servant waged in favour of the State. That Colbert, nineteen years older than his master, should have supplanted Fouquet when the young Louis destroyed that parasite is symbolic of the new time; it was a direct triumph of efficient administration.

Colbert now just over forty came of sound commercial people, a family of Champagne with large mercantile interests. Theoretically these men were, by tenure of some parcel or other, noble, and would have been angry to have been called anything else. In practice they were solidly bourgeois in family tradition. In his early youth he had travelled widely in the interests of his uncle's business. That uncle had put him into a financial firm who were bankers for Mazarin, and Le Tellier presented him to the cardinal. Mazarin spotted the young man at once, took him into a sort of partnership in work, discovered him to be exceptional in his passion for detail, exactitude and long hours: for getting things done. Mazarin, who knew men, knew at once that he had found something valuable. There is a story that the cardinal, a little before he died, told the young king that he owed the crown everything a subject could give, but that he acquitted the debt in giving him Colbert.

Louis, just entering on active monarchy, found thus at his service one long trained in public affairs, dark, spare, reticent, and devoted. He took over this dynamic agent of civil service. Louis, from that twenty-third year of his, after the cardinal had died, when he suddenly announced that he was going to rule single-handed, had Colbert continuously at his side, and for twenty years the two men, the elder and the younger, were at work hand in hand.

Colbert was a man by nature open to discontent—but his eyes alone betrayed that ill-ease which was relieved by a certain French mockery, never expressed in words, but occasionally apparent in his glance.

Colbert had advanced his own fortune as well as Mazarin's. He was alive to the private profits which office can yield. He did not escape that social vanity which is the chief temptation of men who rise slowly into a rank slightly higher than their own. He would allude to his seigniorial rights and wealth briefly but in rather too emphatic a fashion. But as a whole his private habit of speech and gesture was, if anything, too rigid and there was a sort of tonelessness in his voice which made him the less liked by the livelier wits of a brilliant time—especially less praised by the women in proportion to their talents of the drawing-room and the writing desk. He served to the end very faithfully but later on without zeal, rather by routine, and might be taken by a modern for the very pattern of a high civil servant, by a ruler as the model for a minister—apart from foreign affairs.

His effect was immediate. Following on the fiscal debauch of Fouquet he restored all by the magic of method and direction and he changed the whole economic position within two years.

The year 1662 had not ended before he had put the Crown financially upon its feet. There was to be any amount of trouble in the future, revenue was not to suffice for the expenditure of the great wars, in every fashion the Crown would find itself embarrassed and driven to expedients during that ceaseless struggle to establish secure frontiers and to maintain them against increasing coalitions; Colbert himself was to sink under the strain before he died, and, indirectly as a consequence of the strain, lose the gratitude

of the man for whom he had done all. But Colbert's combination of work and exactitude had founded the realm.

What Colbert *was* in the management of finance, those
first few months sufficiently showed. There had been no true
fleet in 1661. Before the end of 1662 there were twenty-four
ships of various rates. Nothing very grand, but a beginning
for a nation which had been helpless at sea in the presence of Holland and England: "the maritime powers." The
United Provinces ("Holland" today) had been developing
their incomparable sea-power during a lifetime and more.
England had kept and trained crews on her ships during
the pressure of the Civil War and after. Charles Stuart
was beginning to strengthen that embryonic navy which
his father had established and which the revolutionary government of Cromwell and his predecessors had confirmed,
which James II, the true creator of English sea-power,
was, first as Duke of York and later as king, to put into
permanent form. But when Louis XIV began to rule single-
handed he had against these two fleets of the Channel and
the North Sea, the Dutch and English, no fleet, one may
say, of his own. Colbert had now given him the beginnings
of one. By 1665—four years after the active reign opens—
Colbert had already *doubled* the number of guns afloat.

For his magnificence in details of building and of furniture the young king had had nothing beyond a few thousands a year in our money. After Colbert had put the
exchequer to rights in those few months, the funds for the
margin of royal magnificence had multiplied *two hundredfold*.
True, this cost of splendour was only a small item out of
the whole expenditure of so great a state, but it was almost
personal in character, and that is significant. Where Louis
had a pound to spend at Mazarin's death in building or
furnishing, he had something like two hundred and fifty
pounds to spend two years later upon such adjuncts to
the throne.

But by far the most important of Colbert's actions in public finance was the drastic curtailment of usury.

The French Crown was not to be free of that curse any more than the English was. The beginnings of banking had got Louis in its grip as it had got his cousin Charles, though France was increasingly a monarchy and England less and less so. But Colbert did at least prevent the crown of France, under its financial strain, from breaking down. No one could say that the crown in France was insecure as it was in England, where the money-power in those same years, 1660-90, got the better of Monarchy for good and all.

It is interesting to follow in detail the way Colbert went about this first wrestling with usury. That indebtedness called "rentes" (what was called later in England "the National Debt"—credits raised by a national government on security of promise to pay its creditors usury out of taxes levied upon its subjects—the system under which we are living, not without difficulty, today) such National Debt was not abolished, of course. Colbert could not abolish it any more than he could abolish war. But it was held in check. A bit was put in the mouth of the bankers, and there was a curb as well as a snaffle. All the latest issues were redeemed by a purchase based upon the actual sums originally advanced to the king, neglecting commissions and cutting down accumulated interest. The mercantile class, who had invested in such "Government Securities" grumbled loudly; but they did not win. In those years when the "restored" Stuart king was hobbling along in debt to his English moneylenders at a rate of eight per cent., Colbert compelled *his* French moneylenders to take five. In everything he did he relied upon that prime instrument, Monarchy, for mastering the plutocratic power.

It was not all this man did. He did very much more. He replaced the press gang by an orderly system of recruitment for the navy which lasts to this day. He demanded everywhere exact accounts. He worked day and night to develop commerce, and in particular to develop manufactory.

It was not possible to avoid wars, but if he could have avoided them Colbert might have made of the French state a monarchy financially superior to the rising oligarchies of London and Amsterdam.

He fell as all men fall, and as all states fall, through the very qualities that had made him rise. Because his whole being was given up to the economic stability of the government he served, because he understood the value of manufactory and orderly finance, because through such understanding he had restored the financial strength of the monarchy, or at any rate prevented its financial collapse, because of all this, his vision, especially as he grew older, concentrated on that one field and failed more and more in general grasp—especially of religious issues and international problems. What a subject's philosophy or race might be mattered little to him so long as that subject had aptitude for commerce and fed the revenues of the crown. He had a natural sympathy with that powerful body, the upper middle class French Protestants, who, being essentially commercial, were averse from agriculture and the life of the countrysides; townsmen; in many towns the principal financial force, and in all towns a great one.

The populace and, naturally, the peasants detested the Huguenots. They were something alien to the nation. But to Colbert that meant nothing. Therefore, when public action was taken against the Huguenots at last and Louis attempted to achieve religious unity throughout the nation—or rather earlier, indeed as soon as it was seen that things were going that way—Colbert for the first time found himself in opposition.

It was a concealed opposition. He hardly knew himself that it was opposition: but there it was. Long before the repressive actions which it was hoped would lead to unity, long before the mutterings of the storm against the Huguenots, Colbert had been half in opposition as being out of sympathy with the Dutch war, and it was the Dutch war that gradually thrust him aside.

Had that war led as it might have led, to a rapid and complete victory none would have weighed his attitude therein. But the Dutch war turned out to be something far from a rapid and complete victory. It half failed after its first beginnings, and since Colbert had always thought it would lead to trouble, therefore, when trouble came, he was the more disliked.

His retirement was voluntary and not without despair. When he was dying and the king sent his honours to so great a servant, Colbert could only ask why the man whom he had thus slaved for during a lifetime could not let him die in peace. Before he died, Colbert, who had no knowledge of Shakespeare, said again: "If I had served God as I had served 'this man' I should be sure of my soul."

It was the fashion of that day to make sure of one's soul before dying. Colbert, who cared little for fashion, followed it in this point of salvation. His life ended on the 6th of September, 1683.

He had seen out the first phases of the great reign: the adolescence, the first wars, the great mid-struggle of France in arms against a growing coalition as the result of a policy which he disapproved. He did not live to see the decline of the king's power abroad. Only after his death came that desperate prolonged and successful resistance to Europe in arms, which resistance is the major glory of his master.

Colbert, the most assiduous constructor of Louis XIV's great France, took less and less delight in the fabric he had helped to raise. He was divorced from it in spirit at the end and therefore he ranks with those many whose heavy labours fail to earn them any final consolation.

There is one last point to be insisted on again about Colbert. He was middle class. The term does not, in French, imply the real and living distinction it implies in English. You would not have found him different in accent and small details of social usage from others at Court. France was not and never had been, as England has so long been, an aristocracy. France had never had a governing class for it had always had a true Kingship. But France felt strongly something which in England died gradually as English religion changed; something which today in England is quite forgotten. I mean "Caste." And Colbert was not really (though technically) of the *caste* called in France "Noblesse": the caste which thought, and thinks, of itself in terms of blood and lineage.

Now it was a chief characteristic of Louis that, from '61 onwards, that is from the beginning of his real reign, he used men of this kind; men who either were not considered equals by the *Noblesse*: men who even when they were technically of such rank were practically, by experience and upbringing, rather of the administrative type. And Colbert thus emerging, intimately bound up with the king at the origin of the king's rule, is symbolical of that professional bourgeois spirit: a spirit which has made the culture of modern Europe, its historians, its scientists, and even its divines. Also its poets: a spirit to which talent is of more interest than wealth. That spirit is today in peril of death. That cultivated middle class is today fast disappearing as a permanent corporate thing in the State and with its disappearance our civilisation now rapidly declines.

COLBERT'S REVENUE

The main matter of Colbert's action being the revenue of France, what was that revenue when Colbert took over and set the national finances right in 1661-62?

It is a question very difficult to answer, so varied were the sources of income,[*] so overlapping, and often, in detail, so capricious. A precise estimate is impossible; but, roughly, the revenue of France at that time was 62,000,000 livres. The gold value of the livre was about one-fiftieth of an ounce, say one-twelfth of an English pound at the old full gold value of that unit as it stood till the crash of 1931. So Colbert and Louis, his master, handled a total revenue of rather over 5,000,000 full English pounds. The English revenue of the day was not quite a quarter of that sum.[**]

The real difference was far greater. Charles II of England's inland revenue was so eaten up with recurrent usury on perpetually renewed advances from money-lenders, that the nett remainder was little more than a fifth of the French real inland revenue. This comparison between the current income available to the two governments must always be kept in mind when we consider their relations one to the other, the continued difficulties of the English Exchequer, and, later, the advances made by Louis to Charles.

The real state incomes are in each case greater as we have seen than the official figures of inland revenue, for

[*] The main sources of French Inland Revenue in 1661 were:
(1) Two-thirds of it the *Taille*: a sort of income tax falling very unequally and missing the noblesse, the clergy and the landless, or small wage earners.
(2) One-quarter of it the Salt Monopoly.
But there were also capricious subsidies voted by the privileged bodies and the sale of offices. Crown rents and dues which in the early Middle Ages had been the main source of all national (i.e. Royal) revenues and expenditure throughout Christendom, had sunk to insignificance. Other capricious revenue there was, notably of occasional grants by the privileged classes, also customs and certain private lands, but the *Taille* and the Salt Monopoly account, as here set down, for eleven-twelfths of what was officially counted Revenue: the King's Income.
[**] In terms of the depreciated English pound today (April, 1938) with gold at seven pounds the ounce, Charles II's revenue was rather less than 2,000,000 of our present pounds; Louis XIV's was over 8,000,000 of our present pounds.

they were increased by customs at the ports, and these in England were growing rapidly. For foreign trade was expanding—especially through the Port of London—all during the Stuart period in England and (much less rapidly) in France under Louis XIV. By the time Louis died—in 1715—the English revenue had caught up a great deal of leeway, though it was still far below the French.

In population we must reckon Ireland and Scotland in with England when making any comparison with France. The total number of Charles II's subjects—at this moment—1661-62—was probably well over one-third of the French population—by the time of Louis's death, more than fifty years later, it was *perhaps* approaching a half.

Now if Colbert's revenue was some 5,000,000 English full pounds (at rather over four pounds to an ounce of gold) what was the social value of such a sum in those days compared with the corresponding value of a similar sum today. By how much must we multiply to get the modern *social* equivalent: what does a million pounds a year in the society of 1660 mean in modern terms?

How do we compare the *social* value of such and such a sum in one epoch—such and such a number of money-units or ounces of gold, or of gold and silver combined—with the same number of units in another epoch? We know, in general terms, what £1,000 a year meant in London just before the Great War. What did it mean in 1660? In 1680? In 1715?

That question of the comparative social value of money at different epochs is, in the merely temporal sphere, the most important question which the sphinx of history sets a man to answer. On that account, perhaps it is the one question which he cannot answer, and no wonder the sphinx strangles us.

You find that question set in a hundred forms and at every turn.

It is comparatively easy to estimate, within a wide margin of error, what a certain unit of currency—say one pound sterling at the old full rate of about four pounds to the ounce of gold—can purchase of such and such a commodity in one epoch and how much it could purchase of the same commodity in another. But the number of commodities commonly in use is very great and their separate prices differ enormously. Wheat may be only three times dearer in our time than it was at some given date in the past; iron much cheaper now than then, small ale twenty times dearer now, but wine not double. Clothing three or four times more. Many widely used articles are far cheaper today than at the past date. Meanwhile the number of purchasable categories increases. Also some commodities—for instance, rye bread—which were in universal consumption are no longer used. Others, once rare, such as tea, are now common to the whole population. Others such as carefully carpentered woodwork, once in every home are now precious exceptions. Try as you will to "weight" the figures given—a high proportion to common necessities such as bread, and a very low one to luxuries, such as silk—and you are confronted by a decline in the use of bread, a vast increase in the use of silk, real and artificial. To clothe, mount and equip an armed horseman cost Cromwell £10 where it cost the nineteenth century £50. But we can transport a ton of ammunition from London to Gloucester at a fraction of what it cost Cromwell to do so.

A general answer, if we reckon by the average prices of a few staples, common to 1661 and 1914, gives a multiple of about five or six for the time of the Civil War compared with our own. That multiple falls as time goes on. You needed at least a £5 note to buy in 1914 the common things you could have bought in 1650 for £1. In 1700 you could not have bought them for much less than 35s.

But one feature does stand out vividly in all these calculations, which is the enormous, the fantastic increase in the

94

cost of public work and expenses. Thus the English population has multiplied in under three centuries by eight, the English public expenditure by eight hundred.

Consider such a point as this. We can still admire one of the great public works which Colbert brought to perfection, the canal which links the Atlantic Ocean to the Mediterranean.

It is 180 miles in length. It is carried across the watershed between the Garonne and the Aude with the most elaborate skill. When it was made there was nothing in Europe like it, and today we look at it as we pass, not exactly with wonder, for we have much greater things today, but with interest and praise. It was a vast national undertaking. It took thirteen years. Colbert, who was still in full power when it was begun, who had been dead nearly a decade when it was completed, had had the vision to desire it on an even greater scale. He wanted to make it a good strategic communication between the two seas, and to take war-galleys rather than barges only. Such a waterway between their Mediterranean and their Atlantic coasts is an enterprise the French ought still to undertake and would undertake tomorrow if they had a strong national government instead of the unhappy system of Parliamentary politics which is dragging them down. Well, that great work cost only seventeen million livres—much less than a million and a half English pounds! Vauban, the greatest mind of his time in engineering and in the larger strategies, estimated the cost of enlarging that canal sufficiently to carry men-of-war from the Mediterranean to the Bay of Biscay. He found he could have done it for another 6s. 8d. in the £. Twenty-three millions of livres, barely two million English pounds, would have sufficed all told.

But as that is only speculation, let us confine ourselves to the actual work. The riddle presented is sufficiently striking. Seventeen million livres in those days, which overlapped the reigns of Charles II of England, James II and William III, represented in English money less than one and a half million English pounds. It represented barely one million, four hundred thousand English pounds. Now whatever multiple you take for the value of money in comparing those days with these, how on earth could the thing be done now at such a cost? Between three and four is the multiple commonly given to represent the average social value of money at a middle date of that time—say, 1680-85—compared with the social value of money before the Great War in 1914. Let us take the largest multiple, four. Can anyone conceive today the making of such a thing as this canal for six million pounds?

Further examples might seem wearisome, but one is worth putting briefly because the thing is of such high importance to the understanding of history, and yet so bafflingly difficult to judge. A prince promises an ally a contingent of 30,000 men, but he says if he cannot furnish them off his own bat, will his ally, to whom he is sending them, pay the cost? It will come, says he, to five livres a man for initial expenses, and seven livres a day for current expenses during hostilities, say twelve livres a day per man all told during the course of the campaign, and that is in modern English money a pound a day. Multiply by over three—by four if you like. How can one make sense of it? How could you equip and supply an army of 30,000 men in all arms on an estimate of 120,000 odd pounds? How keep it in the field for a year on a credit of £17,500 a day?—say six million pounds for the whole fifty-two weeks?

Here is another example. The French Revolution of 1789-93 sprang, as to its fiscal causes, from a deficit of two million pounds on a revenue of, say, twenty. Two million pounds adverse balance was mortal to a nation of perhaps twenty-five millions at the most. Today with a population not double in size and not trebled in economic power of demand, the French State, though imperilled, survives a revenue *thirty* times as large and a debt fantastically uncertain because disguised, but anyhow fantastically larger—sixty times at least. How are we to account for such a contrast?

But indeed the whole question of money's social value at distant periods is baffling and perhaps insoluble. A man of any social class above the labourer and small dealer in England today is cramped on double the real income (measured in goods) that sufficed his father—thrice at least what sufficed his grandfather. Why? No one has answered that question.

It must be enough for us to remember as we follow the effect of monarchy on Louis XIV and his contemporaries in the early part of the reign that we are dealing with figures whose real meaning has wholly changed. We must accept currency units at the social values of their day and see Colbert and his master handling, all told, annual receipts of certainly under eight million of our modern pounds, Louis's cousin Charles II of England meeting expenses, though with difficulty, on an income a quarter of that amount; and on such a basis the public service of the state, including its armed forces, could carry on!

7

*Michael Le Tellier
and His Son Louvois*

NEXT IN IMPORTANCE AFTER COL-
bert as a founder of the Reign comes the Le
Tellier family, father and son, who do for the
army what Colbert did for the revenue and the fleet.

The Le Tellier family, of which Louvois, in the second
generation, became as companion and contemporary of the
King the most famous member, is a capital example of
the dynasty in public life. There are always dynasties in
every form of successive human effort. Under an hereditary monarchy, where the principle of dynasty is accepted
and the example is set for everyone by the nature of the
government and of society, the action of family continuity
in the lower as in the higher forms of administration is
especially strong.

That social principle of family continuity which has
always been and still is characteristic of the French in all
ranks of life, must be carefully distinguished from the aristocratic principle. I repeat, it was founded on the dynastic
principle of which the king was the model. Aristocrats,
even when they do not govern are naturally attached to
such continuity. The very wealthy families who, with their
dependants and lesser relatives, are the components of an
aristocracy always maintain continuity. They make every
effort to do so. It gives them security and eminence and
in countries such as France where lineage in every class of
society holds so high a place it is absolutely vital to the

social prestige of the nobles. Titles count for little with the French and mere wealth is not respected. Blood they understand. But that has nothing to do with the form of government.

Where the form of government is aristocratic, as in England, lineage counts for much less. It is membership of a class (which is carefully kept ill-defined) that gives a man and his relatives governing power side by side with the power of mere wealth. To be what is called "a gentleman," a social product peculiar to England, has little to do with ancestry. The trick can be acquired in one generation by training in special schools, and England today swarms with unmistakable gentlemen whose fathers are odd and whose grandfathers were "impossible." There was and is no parallel to such a class in France, because France has never known that very rare and exceptional thing, class government.

The choice of middle-class men for public office deliberately made by Richelieu to begin with, then continued by Mazarin, and later carried on with such vigour and intensity by Louis, was the very opposite of the aristocratic method of government. The men who acted as ministers and agents for Louis XIV were in mind and tradition quite different from the men who could boast of great family and long descent. Many of those agents were of territorial birth, all of them were technically "noblesse." Many of them had fortunes before they were taken up by the government. All of them (of course) acquired large fortunes once they had an official position. But the core of that position was service, not a mutual understanding with their fellows. In the scheme of French political power you find public men directly attached to the Crown. They were arranged not horizontally as powerful men are in England, with the big mercantile fortunes, the big bankers, the big landlords and the rest of it forming the governing group, but vertically, from the Crown downwards.

It is this peculiarity in French administrative tradition which is such a puzzle to English historians and contemporary observers when they deal with French affairs and particularly when they deal with the reign of Louis XIV, in which French affairs were at their most intense and at their most national.

To understand that principle of continuity by heredity which the French monarchy so greatly strengthened, the mere statement of dates is sufficient. The Le Tellier family, father and son, covered much the same space in history as the Cecils, father and son, had covered in England nearly a hundred years earlier—all the active part of a human life— over fifty years. Only we must remember that whereas the Le Telliers were subordinates and served, the Cecils were masters and commanded. Burleigh controlled Elizabeth. Louvois never controlled Louis.

Of course continuity in administrative power was far easier of attainment in the France of the later seventeenth century than it is anywhere under modern conditions. Today we obtain continuity either through class government or through despotism. In the time of the Le Telliers continuity was unconsciously imposed by the doctrine and habit of national monarchy. Absolute in theory, that monarchy in no way resembled a despotism. It was counterbalanced by a hundred national institutions, by a long dynastic tradition, and by the easy access of all to the presence and converse of the ruler.

There is another point which many have remarked—and I shall follow them here for it is of capital importance. Today, whether under the artificial and ephemeral machinery of despotism or under the more natural machinery of aristocratic class government and especially under that moribund diseased effort at parliamentarianism which is ruining the French today, speechifying and all its deleterious accompaniments are not only the rule but a necessity. In proportion as speechifying is a necessity, in that proportion is public life unreal and troubled. All use it, the despots talk as much and as loudly as romantic actors. The public members of a governing class speechify in their senates and outside without ceasing—and dreadful stuff it is. But it is expected of them and goes with the "publicity" of photographs taken years before the time when they appear (so as to represent these figures as full of youth and vigour).

Now the Le Telliers, father and son, never made a single public speech. It was no more their business to saw the air than it is the business of an admiral or a general in active command to do so. That consideration alone is sufficient to show the difference between their time and ours.

It has been said that the French are made of flint: a sound metaphor. They have the edge, the glint, the hardness, the impenetrability, which go with the word "flint"; but this applies to the core of them, not to their externals. Both the older Le Tellier and his son Louvois were made of stone and of *that* stone; but both would, and did, play a part.

Michael Le Tellier, the founder, as having risen from much less—whereas his son Louvois was born in the purple—had learnt the lesson of subtlety from the beginning. But his service to the royal party was genuine indeed. It was he who reconciled during the Fronde the highly-placed rebels, on one side with the Queen Mother and with the Cardinal on the other. He did more; he reconciled the King with his mother when there was friction. He had through years of such service acquired a reputation which greatly enhanced his value with the royal family to whose interests he was devoted.

It is to be remarked that in social manner Michael Le Tellier was suave, or at any rate gentle, which his son never was. Had not Michael Le Tellier restrained himself in this manner he could never have reached the height he did. His son could carry on, having inherited the fruits of

his father's efforts, but that father could never have become
what he did had he shown his son's temper. Another thing
we must remember in connection with the Le Telliers is
the nature of the rivalry between them and Colbert, a
rivalry which continued during the whole of Louvois's life.
It was Michael Le Tellier who had made Colbert, and
not only did he and his son never forget that fact, they
over-emphasised it. They were slow in understanding how
necessary Colbert had become and how immensely valuable.

Louvois had in his rivalry with Colbert the immense
advantage of being on the winning side in general policy.
When he and his father prepared and decided the Dutch war
they had the tide under them. Colbert in opposing it was
not only on the unpopular side (and, by so much, out of
touch with the King and with the people) but was also less
in touch with reality than the Le Telliers. Although it was
to prove ruinously expensive and although it was to bring
no final victory, yet the Dutch war, from its preliminaries
in Flanders to its last results on the Rhine, was a necessity
to the new strength of the country. In that choice between
"eat or be eaten" there could be no doubt on which side
national policy should lie. To dominate the Netherlands was,
as we shall see when we come to these campaigns, a matter
of life and death to the French monarchy, and therefore to
the French nation, for therein lay that open frontier whence
invasion perpetually threatened and through which hostile
armies had poured into France ever since the Hapsburgs had
inherited by marriage the marches of the Rhine and the rich
mercantile cities and harbours which mark the delta of that
river: for the Netherlands are but the delta of the Rhine.

Louvois might have advanced as Colbert did, by individual talent and pertinacity. He did in fact advance by
inheritance; for the Le Tellier family had already become,
when Louvois himself was only a boy, one of the props of
the monarchy and therefore of the state.

They were legal. Their avenue to great wealth, responsibility and power was through the Lawyers' Guild. Michael Le Tellier, who was his father, became at last Keeper of the Seals through devotion to Anne of Austria and to Mazarin. It was his fidelity to the Queen Regent and the Cardinal, his steadfastness during all the troubles of the Fronde, when his own profession, the lawyers, were in open revolt against the Crown, that earned him the permanent gratitude of those whom he helped to victory. And after Mazarin and the Queen had reached undisputed primacy—that is, after 1653—after Mazarin had acquired complete power over the French State, to be exercised during all the last eight years of his life—Michael Le Tellier was more and more chief organiser, and in particular looked after the raising and training of the army. He was also the most sober and the most responsible, the weightiest and the elder in the group which surrounded Louis at the opening of his direct reign, in the spring of 1661, after the Cardinal's death; and though it is with his son Louvois that the great armies of Louis XIV will always be associated—for Louvois was the maker of these—yet in the first preparatory years, those first six years of young glory before the opening of wars, Louvois was only going through his apprenticeship. It was his father who did all the main work. The army that was put into the hand of Louis for the invasion of Flanders in '67 was the creation of the older man. But Louvois is the name already associated with the new army, and though to think of him as its creator is to belittle his father, yet he continued his father's work and greatly enlarged it, confirmed it, and was the true maker *in action* of what his father had prepared.

Since we shall later follow Louvois as the war minister from the first campaign in Flanders onwards, let us appreciate at the outset what kind of man he was, and first, let there be no error upon his greatness. He was great in decision, in breadth of planning, in that supreme quality of industry which marked all these men, the early architects of the reign.

He was great in intelligence and especially great in his power of command. But these phrases are abstract. You can better understand the man himself in the concrete by saying that he was a mixture of ferocity and high talent. The ferocity was so violent, sometimes so extravagant, and very often so repulsive that it makes posterity misjudge him, because men have difficulty in accommodating their minds to a combination of good and evil. Hearing that a man has in him something which they hate, they will deny in him qualities which they should admire. And so it is with Louvois. He was not only a relentless persecutor of men and opinions which he thought bad for the State, but of men and opinions with which personally he disagreed, whom he found personally antipathetic.

He was, apart from the persecution of men and opinions, abominably indifferent to the sufferings of mankind, with no pity for the disarmed and helpless. The terms in which he talks of victims in his letters are not only, as might be expected, odious to us today, they were exceptional, and, if not odious, at any rate inacceptable, to his contemporaries.

With all this went of course a violent temper; at times it became (when he had full power, unchecked) almost insanely violent. It broke out but infrequently, not because he was self-controlled, but because the fits were intermittent—which was lucky, for when he was under the empire of such fits he was hardly responsible. All this went of course with great energy, but it detracts from him. It lessens him.

His political judgment was, on the whole, bad. But where he specially went wrong was in his conviction that blind force in the hands of the better armed could solve every problem. Through the unbridled and excessive use of such power Louvois left behind him evil effects which outlived him for generations: effects in the Low Countries, effects among the French Huguenots both at home and in exile, which effects we feel to this day.

He is not a little to blame for the false picture of the reign which the victims of the reign handed on in Germany, in Holland and in England, as in the provinces of their own country. Louis XIV, the ambitious tyrant of legend, is in some large measure a Louis XIV seen through the medium of Louvois; an illusion, but a powerful illusion. Thus, the "Dragonnades"—the quartering of troops on a rebel population—though a practice common among Germans was in France the special policy of Louvois.

Yet the qualities wherewith Louvois served the State and wherein he may also be morally admired, outweigh these defects or crimes.

In the first place he was loyal and more than loyal. He was more than devoted to his master, which is as much as to say, more than devoted to his country. For we must always remember in talking of this reign that the Crown and France were one—that ideal figure of the nation, which is everywhere an idol for modern men, was under Louis XIV alive and present in *him*. France was indistinguishable from the actual human being who was crowned and anointed, the incarnation of his people.

Louvois had this passionate personal devotion to his King which is well proved by the familiarity of his approach, the licence which he permitted to his intercourse, but still better proved by his intense emotion when he pleaded to the King himself for this or that, urged this or that policy, or, to third parties, defended the throne against all attack. This was his prime moral advantage: the good and faithful servant, the intense friend as well. He had, however, greater qualities on the intellectual than on the moral side. He would not have made a great strategist, but he made a

very great contriver and producer of all those things which
the captains of armies need.

He had both inherited from his father and learnt by
his father's example, not only the machinery by which the
French society of his day could best be dealt with for the
production of troops, but also the prime importance of
detail *and of its instant accommodation to changing circumstance.*
For there is in military affairs a virtue in mere organisation
which corresponds to the virtue of rapid action in tactics.
Every new invention, every new suggestion, as the art of
war developed before his eyes under the practice of the
field, Louvois seized upon and used. He may be distantly
compared in the campaigns of Louis XIV to Carnot in the
early campaigns of the Revolution.

Let it be remarked in this general view of so outstanding
a man, that he was essentially fitted to be the companion
and sustainer of his master.

They were much of an age—only three years between
them. They had known each other from childhood. They
had come into public life at the same moment. They had
married very early in the same fashion—that is, conven-
tionally: the one with a royal marriage for monarchy, the
other, with a marriage of good birth and great fortune
for the strengthening of a name already powerful but still
rising. To each that marriage was mainly official, each was
engrossed upon the business of State, each particularly, and
Louvois even more than Louis, upon the State at war: that
is, upon the recovery of France which could only be effected
by force of arms. For in that long duel against a ring of
surrounding, actual and potential enemies, who had in the
immediate past all but destroyed the French State, Louvois
was, as it were, the "second" to the protagonist, the King.

He and Louis also were of the same complexion, dark,
with a determined darkness. Each of the same energy,
though in Louis that energy was far more controlled, both

by nature and by calculation. The two men were made one for the other, and especially so because the inferior was made for such service as he gave so amply, and only for service to the highest. He possessed in a singular degree that which has always endeared a man to French armies, that to which the French character particularly lends itself, the Power of Command.[*]

This is a thing one cannot define any more than one can define a savour. Moreover it is a thing which varies with the varying social temper of varying societies. Many a man displays power of command over English subordinates, being himself an English gentleman, who, attempting the same effect upon men of another nation, would only make himself ridiculous. Conversely, many men exercising power of command over a French troop would so offend an English one as hardly to be obeyed. There is, however, this in common among all such men: that in some mysterious fashion the decision they have taken and the will behind that decision is transferred to those whom they order: so that these are "informed" (as the old word went) with the spirit of the one in authority or even with the one advising them.

Now Louvois, for all his defects, which were often much more than defects and became in their intensity thoroughly evil, was filled, especially in moments of crisis, with this supreme talent. He had no occasion to exercise it in war, for he acted throughout as a civilian. No doubt had he entered the Career as an officer, subordination, responsibility and routine—the three marks of military command—would

---

[*] Napoleon, who himself possessed this talent in a high degree, made two remarks about it which, among others, are specially memorable. The sense of them I here give:
The first was that the common saying "One cannot learn to command until one has learnt to obey" was nonsense.
The second was that dozens of men who, from their reading and even their experience, know all about the matter in which they have to command, are by character not fit to command a platoon. He was plumb right as usual.

have moderated and perhaps lessened his power in this respect, as it would also have tamed what was too violent in him. In his place, however, and for his purpose, his power of command did its work very well. It enabled him to impose, civilian though he was, a military discipline upon the finances of the armies; it enabled him to get reforms carried out exactly and at once. It also had this advantage to himself which was sometimes an advantage, but sometimes a disadvantage to his master; that it enabled him to drive his constant advices well into that master's mind.

It would be foolish to apply the term "power of command" to anyone addressing Louis XIV. Neither the King's own character, nor the atmosphere of the time, nor the nature of his office could make such a thing conceivable. *He*, supreme example of monarchy, was there to command and in his presence none could do more than advise. But Louvois commanded others, and even with Louis himself advised with such firmness and in such clear outline, that his advice weighed more than that of any other man in the King's surroundings. Of the many elements in Louvois's greatness, this was not the least, and a soldier would understand it best of all men. But let it be remarked that Louvois's power of command, though springing perhaps from the same root as the other forms of his energy, was altogether separate from his extravagances. In command Louvois was never a bully, though such characters as his often degenerate into bullying what they command.

Amid a thousand instances of his power of command, I select these two as capital, though they appear not in the shape of command but of advice. The first: his ardent support of the Revocation of the Edict of Nantes; the second (much earlier in time): his action on the field at Heurtebise, of which detail will be given in its proper place.

Louvois's advice and support for the policy of ending Huguenotry—a policy inherited from his father and so certain in his own mind as to be beyond discussion—was far from being the chief factor in the decision which Louis took when he determined on the final revocation of the Edict of Nantes. What the main factors of that very important Act were, and the order in which one should place them, will be discussed in the next section. Louvois's attitude, following on his father's equally strong conviction, counted. Though the Revocation would have taken place without him, his more than approval confirmed the King. This was an example of Louvois's mastery in advice, used for what proved ultimately to be to the disadvantage of the State.

Heurtebise (which I think you will not find under that title in any index or summary: I use it here as the most convenient name), Heurtebise, what happened on the field of Heurtebise, may or may not have been to the advantage of the State. That we shall never know. The decision taken at Heurtebise in the midst of the King's first great war may have missed its supreme opportunity for placing Louis XIV and his triumphs in security for ever. It may, on the contrary, have saved Louis XIV from a great disaster. The opposing arguments shall be weighed when we come to the year '76. But whether the advice given were wise or unwise, there is no doubt that it was of capital import. Heurtebise was a moment full of fate, and the decision of Heurtebise was mainly the creation of Louvois. It was he who persuaded the King in those few minutes to determine all the future. For if the decision at Heurtebise were indeed wise, then we must conclude that it saved Louis XIV from disaster and perhaps from death and (who knows?) from the breakdown of the monarchy itself. If, on the other hand, it were unwise, it must be called the seed of such failure as attended the plans of the great king. For if the decision of Heurtebise were unwise it meant that this chief opportunity for destroying the main forces opposed to French power was lost.

Though of all the group Louvois was the one who had the most direct influence upon the king, this influence has been exaggerated by the malice of Saint Simon, but this very malice proves that the influence was considerable. Saint Simon was embittered, we must remember, as were all the men of his rank, by the vastly increased power of the Crown, his dependence upon men whom he regarded as social inferiors. He was particularly bitter in such points because he was a vain and touchy man, always absorbed in rank and precedence. He had been mortified from early manhood. When, therefore, he saw anything have real effect upon the mind of Louis—such a powerful effect, for instance, as the second wife had over the last half of his life, or such influence as this of Louvois—he was especially moved to annoyance and depreciation.

This is not to say that Saint Simon is negligible. He is negligible neither as a witness (though he is often very doubtful in that capacity) nor above all as a writer. But he is a bad guide.

He is doubtful as a witness not only through his bias but through the more physical impossibility of his having acquaintance with many of the things which he professes to describe. He came very late into the period of Louis's reign (not himself a witness till 1695 when he was twenty and Louis fifty-seven) and though he often tells us from which of his elders he heard this or that one cannot call the narrative documented in any full sense. It was true also of the spirit and the place and time in which he lived that he would sacrifice reality if not to epigram or to anything to be called real wit, at any rate he would sacrifice it to effect.

Take for instance the famous passage about the window; how Louvois and the King had a quarrel over the width of a window when the Trianon was being built; how the King had seen that the window—one of three—was wider than its fellows; how Louvois denied this; how the King had it measured and turned out to be right; how the private quarrel affected public policy, etc., etc. The story is on the face of it absurd. There could not have been a difference in the width of the windows, terminating as they did in semi-circular arches, of exactly equal height supporting a straight line. Nor would an architect have made an appreciable error in such a thing, since all his design was based on repetition. There may indeed have been a quarrel about some detail of building, but whatever it was Saint Simon has got it wrong.

Still more dubious and indeed frankly incredible is the story of Louvois dragging himself about on his knees to persuade Louis against recognising his second wife as queen. It is quite inconsequent with anything that we know of Louvois, and equally inconsequent with anything we know of Louis; one may add, still more inconsequent with the well-founded historical picture of Madame de Maintenon herself.

As a writer his style is admirable for its purpose, and it not only leaves a permanent effect upon the reader but often enough it engraves for us a vivid false impression of reality. Everyone must value it who desires to visualise, for instance, the famous death days, and in bulk it properly projects all the last years of the reign.

One may say of Saint Simon's style that it is like his handwriting, not only secure and clear and level but after a fashion convincing. The trouble is that it is a little too convincing and that just because he was so excellent a writer Saint Simon has been overrated as an historian.

But Saint Simon was inevitably and even heavily affected by the spirit of his own society at his own time, and that must be discounted.

But I will put off Saint Simon to a later page and now return to Louvois.

There was yet another thing about Louvois which gave him his position with the master. He was vigorous in the overlooking of accounts, keeping down all expenses and getting the full money's worth for whatever he ordered.

We have seen how a desire for this was characteristic of Louis XIV as it was of Napoleon. Neither of these great rulers could tolerate waste and both of them hated the waste that goes with carelessness. Louvois did as much to create an army immensely large for those days at the least expense as Colbert did to create a revenue very large for those days with the greatest economy and at the least cost of collection. There was, however, in this man an element lacking in all the others who surrounded the King. It was that odd mixture of organising talent with brutality. He advised, and he was the instrument of, something we shall come to later, something not to be forgotten and of profoundly evil effect upon the fate of Europe: the ravaging of the Palatinate. He organised it on a plan in military conception sound enough; he had it carried out most horribly.

In this he was rightly opposed, though with great discretion, by Madame de Maintenon. She, who never interfered with policy of any kind, was moved to show—without emphasis and with we know not what restrained gestures or hints—her dislike of the affair. She complains also that Louvois could never bear her; nor could he, for he felt instinctively the balance and the strong sense of virtue in that woman opposed to his callousness and gusts of fury. It is to be remembered, while we are on this head, that he would, if he had had his way, have burnt Treves on the Moselle as he burnt so many of the greater and lesser places on the Rhine.

8

Lionne

THE THIRD ELEMENT OF THE GROUP was Lionne. As Colbert meant finance for twenty years and the Le Telliers—especially Louvois—meant the armies, so, for half that time (the first ten years) did Lionne mean what we call today in England the "Foreign Office." He it was who presided over the diplomacy of a moment when diplomatic skill was consolidating the new period of French advance and was making all ready for the later action of arms. The taking over of power by the young King found Lionne already busy at work in the business of foreign affairs. He had acted in them for the last dozen years of the Cardinal's rule, ever since five years before the end of the Fronde. He carried the momentum of such experience with him when he sat at the first councils of Louis after the Cardinal's death. Like his colleagues, his full effect was only felt after the strengthening of all French action by Louis's indefatigable application and unflagging control, but Lionne brought into that new era a middle-aged cargo of things said, done, and known in negotiation with foreign courts.

It may be said of him that he "caught decision" from his junior and master. But for the steady plodding of Louis XIV in daily work Lionne would have been too erratic. The King was his flywheel, and therefore with Lionne, as with all the ministers of that most effective opening of the reign, it may be said that Louis was co-operator and even main author of whatever was done.

Hugh de Lionne did not create the foreign policy of the new reign. That foreign policy was a legacy of Mazarin's and in the main point of it, the determination to master the Netherlands, it was erroneous because overdone—but the root of that error was Mazarin's.

It was not an error in principle. The Netherlands were the key point of all French defence and to be the chief foreign influence over them was the necessary aim of every wise and continuous foreign policy. But it was an error to be abrupt in the pursuit of that aim and to underestimate the power of mercantile oligarchy so rapidly rising in wealth and organisation. So far as we can pierce the veil of Mazarin's suavity and secrecy, it *was* Mazarin who had first envisaged the ultimate recapture by the French monarchy of that north-eastern "bastion" which in the early Middle Ages had lain under Gallic influence.

Lionne then did not invent the idea of grasping Holland. He is not to blame for its preparation nor, of course, for its final failure which came after his death.

What Lionne did do, and what is most remarkable about him, was to preside unbrokenly, in spite of his inconsecutive character, over all the major things that were done internationally by the government of Louis during those first ten years: the more remarkable, I say, because he was inconsecutive. He was by nature a sensualist. He was therefore lazy, only driving himself to work by fits and starts. He trusted much, as do such men, in his spasmodic energy. He trusted also in his clarity of vision. He foresaw the consequences of action—or at any rate its immediate consequences—as vividly as a man with a microscope before him.

In all the minor things, therefore, he eminently succeeded in spite of a poor presence, which is a handicap in diplomacy. If in the major things he did not wholly succeed, not so much he as the inheritance of Mazarin is to blame; but Mazarin is to be praised also, and highly praised, for having bequeathed him, as he did, his royal pupil. Mazarin had discovered him and used him in the essential Peace of Munster, one of the twin peaces of Westphalia which had completed the Cardinal's work and had founded the new hegemony of France in Europe. Mazarin had discovered the value of Lionne in diplomacy, had attached him to the household of Anne of Austria and made him before his own death a Councillor of State, and it was he who played the chief secretarial part in the arduous business of the Pyrenean Treaty just before the young King's marriage, the final settling of the southern frontier of France. Mazarin at the end of his life pointed him out to Louis as the man most capable of conducting foreign affairs, just as he had pointed out Colbert as the man most capable of conducting finance and domestic government: what we should call in England today the Treasury and the Home Office combined.

Lionne was a quarter of a century older than his king. He descended from a minor territorial family of the Dauphiné which had behind it perhaps two hundred years of good lineage. But like all the men whom Louis gathered round him, or himself chose for public office, Lionne, though a noble, had no great inherited local political power or wealth. He had been trained at first in finance. His office was little more than that of a clerk until he was gradually appreciated and promoted by the Cardinal. He was already fifty years of age when he was for the first time called Secretary of State, just at the beginning of the active reign.

Though the story of his achievement under the active reign covers only the first ten years of it (he filled the office until the eve of the main Dutch War, that is, until 1671) yet he started all that followed, and his first field of action was the Stuart restoration in England.

It was he who negotiated the sale of Dunkirk by the English—that major stroke of policy was entirely his doing though perhaps the financial details of it were rather Colbert's than his own.

The English Government sold Dunkirk for rather less than half a million pounds, say one and a half millions of our money today or perhaps nearer two millions in total value. It was an exceedingly wise move and therefore desperately unpopular in London. As everybody knows, Clarendon was unjustly saddled with the responsibility of it by public clamour, so that they called his big house in London "Dunkirk House," etc. It was a wise stroke of policy because it got rid of a liability which not only cost the English State a heavy annual loss but was held precariously. Dunkirk could not have "stayed put." Cromwell took it in a most ill-advised moment, as though the enormous revenue which he disposed of through despotism and got in part by confiscations could last indefinitely and could afford such luxuries.

When I say that Colbert probably negotiated the financial side it is to be remembered that there was trickery in this.

The bargain was for the three million livres to be paid in three annual instalments. Colbert was rapidly accumulating a balance which left plenty of money in hand for the payment to be made at once. But the English Government could not suspect this. They inherited the traditional view of a French exchequer even more embarrassed than their own. They, therefore, accepted the scheme of deferred payments. The French Government paid in bills which were discounted on London and then bought up by one whom London took to be a French independent banker—really an agent of Louis. In this way the King saved half a million livres on the purchase price, paying in cash two and a half million livres only, instead of three.

Lionne's work covered all Foreign affairs, of course, apart from the arrangement with the Court of Westminster. It was Lionne who negotiated Breda in '67 and Aix-la-Chapelle the next year, and it is to be remarked that he, more than any other man—though it was not strictly his province—negotiated the first truce with the Jansenists in 1669; but all that was done in these first years turned on the supposed "management" of England. As we shall see there was quite as much work being done on the English side, *and better done,* for Charles II knew how to use the French desire for his friendly neutrality and support; but half the complicated bargain arose from Lionne's initiative.

Even before Mazarin's death there was the brilliant stroke of Charles II's Portuguese marriage. In the ceaseless vigilance upon and intrigue against the still splendid but declining power of Spain one main activity was the playing against Madrid of the Portuguese card. Madrid had held Portugal for sixty years under Philip II. That annexation was held by contemporaries to mark the summit of Spanish power—it marked as a fact the descent thereof. While Louis XIV was a little child the Braganzas had led a rising which restored Portuguese independence and thenceforward the main concern of Paris was to support Lisbon, now almost openly, now secretly, but untiringly, as a continued drain on Spanish resources. The French lent commanders and volunteers to the weaker side, and now, in the last days of Mazarin, strengthened it further by supporting the marriage of the Portuguese Princess Catherine of Braganza to the newly-restored Stuart king. The final success of that policy was sealed when the new queen was established in London, almost coincidentally with the death of the Cardinal.

Thenceforward Lionne watches, with his master, every opportunity for working in with the power of England. Though Louis was the ally of the Dutch in order to put pressure on the Spanish Netherlands to the south of them, though he was still their nominal ally when war broke out between them and England, he mixed as little as possible in that affair. He and Lionne saw with content the naval triumph of the Duke of York and the new English fleet which the Stuarts had made, which the Commonwealth had confirmed and which as a modern and fully organised force the Restoration completed. The French revenue was always at hand to help Charles II with occasional small but useful contributions to help him against his domestic enemies. On to the end of the Stuart dynasty its intermittent connection with Louis is one not major, but important, factor in the fabric of French international power.

It has often been remarked that the change in the fortunes of Louis came with the final victory in England of the Money-power over the national Monarchy, with the triumph of that wealthy oligarchy of great landowners, great merchants, and the new banking system behind them; with the failure of James II and with his exile.

The cause of this is not obscure. All that side of European culture of which Louis was the chief figure was opposed to the newer culture produced by the Reformation. Louis stood, in the main, for the peasant, the traditional bonds of society inherited from times before the great religious revolution. Opposed and rapidly increasing in power was that other spiritual force which was to make Capitalism. Now London, rapidly expanding in numbers, wealth and consequence was, with Amsterdam, the pole or focus of that new force. When English Government was captured by that rich class which became the leaders of the nation, when the English yeoman began to disappear and the townsman to replace him, above all when the ruined English *monarchy* at last collapsed, in 1688, the balance of Europe was changed: the scales were tipped *against* what Louis represented and *towards* plutocratic oligarchy.

Instinctively, therefore, in the background of all the immediate and detailed reasons for supporting Charles, his cousin, the French king was moved to that support. As always, religion was the ultimate root of the affair.

9
Charles II

THE CHARACTER OF CHARLES II himself played at least as large a part in the issue as did Lionne and the advisers and agents of Louis XIV. For Charles was a man not only of high ability in general but of special aptitude for diplomacy. His object—difficult indeed of attainment—was the preservation of all that remained real in English Kingship—even, if possible, to restore some solid part of the power that had slipped away from the throne in the issue of the civil wars. Wholly restore it he could not, but might he not by careful interplay of the pieces on the board re-establish enough kingly power to check the change that had already so widely affected his country?

Our official history has created on Charles and his effort a myth puerile in its simplicity and thoroughly false in its proportions. He has been represented as indolent, centred on personal enjoyment and without plan: the overwhelming difficulties of his task, the cancer of usury eating up the revenue, the absence of an armed force, are minimised; the enemies of the Crown are called "The People" and modern national feeling is called in to ridicule what had been the most national thing in England, the Throne—supporting the weak against the strong, checking oligarchy and permitting the survival of a peasantry.

Nor does this false picture of Charles allow for the inevitable defects of his own view of his own time.

Men are always obsessed by the immediate past. However great their talents, however strong their sense of reality, they always exaggerate the last experience. Much as we do today make the Great War our chief memory and spend most of our energies trying to prevent that disaster happening again, so the killing of Charles I obsessed the generation of his sons. They missed, in part, the true meaning of their time: they thought that the essential was to save the name of Monarchy and a Dynasty, whereas the essential was to preserve some active power in the hands of one man, whether he be called King, Protector or President.

Moreover, men can never foretell the future. The creations of some men, such as Richelieu and Bismarck, outlast them in the most surprising way; the creations of other men, equally able, are lost through causes over which they could have no control. It was so with the efforts of Charles II to restore in some measure the English crown, to erect something of a true monarchy again in spite of the disasters of his father.

He failed: after his death the effort broke down. We, now looking back on it, can see more or less why it broke down. It was in part due to defects in judgment of his brother James who succeeded him, but also to the fact that there was no longer a large organised body of wealth ready to support the ancient tradition of active national monarchy in England.

Charles II's every important action, from the moment when he sets foot in England until he dies, is an example of how much he excelled in negotiation and statecraft: that is, how well he knew the art of playing one hostile faction against another, using allies almost against their own will and always more than they intended to be used.

His standing difficulty was lack of funds. The government was always heavily in debt, and more and more in debt, to moneylenders who were in the same camp as the larger landowners and merchants now beginning to take over real power. Parliament was a committee of the wealthier classes and would not even vote enough money to keep up the navy which his father had created and which he himself had so thoroughly well continued. They would not even vote him enough money to carry on the ordinary affairs of the State. What he did was to play them against the support of the French monarchy. The French crown, with four or five times as large a revenue as Parliament provided for Charles, had plenty of money to spare for supporting its policy in foreign countries. French agents bought up English Parliamentarians and at the same time *tried* to buy for Louis the support of the English crown; but Charles was always too clever for those agents.

He took the money offered, but the moment Louis presumed on this and thought he could impose his policy on England, Charles would skilfully change over and fall back on the Dutch or even on his rich rebellious subjects in their Parliament.

There are two first-rate examples of his ability in manœuvre. One was his formation of the Triple Alliance to show Louis XIV that he could be independent of French support if he chose; the other was his marrying his niece and heiress Mary to her cousin William of Orange, the fixed enemy of the French king.

He was equally clever in manœuvring the religious factions. When there was a wild outburst of fanatical anti-Catholic feeling in London he yielded to it. He gave the runaway horse its head. When the Established Church proposed to balk him of his natural allies, the dissenting Protestant churches, he did not openly support these against bishops, but he shaped his whole policy towards a toleration of the Nonconformists. They knew that the King was their friend. He saw that open support of the larger English Catholic body with its equally large body of sympathisers not openly Catholic would have ruined him, so he went very slow on that although all his sympathies were with Catholicism. Could Charles's ghost have warned James in this regard what a difference it would have made!

Of course, a life of this sort, passed in perpetual dissembling, is reprehensible. Charles can be as heavily blamed on the moral side for this perpetual shifting and manœuvring as can his elder contemporary, Mazarin. But regarded as an intellectual effort and as a piece of political ability, it was first rate. It was all the cleverer because he was one of those men who never give the impression of working hard and yet who manage to get through an enormous amount. Such men have the same advantages as have those who look stupid and dull but are really subtle and intelligent.

When he came to die, Charles certainly thought that he had saved the crown for good and all. It was, of course, an error; but it was an error which every contemporary shared and which might not have proved so complete an error if his brother James had been one-tenth as fitted for intrigue as he.

Permanent Parliament in England

Of all this Lionne—and much more clearly Comminges a little later on—had a conception, but a conception hardly full enough. Lionne was familiar with kings: of oligarchy he knew less, and that typical and chief example of the new oligarchies, the new *permanent* Parliament at Westminster, he, like Louis, had an imperfect comprehension. It was a revolution in English politics when the House of Commons, in 1660, at the return of the King, remained, with the House of Lords, permanently sitting.

The House of Commons was, as I have said, a committee of the wealthier classes. It was obviously a committee of rich landowners, but there was also a mercantile element and an element of lawyers who, by this time, were part and parcel of the new governing class.

Until the quarrel between Charles I and the bigger taxpayers (supported by a large number of the smaller taxpayers) Parliament had never been permanent. It was not a standing institution. Parliaments had been summoned for particular occasions in England, as in all other western countries. Parliaments were summoned by real kings in active power to inaugurate the beginnings of their reigns. They were also summoned when the King wanted to ratify some proposed laws which he had in mind. A notable example of this was the so-called "Reformation Parliament." Henry VIII got it together to support with regular forms his loot of the Church—and nearly all the members of that Parliament got something out of that loot sooner or later. But Parliaments were especially summoned when the King needed, suddenly, unusual supplementary money, over and above the regular national income with which (of course) Parliament had nothing to do, and which was entirely in the king's hands.

Thus Parliament had been repeatedly called upon to provide voluntary grants during the Hundred Years' War in the Middle Ages. Men thought of Parliaments in the French provinces, in Scotland, in England, as occasional, exceptional gatherings wherein the representatives of townsmen and the countrymen met to offer the king, not without grumbling, quite irregular novel and *temporary* gifts—"tips" as it were, *not* income. There were no "taxes" in our sense; no regular revenue voted by Parliament. The regular revenue came from the property, the estates and dues of the king, and everybody took it for granted that the king ought to make that personal income of his suffice for his duties and expenses of administration. But by 1660 the English crown was financially ruined. It had nothing to speak of as its own. It could get nothing with which to carry on but what Parliament chose to give it—and Parliament gave it less than half the bare minimum required for governing and defending the country: nominally £1,200,000 a year: really less than half that. Thus did this new plutocratic oligarchy arise over against and at last supplanting Popular Monarchy.

After 1660, then, it became a sort of accepted novelty—soon to be no novelty but a routine—that Parliament should sit permanently, and this made it, even in outward appearance, a partner with the king in the government of England. Such a partnership had never been dreamed of in the olden days.

Henceforward, through that first very long unbroken session of seventeen years men had grown to think of this body of rich squires, rich merchants and rich lawyers as co-equal with the king.

But really, of course, Parliament was now on the way to become much more than that. It was becoming government itself, with the king as opposition. The king retained his power to nominate ministers and agents; his Council also was of his own nomination and he, in his Council, decided on Policy. But he had an income not half large enough for the national needs—and only Parliament could provide the balance. It refused to do so save on terms of substituting its own power for the Monarchy.

With such a new factor in foreign affairs—a factor puzzling to them—were middle-aged Lionne and young Louis faced at the opening of the reign; and meanwhile another Money-power had long arisen in the field of international politics: that of the Dutch Merchants. The French Government had to use both Dutch and English as makeweights to its main rivals, the Hapsburgs—Austrian and Spanish. It had also to prevent either the Dutch or the English from getting too strong; therefore it had to foment quarrels between them: moreover it had to prevent either of these maritime mercantile groups, centred in London and Amsterdam, from leading the other in a coalition of naval force. France was building a navy, but not for years would it equal England or Holland at sea, and never come near to rivalling the two combined fleets.

Sea power was not at that moment of the prime importance it came to be in the later eighteenth century. It was mainly an adjunct of, and protection for, merchant ships and carrying-trade, colonial and foreign. England and Holland were rivals, so it was not impossible to divide their interests and prevent coalition. But the situation had to be watched, though what ships did by sea could not yet compare in political importance with what armies did by land. The French king would always be vastly the superior of England, still more of the Dutch, by land.

The critical moment for French Policy, for Lionne and Louis balancing the two maritime powers, came four years after the opening of Louis's active reign.

The dates of this critical moment should be closely watched and remembered: the dates of the fighting season of 1665.

The rivalry between England and Holland, the two maritime powers, reached a head in March, 1665, when England declared war on her commercial and naval rival. France, to balance Spanish rule in what is now Belgium, had a standing alliance with Holland. Holland now claimed from the King of France the redemption of his promise—but he did not carry it out. He was only too glad to let the two maritime states lock themselves in war. He desired the supremacy of neither, but it was for the moment an advantage to him that the English under the excellent leadership of the Duke of York, who was later to be James II, won that great North Sea battle of his in the June of that year. Louis certainly did not want the English to obtain a complete mastery over Holland: that would have meant an alliance between the two maritime powers; it probably would also have meant that the Orange faction in Holland would have had the future in its hands. Though he did not want a complete English victory he was glad to see one of those two naval powers crippled by the other, and both perhaps exhausted.

In the August of 1665 he had promised the Dutch to help them if England refused their offers of peace. While he was still thus occupied there came in December the thing which changed all. Philip of Spain died: and at once Louis prepared to claim the Netherlands by right of his wife.

This was the moment which had been so long discounted and awaited. A wretched infant (now Charles II), four years old, too weak to stand or walk, too dull to speak, was left on the throne of Spain. All that the Spanish throne had inherited from the House of Burgundy—*and this included the Netherlands, the Delta, the flat rich country of great merchant towns and ports whence invading armies had struck down towards Paris during two lifetimes: Artois, Flanders and the Hainault, Lille, Arras, Antwerp, Ghent, and Brussels for capital*—was to be challenged by Louis in order that such a threat to Paris should be ended for good and all.

Had Louis a legal right to advance such a claim? His wife, the Queen of France, was elder half-sister of the puny baby now called King of Spain: she was the issue of Philip IV's first marriage. By the custom of the Low Countries the children of a first marriage had priority of succession to land over the children of the second. The Crown of France had renounced the Queen's claim at the moment of her marriage, but the lawyers could plead that this renunciation was void because her dowry had not been paid.

It was but a pretext. The underlying motive of the coming war was necessity: to occupy and close that open frontier to the north-east which had given entry once and again to invasion and twice imperilled the very heart of the realm. It was certain the pretext would be used: it was certain the Spanish Government would refuse it. It was certain from that date, the last days of 1665, that the first radiant opening of the Great Reign, its young peace, was to end.

❋   ❋   ❋

Before we conclude these first (and high) six years of peace which introduced the great wars, let us see the general plan of that Europe in which the King—in his thirtieth year—was to confirm the State by arms abroad as he had already consolidated it by industry at home.

Louis had not acted on the offensive during these first years, although the time for an offensive on a grand scale was approaching. He had lent certain armed forces to foreign powers, he had shown his strength in claiming—with threat of action—special diplomatic immunity for his embassy at Rome: showing in this some insolence in order to advertise his new attitude and power abroad.* He had required and obtained apology and submission. He had shown his new fleet in the Mediterranean. But all these preliminaries were trifles. His concern was with much greater things.

He already knew that the main business of his reign would be the consolidation of French territory through the re-establishment of French Power. He knew that

---

*   In this first brush with the Papacy Louis did not vacillate—he never vacillated—but he was moved to incongruous acts. While desiring peace he did violent things. For instance, he occupied the Pope's town of Avignon. He strongly backed up his ambassador in Rome against the Pope's very reasonable reform, whereby the immunities of the districts round the foreign embassies were to be removed (an embassy is always inviolable, but in Rome whole districts round each embassy had been closed to the police and the good government of the town, an abuse which the Pope was rightly determined to end). Some talked of an expedition into Italy, but we must remember that on both sides the quarrel was not so much invented as exaggerated by big talk and over-emphatic phrases. Let me say it again, neither party was prepared for the last step. Rome would not risk schism. France would not risk heresy. Three lifetimes of experience had warned each against such catastrophes.

thoroughly, though so young, for it was the permanent legacy of Richelieu and Mazarin.

There is a pentagon of fertile, well-watered, well-ploughed land between the flats of the north-east (the Rhine Delta), the main mid-stream of the Rhine itself, with the Alps of Mediterranean; the Mediterranean coast and the Pyrenees; the Atlantic, and the Channel, which pentagon is Gaul. It is the necessary meeting place of travel from Britain to the south, from the Germanies and (by land) from Italy to Spain. It is permanently wealthy from the energy of its people applied to such a soil, and it naturally supports a host of towns set on its main rivers: it has but one mass of barren upland set in the midst of it and severing no communications.

The pressure upon such a situation is continuous. Gaul had been organised, and for ever, by Rome, from which act onwards for fifty generations it dealt with invasion at the hands of North Sea Pirates, of Slav, Mongol and Germanic armies, and of Islam from the south. Such a history has not produced but has well suited a race of military temper, and all that long story, which is also the central story of Christendom, has been filled with passionate internal conflict alternating with intervals of abrupt internal cohesion during which Gaul invaded others in its turn and affected all Europe with its tradition and its arms.

Louis came at the end of one of those ages of disunion which periodically threaten the life of Gaul. He was the heir to, but also the architect of, a new national unity which, after 150 years of invasion and peril, was to restore the State and to turn the tide of Gallic energy from domestic conflict and from anxious defence of the boundaries weakened by such conflict, to an external offensive in which Gallic influence in arms and ideas should radiate throughout our civilisation.

There had come a moment, a century before the birth of Louis XIV, when all that surrounded the French realm had fallen into one hand, the House of Hapsburg. The great Emperor Charles V, feudal head of all the Germans and of many Slavs to the east and the paramount power in Italy, was also, by inheritance from the House of Burgundy, sovereign of the Netherlands. He was further King of Spain and of the vast new Spanish conquests beyond the ocean in the New World. In that day the French were surrounded by a sea of Hapsburg Power, to which they might succumb.

At the abdication of Charles a long lifetime before the birth of Louis, this enormous Hapsburg Empire was divided between a Hapsburg at Vienna and a Hapsburg at Madrid. The Spanish Crown inherited, with Charles's grandson, the lands in the Delta of the Rhine and Scheldt, the Netherlands as well as what lay beyond the Pyrenees to the south of France, also the Americas, their new commerce and wealth of all kinds, much of Italy.

The other branch of the Hapsburgs, known as the House of Austria (since Vienna was its centre) held the complex feudal lordship of the Germanies with Slav intermixture. The two Hapsburg Empires, though no longer in one hand, were still in one family whose territories surrounded France everywhere. To face such an encirclement would be the task of the new French reign—and especially to close the entry from the north and east, whence armies had come again and again into France as invaders.

They had reached St. Quentin in the sixteenth century, and again, later, in Richelieu's day, had all but reached Amiens and the barrier of the Somme.

Austria and Spain, Hapsburg Austria and Hapsburg Spain were, in combination, the weight—overwhelming upon the *map* at least—under which France still lay. Both parts of that family combination were already less powerful than they seemed. It was to be the task of Louis to lessen them still further and to dissolve the elements so

opposed to the country with which, as King, he formed
one thing; for he made of the Monarchy and the State it
ruled a single person.

THE WARS BEGIN

All 1666 was preparation. In the first days of May, 1667,
there was handed to the Government of Madrid a formal
document setting forward the claims to the Netherlands
of the Queen of France. It was called "A Treatise on the
Rights of the Most Christian Queen over divers States of
the Spanish Monarchy."

Already the armies which old Le Tellier and his son
Louvois had recruited and trained were stretched out in a
string of detachments along the line of the Somme, facing
the frontier, ready for their concentration and the attack.
The peace was at an end.

III
The Founding of All
(*Within*)

1661-1667

*"Vous qui passez, venez à
Lui, car Il demeure."*
Victor Hugo, on the Crucifix.

10

Louise de la Vallière

S O MUCH FOR THE EXTERNAL LIFE
during the first years of active monarchy. It is all
directed—even in such very early youth and the dis-
tractions thereof—to the king's office and his function; that
is, to Duty. He must be king—for an example to others in
deportment, manner and authority, for the good ordering
of a vast community incarnate in himself, for the glory
of the State, which was also his own glory, and for the
betterment of Christendom.

What of the Life within—which is the very man?

It is to be measured and judged by his relations with
women, for all the life of a living soul lies in such relations
to creatures or to God.

There had been but one deep emotional experience or
vision in his life: the episode of Mary Mancini.

His marriage was to one side of his real being: it was
official, and ceased at once to be anything other than official:
the provision of an heir, the setting up of a second royalty
at his side, a queen as was befitting, but nothing else in
any sense his own.

For the rest, though love and its test, self-rendering, never
touched him again, three main episodes mark his personal
and intimate experience. There were others—but they were
ephemeral. Three women only made impress upon him and
remained in his memory at the end.

The first was a lover indeed, a lover of him (to his delight)
but not he of her. The second was that common thing, a mistress, though a mistress most exceptional. The third was a wife.

The first was Louise de La Vallière, young of the young, the very air of his own youth. Their connection lasted six years: from 1661 to 1667—while he was still in his twenties. It coloured all the launching of the reign, its morning glories and its only episode of peace. In his thirtieth year came the wars and the fading of that original attachment in the occupations of maturity.

The second was a daughter of that great house called Rochechouart Mortemar; she was the Marchioness of Montespan, omnipresent in his court and dominant for a dozen years, from the first campaign of '67 to the change of '78-'80. When he finally and abruptly broke from her his fortieth year was past.

The third was Frances d'Aubigné, who increasingly guided and rightly guided, his inner life. After a rapidly ripening acquaintance of three years, Louis (on the death of his poor queen) privately married her. She had the title by which she is known to history, that of Maintenon. This permanent and solid business lasted, as marriage should, a lifetime. From that first approach and marriage, on for thirty-two years, she was the companion and the necessary friend. Only death, at the end of old age, divided them: he seventy-five, she two and a half years older. She survived him by less than four years when, during the spring of 1719, she in her turn also died, the sober widow of so great a man.

First, then, of Louise de La Vallière.

She was but a girl of sixteen when first she saw the king (he retaining no memory of it) on his way south to his marriage. He passed by Blois, her countryside in which the small stone country house of her dead father stood.

She had seen Louis again—a distant glimpse—when he went through the streets of Paris in state on his return. She was already at court as maid of honour to Henrietta of England, Duchess of Orleans, sister-in-law of Louis,

Charles I's daughter. Louise de La Vallière, now thus at court, was poor enough and but one in a crowd; she could not have held even such a post save as being of the *Noblesse*, of that caste system to which, though it was but half real, the Gauls have been wedded since Gaul was Gaul.

Yes: she was of the Noblesse, but of what petty Noblesse! Her step-father, her widowed mother's *third* husband, was but a sort of appendage to the Duke of Orleans's house-hold—by title "Master of the Kitchens," in actuality a sort of gentleman-steward. It had been at his request that his step-niece was attached to the train of the Duchess of Orleans, "Madame."

The early summer of 1661, just after Mazarin's death and the change, was, at that court, a season of great gaiety, full of the music, the violins, which the young emancipated king had come to adore, of gala, of feast—and in the midst of this incipient affair between Louis and his sister-in-law Henrietta, "Madame." She attracted and loved to attract, it was no more; but the queen mother disapproved; Louis was too much at Henrietta's side and the young woman, to silence scandal, took the youngest, the most simple, the most innocent of her attendants, Louise de La Vallière, for a constant companion. She was always present when Louis called on her mistress; soon he noticed her. She was silent, timid, of an exquisite complexion and already, I think, in love; constantly watching the king. She yielded to him. He had charmed her and he (to put it plainly) seduced her. So this thing began.

Now here we learn a lesson in monarchy and its effects. Many a man powerful through wealth or station has acted thus, but with Louis it was a special case; the sacrifice of a soul to Monarchy. Already he judged himself not by the common standards of men—nor she him. He was a sun shining in mid-heaven: much more than her master, her God, and certainly at that time her heaven. He for his

part took all as of right. The flower was in his garden
and he plucked it.

We cannot know the exact date, but it must surely have
been sometime during the July of 1661, in the full festivities of Fontainebleau that she fell. She would be seventeen
in August, he twenty-three a week or two later.

Let there be no error; it was an abomination. Here
was not one of those innumerable introductions to life
of a lad by some woman in the common tradition of the
rich and hardened. Here was not even a mutual flame of
youth to youth, she knowing her way and he his. I repeat,
she was innocent. He destroyed her innocence without a
scruple and as a thing of course. He desired and did. He
made her wholly his—but not himself hers. It was to be
enjoyed by him, so long as it should be enjoyed, but *she*
was possessed nor ever could be at peace again.

How much does he stand excused? We do not know,
for such things are known only to God. But it behoves
us to see with his eyes. He felt without question that all
around belonged to him, and he had here refreshment in
the aridity of a very wealthy, too satisfied world. Even
young men soon learn to know the dryness of that dust.
He was loved at last for himself alone, though he himself
had ceased to love. His young spirit needed little support, for it was in the full tide of vitality—but in so far
as he obscurely needed the couch of passionate devotion
from another, why, here it was for his repose. Goodness,
essential goodness, in her light blue eyes and tender face;
unswerving fidelity; no edged words to disturb him, no
obstacle in her self-effacement; presenting what was—for
the world of that day—beauty, for any world and any day
freshness, the health of the heart and complete abnegation:
what a gift freely given to his youth. Now the gifts of
youth misused never return save in such aching memories
as may, in the very end, purchase beatitude.

Her portraits are not of a singular loveliness in our eyes. The ringlets of her very fair hair, not over-abundant, are of a fashion that does not meet our own; they fatigue us in Lely's pictures, as in those of Mignard, falling on bare necks and shoulders generally insipid. It was herself that captivated all and even women praised her.

The elder women and the wiser loved her in proportion to their wisdom. Louis himself was indifferent to such attraction in her—but not indifferent to her adoration. This it was that moved him and this which bound him. He sought that passion for himself alone, which he did not reciprocate.

He needed, as it were, daily proof of his supreme office, even so early in manhood, even in so intimate an affair. The Vallière supported him in her weakness, and her devotion nourished him for a little while.

So did he purchase for nothing what is beyond price and esteem it, after six years' use, as of no remaining worth. But she to the very end of a long life knew nothing but that intense adventure of her girlhood and her repentance; keeping two gods, one human, departed, unforgotten; the other the very God of heaven and earth, God everlasting to whom she did expiation for nearly forty years. Hers was the greater part.

She had no wit—which was as well for wit is dangerous in women, being not native to them; and the King, though he admired wit in others and was too strong to fear it, both knew it ill, and made no service of it. He was later to be proud of wit in a companion, but paid wit no honour in anyone and himself required it not at all.

Her very slight limp—unseen and unfelt when she danced—perhaps endeared her somewhat to him as slight physical defects, being personal to them, will often endear women to men. Her usage and constancy certainly endeared her to him—so long as he remained, which was not very long. She felt his every neglect, and this so strongly that their first quarrel in the early months of the business drove her to her first despairing repentance.

Generations have sentimentalised over that first flight to a convent whence Louis brought her back in the haste and eagerness; over her second later flight for refuge whence she returned not sought by him in person but by dependants at his orders (and she said: "Once it was the King himself who came for me!").

But the emotions which the romantic find in the lapses and the returns are wholly unworthy of the tragedy: that tragedy was too great, even for pity of the common sort. Pity is out of place before so vast a thing as the war between two burning devotions, one human, one divine, in the simple heart.

Rather is such a conflict the deepest theme meditation could choose and perhaps beyond human power to treat at all.

I have said "Hers was the greater part." Indeed to the clear eyes of Eternity, the pageant and the splendour of the age, the wars, even the high letters of that great day, even Bossuet, even Racine, are but lesser incidents of an incomparably greater spiritual passage, the agony and redemption of a soul.

❋   ❋   ❋

So long as the queen mother lived the connection between Louise de La Vallière and the King was not publicly admitted. The first child was born secretly in that house of the Palais Royal which had been Brion's. Colbert was the confidant to whom all was entrusted. The servants were told that the young mother was some lord's mistress and the boy (for it was a boy) was handed over for guardianship to a family of the people.

It was the Christmas week of '63. The King was away. She was alone. Yet such was her frail courage that four days after the birth she showed herself in public at midnight Mass, to silence, in part, the whispers and the half ridicule of the courtiers.

Then, there was the throne to be remembered. The queen had given Louis an heir many months before and a Dauphin of France was in another brilliant heaven infinitely above that obscure baby of the unknown name and hidden home. *He* the son of France, the inheritor of the blood royal was in a blaze of light—the poor little half-brother was not heard of—and soon that infant died as did the next, also a boy, also doomed. Louise and Louis hardly had seen their children, or known them, when they were gone.

But when this amorous business of the King's was in its fifth year, in the January of 1666 the queen mother died. Louis who had so observed the exalted tradition of the crown and had also a deep personal veneration for Anne of Austria, her fine firmness and self-sacrifice in what since Mazarin's death had been a widowhood, felt himself free at her death from a bond that had restrained him.

Before the spring he knew that a third child was coming. A decent veil was still drawn, but when the child— a daughter—was born, in October, he was prepared to acknowledge it and its mother. Louise was given her duchy as though half royal already, and the little girl grew up to be more and more a princess: she was to be known by the Royal title of Blois and later legitimised.

A new phase of Louis's Kingship had opened, that novel transition during which the bastards gradually took their places fully as sons and daughters of France—after a fashion. Louis, nearing thirty, could do this. He was already a god, greater than custom, itself strongest among all the iron chains which are most binding on men.

By that irony which is the salt—but often the poison— or our evanescent human life and in particular of women's most ephemeral happiness, that very moment when Louise,

Duchesse de La Vallière, was elevated by her lover to a sort of throne, her romance was leaving her. Child-bearing had already taken toll of her simple and pure beauty. The "Rose leaf" was fading and, alas! that by which she had lived these six enchanted and embittered years was ebbing from her. She was still necessary to the King, but not supremely and no longer uniquely so.

The air of her soul grew chill and that certitude in mutual love which is the sustenance of such souls was abandoning her. *She* never changed at all. The very high and steadfast flame burned on and would so burn for ever. It is wise to believe that this utter love she had for her royal divinity survived the incomprehensible boundaries of death and that her eternity stretched out its arms for him as had her mortality. But *he* was no longer there—not he himself.

Louis, his very self, had never been hers; for after Mary Mancini he could never so merge into the very being of another. He had but stood by and followed an attraction, separate always in spirit from the human being at his side. Even so much of him as had been at her side was passing, and another bond was ousting her would-be unending claim. And she was not yet twenty-four—the child!

What had come in to change him will be told later; it is enough here to conclude the play.

The central business of the reign, the triumphant wars, had opened and a new preoccupation altogether. Side by side with the queen and her new rival she followed the armies in Flanders. She returned to a mortal fatigue. Once more she fled for repentance and was a last time summoned back. Within three years she found the cloister again, and this last time for ever.

IV
Maturity and the Wars (*Without*)

1667–1681(83)

II

Maturity

THE MATURITY OF LOUIS XIV, THE principal moment of his public action and effect upon Europe, the most triumphant epoch of his wars while he was still in the ascendant and before the inevitable final coalition had formed against him, covers some sixteen years, 1667 to the middle or end of 1683.

The core of those sixteen years is two sets of wars: first the preliminary attack on Flanders, 1667–1668; second, the main war, beginning against Holland alone and then spreading to a coalition.

That main war begins in 1672 and ends with the group of treaties generally called after the Peace of Nijmegen in 1678-79. During the end of the period, from 1678-79 to the end of 1683, four to five years, the results of victory are confirmed, the gains consolidated—notably the acquisition of Strasburg in 1681, a fortress which bolts the door against invasion and completes the frontier.

Immediately after this the storm of Europe against the French monarchy is gathering but has no direction. The atmosphere is still that of a climax and of a full success. With 1683 the tide turns; all changes; and soon the long, increasingly difficult, defensive begins.

12

Flanders

WHY DID LOUIS XIV IN THIS
spring of 1667 move on Flanders and the
southern Netherland provinces still under
Spanish rule? Why did he next move against the rebel
Northern Provinces which Spain had failed to hold? Under
what conditions was either advance to be made?

These two motives joined: first the setting up of a barrier to make invasion from the north-east—the mortal peril
of the last 150 years—in the future impossible; second,
the winning in the whole international sphere of that duel
between Monarchy and Money-power which had begun at
home with the affair of Fouquet. Holland was the effective
symbol of the Money-power as was Louis of Monarchy. For
both purposes the instrument ready to hand on the death
of Philip IV of Spain, was the claim of his daughter, the
French queen, to inherit the Netherlands.

If you read history the wrong way round, that is backwards, thinking of the past as though it were today, the
Netherland Wars of the King's Maturity are not comprehen-
sible. They seem no more than aggressions with irrational
greed for more territory or military glory as their motive.
They have no historical origin. They fit into no scheme.

We moderns, in Western Europe at least, think in terms
of nations—and of nations as we know them, under their
modern names and with their modern, or recent, boundaries. When we heard the words "Holland" or "Dutch" we
think of a modern nation with its capital at the Hague.
When we hear the name "Spanish Netherlands" it sounds

to us a contradiction in terms. We have to be told that "Spanish Netherlands" meant in Louis XIV's youth much what "Belgium" means today. We have further to learn that the legitimate government of *all* the Netherlands had lain in the Spanish Royal House, unquestioned before the religious revolution which dislocated all Europe. When we hear of "Franche Comté" or "The Jura" we think of an old French province or a modern French department (one of many French departments) up against the Swiss frontier.

But the men of 1660 did not think in these terms. The territories with which they had to deal were local *Lordships*, some large, many very small. These had gradually coalesced to form whole provinces and kingdoms, but the process of unification was not yet complete. Most of these Lordships were in lay hands, but not a few were church lands—Lordships the Lords of which were Bishops; for instance, the territory of Liege.

A man held a Lordship by hereditary right and the local customs of inheritance differed widely. Also one acquired a Lordship by marrying the heiress thereto, and the more fortunate or ambitious of the great houses extended their territories mainly by carefully planned marriages of policy often continued for generations until a district as large as a modern nation had come into one control.

When Feudal Christendom was growing up in the west (from a thousand to eight hundred years ago) it was all a dust of little village Lordships, of market towns also, each under a Lord but gradually becoming independent, and of larger Lordships, combining many villages, to which the lesser Lordships were attached by feudal bonds. In theory every Lordship was answerable ultimately to some superior Lordship; even the highest, such as the King of France, sent a symbolic token of fealty to the Emperor. But, in practice, about a century and a half before Louis XIV was born, the chain of Lordships broke off in its upper links and went no higher than some great over-lord who was virtually a sovereign. The Duke of Brittany was, in power, king over Brittany, though he admitted a feudal link with a nominal superior, the King of France. When the King of France wanted to get back power over Brittany the only way he could get it was by marrying the heiress to the Duchy.

The Kingdom of France itself, the largest and strongest of the groups which were to become modern nations, had been built up bit by bit through marriages and feudal lapses. If a feudal inferior failed in his feudal duty, his Lordship lapsed (in feudal theory) to his over-lord; it was by proclaiming the Duke of Normandy thus defaulting that the King at Paris had acquired Normandy from the Plantagenets.

What no one ever did was to claim territory by force. Such a title to overlordship would have sounded shock-ing and criminal *except* in the case of land conquered from pagans or Mohammedans. Of course the claim by descent or forfeiture was often a pretext only and, at the end of the system, was nearly always a subject of dispute, settled by arms. But *some* claim had to be made and it had to have a backing in custom and feudal law to have any chance of success. Mere force was never a title to political power over any stretch of territory until the religious revolution had done its work of breaking up Christendom. Till then claim from conquest by force over fellow Christians was unknown. *That* idea was the product of modern minds and well reflects modern morals.[1]

Now at the end of the Middle Ages, about two long lifetimes before the age of Louis, in the days of the first Tudors and the last Plantagenets of England, there had stood a large agglomeration of Lordships, market and larger

---

1 Phrases like the "Norman Conquest," the "Conquest of Ireland" by Henry II of England, did not indicate mere seizure by force. They were used to mean "enforcement of a just claim."

towns, seaports, etc., under the House of Burgundy. The Dukes of Burgundy were the sovereigns of that agglomeration. It was not one connected territory but a number of pieces of village overlordships and city-territories, some joined together, some standing apart like islands, cut right across in some places by belts of land (like the Bishopric of Liege) which were quite independent of the Dukes. But, roughly speaking, this virtually independent state called the Duchy of Burgundy had covered nearly all of what we call today Holland, most of what today is Belgium (with Brussels and Ghent for chief towns), a belt of what is today North-Eastern France (with Lille and Arras as important towns therein), a district of central Eastern France (with Dijon as capital)—and so on.

By various arrangements the Duchy's direct rule had been somewhat diminished; for instance, it lost "French Burgundy" (the Dijon part); but it still meant, rather over a hundred years before Louis was born—say when Calvin's book had appeared and the Reformation was in full spate— what we call today Holland and Belgium with a strip of Northern France (these were *the Netherlands*) and Luxemburg; while, separate, some way off to the south, the Jura hill district ruled from Besançon and called the "Franche Comté" came under the same "House of Burgundy."

But long before Louis came to the throne there were no longer reigning Dukes of Burgundy. The House of Burgundy had ended in an heiress. She married (in 1477) Maximilian, head of the great German House of Hapsburg ruling at Vienna who also became by a half-hereditary tradition Emperors. Therefore their son would be heir to the Burgundian ducal lands as well as to the Hapsburg lands of Slav and German origin to the east (Bohemia, Austria, Styria, Carinthia, etc.); but before that son inherited he married the heiress of Aragon and Castille—that is, of the Lordships which had built up Spain; so *his* son, Maximilian's grandson, would be heir to the lands of the Hapsburgs, *and* of Burgundy, *and* of Spain—and that meant by this time all the immense new Spanish territories in America.

This grandchild of Maximilian was born in 1500 and called Charles. He came into all this vast world-heritage in 1519, just at the moment when the revolutionary storm of the Reformation broke. He is known in history as the great Charles V (or "Charles Quint"). He held directly or as overlord much more than half the Christian world, for he was sovereign over much of Italy, he held the Imperial rights in Germany, as well as the Hapsburg lands and all the Burgundian Duchy's lands; he was king of all Spain and the Americas; never was so much rule concentrated in the hands of one man.

When this mighty Charles abdicated after the late middle of a long life (in (1556) his immense territories were left by him in two halves. His son Philip, had Spain and the Americas (called "The Indies") and the lands of the old Duchy of Burgundy; his brother, Ferdinand, had the rest, in the Germanies and to the east thereof. These two stand at the head of the two branches of the Hapsburg House.

Men still thought of this enormous mass as Hapsburg land. The Austrian Hapsburgs and the Spanish Hapsburgs of the next generation were cousins strongly supporting each other and France seemed at their mercy in the days when Louis was born.

But the two Hapsburg powers thus surrounding France were both politically in decay. Had it not been so the French action under Louis XIV could never have been launched. On the other hand had it not been so that action would not only have been impossible but unnecessary, because had it not been so the French State would have disappeared. Those who read the matter in modern terms (which are, of course, inapplicable) might say that France was "encircled." The French monarchy appeared to be geographically at the mercy of its Hapsburg rivals. If you judge the thing by the map only it looks, to modern eyes, like the assured destruction of the enveloped power. Here are the Netherlands, the Germanies, the Italian Duchies, the whole of Spain, in the hand of the Hapsburgs, and the French Realm pressed by them on all sides.

But the seventeenth century did not think in those terms. The Netherlands were Hapsburg. The southern half of them (what today we call Belgium) was directly ruled by Spain; the northern half (what we today call Holland) had, with the help of the Cecils in England, and much more by the support of the French kings, precariously founded a claim to independence.

But in the days when Louis of Bourbon was about to begin his military effort everyone still thought of *all* the Netherlands, if not all of them in fact yet all of them in judicial right, as belonging to the crown of Spain. The old men could all remember the time when there had been no question about it. *All* the Netherlands had been under Philip II as heir to Charles V. And though the northern, most distant, lesser half of that flat delta no longer paid taxes to the Spanish king, all the southern half, up against France, was held by Spanish garrisons and was under Spanish rule, from Antwerp and Brussels to Lille and the further side of Flanders. The same Hapsburg power ruled Luxemburg and the Ardennes. Under the Empire lay the Alsatian plain. Then, again Spanish, came the Jura mountains, i.e. the Franche Comté. Beyond the barrier of the Alps you had, apart from Savoy, the Spanish crown holding the strongest bases in the Italian Lombard plain. To the south, all along the Pyrenees, the Spanish Power ran from sea to sea. All this map was daily present in the minds of Louis and his advisers, as it had been in the minds of Mazarin and of Richelieu before them. Hapsburgs up against them everywhere.

❁   ❁   ❁

This "encirclement," remember again, was not a modern "encirclement." No nation was then morally independent in what was still Christian Europe; nations did not murder nations in those days as they propose to do in ours. The quarrels were family quarrels so far as territory went; if there were one serious division in Christendom it was a religious cleavage not a territorial. Still the political preponderance on the map of these two Hapsburg groups of territory was overwhelming. It was evident that the Power so surrounded would attempt to relieve the pressure upon it.

Here remark that the pressure against France was unevenly divided. Between the North Sea and the Alps there was an open frontier. Invasion had threatened Gaul across that frontier from the beginning of recorded time and Gaul had reacted against that threat perpetually. There was fixed in the French mind, and has remained there fixed, the conception that their community could only survive by perpetual vigilance and effort directed against attack from the north and east; Hapsburg Spain in Flanders and all the Lorraine Hapsburg fiefs south of that—these were the active threat.

The Jura, in Spanish hands, was not a base for action against the French crown. No main line of invasion crossed it.

But to get hold of the Franche Comté would mean possession by Louis of a firm bargaining counter when it came to negotiating a peace.

And it was easy for the French power to enter Franche Comté at will. All its issues were towards the Rhone, and its daily life was French. It was a grid of limestone ranges, not accustomed to invasion, still less to invading. It was not wealthy. It was difficult of access even for its legitimate monarchs, lying open rather, and easily so, to infiltration from France. A man going into the Jura from the Rhone

Valley found no change in culture, speech or manners, any more than he does today.

Why did these two branches of the "encirclement," the Austrian and the Spanish, each fail to pull its weight? Why would each prove weaker in the presence of a French offensive than the French themselves at the beginning of the conflict believed?

For two very different reasons. Spain was politically in decay, its strength was passing from one set of causes. The strength of Austria and the Empire had long passed for quite another set of causes.

We must not exaggerate the loss of strength in the one or in the other. The Empire was still regarded as the equal, many still thought it the superior, of the French in arms. And the two combined, Spain and the Empire, were thought, in Louis XIV's youth, a continuous menace. Looking backward upon it we can see that neither was now on a level with the French monarchy as Richelieu had made it and Mazarin confirmed it. But in 1667 when the French attack begins the name of Spain especially stood high. Men are always gravely affected by the tradition of an immediate past.

The Kingdom of France and its policy had lain under the great shadow of Spain even so late as Rocroi. Men saw indeed by now, with Rocroi over twenty years behind them, that the ancient glory of the united Spanish monarchy was dimmed; but there was some delay in the recognition of the full reality. The same man who would have admitted or even contemptuously affirmed the decay of Spain in 1660, had at the back of his mind that Spain which his fathers had known and of which he had himself heard so often in youth. Spain so bestrode the world that her immediate tangible wealth, the fame of her possessions and above all the invincibility of her soldiers was something taken for granted right on into the earlier years of that generation.

A man born in 1600 and elderly in 1660 still thought of
the Spaniards as the premier people.

There ruled from Madrid or its neighbouring palaces
a crowned Figure whose undisputed word ordered armed
forces throughout the New World and all round the globe;
in Italy, in the Spanish peninsula itself. There poured into
the treasury of this monarch the actual gold and silver of
the New World in streams. His ships were on every sea,
his Navy was splendid with triumphal record. Spain had
been the victor at Lepanto, the one great naval battle—
and the only one—which had been decisive, in a hundred
years, and the one in which Europe was most concerned.
For Lepanto had meant the throwing back of Islam with
its threat to all our lives.

Men still thought of Spanish sea-power as we think
today of English banking power or Russian man-power.
As for the infantry of Spain, its invincibility was as much
a commonplace before Rocroi as was English naval invincibility thirty years ago, and though the few years since
Rocroi had already appreciably lessened that impression,
it had not disappeared.

With all this, the unity of Spain impressed the mind
of the time as does the unity of England impress men
today. Elsewhere there had been the violent religious wars
in France, then the horrible, savage and destructive religious wars among the Germans. In France, again, there
had been the rebellion of the princes and the plot of the
nobles and the flight of the boy-monarch and of the regent
mother and her advisers from their capital.

In England all the political scheme of things hitherto
associated with the name of England had crashed in ruin.
In England subjects had murdered their king! In England
a chance usurper called Cromwell had suddenly appeared
as despot to the astonishment of Europe! His government
had looted private fortunes right and left, had transferred

wealth on a vast scale from his opponents to his supporters, and, even in the ordinary way of taxation, had levied
such huge sums as to draw from a population still limited
compared with its rivals the best army and one of the best
navies of its time.

There was no Italy, for Italy was but a congeries of
small states essentially under Spanish domination. Even
Portugal, the old and proud, exceptional local monarchy
separate from Madrid, had been absorbed in Spain for sixty
years and was only shaking off that yoke in the years of
Rocroi.[2] The one overwhelming example of steadfast unity,
unchanging, had been and still was Spain.

Now we have only to look round us today to see of
what great effect is political stability upon the minds of
neighbouring nations. The adamantine quality of the Spanish throne was like the granite of the Escorial: it seemed
unshakable; a permanent monument, stable in the midst of
unstable things. Remember also especially this, the most
important thing in the reputation of Spain: Spain alone
had kept intact the Faith of all her people.

Everywhere else the great Religious Revolution—the
Bolshevism of its day—had bred furious massacre, the
deposing of kings, the break-up of society, the ruin of
the poor, the rise of the Money-power. Spain alone had
fended off that hurricane.

But there was even more than that. There was a long
tradition, a legend pictured in the mind, of all that Spain
had done; achievement that still remained present to the
eye and to experience.

Spain had triumphantly cast out the Mohammedan.
Spain had tackled and almost seemed to have solved in
her own case the perennial Jewish problem, although Spain
had a larger, wealthier, more active and more treasonable

2   "The Captivity," as the Portuguese have called it, is generally
dated from 1581 to 1640.

Jewish population than any other Power. Spain had stood
up to that menace and seemed to have won its battle. Spain
had given her vocabulary to the business of sailors and to
the business of soldiers: to this day we have the Spanish
terms embedded in the one profession and in the other.

There was yet more than that. Spain had set up in stone
upon her own soil the most glorious buildings that Christendom had ever known. We today come upon them as visions,
whether at Salamanca or Saragossa, whether at Santiago or
at Burgos, where the tombs of the kings proclaim Spanish
glory; chief among them the masterpiece of all Western
work, the Cathedral of Seville. In her palaces, in the innumerable sculptures of her private houses, in all her luxuriant
woodwork, in her pictorial art, in her shrines from Oviedo
to the cubic cavern of a nave, all darkness, at Tarragona,
Spain everywhere proclaimed herself—and does so still.

Behind all this was that unique achievement to which
no other European people can show any parallel—the capture and transformation of a continent by a handful of
heroic adventurers. All the seaboard of the Pacific, from
the Californian deserts to the beginnings of the Antarctic,
the islands of the new American sea and those eastern
plains north and south of the Amazon basin—these had
been politically the creation of Spain; and all within the
lifetime of a man.

Never shall we understand what memory occupied with
its menace the rivals of Spain in the mid-seventeenth century unless we bear in mind that picture of an active past
not yet deposed.

Spain, overwhelmingly the greatest thing in Christendom less than a lifetime before, had sunk under the weight
of three glories which promised to last for ever—unity,
world-wide dominions and supremacy at sea.

Sea power had bred a sense of invincibility and therefore
a false security. Tribute from abroad had lowered energy at

home: complete unity had atrophied life and made political debate a sham.

And what of the other Hapsburg king, the original stem, the personal direct rule from Vienna over the mountain Slavs, and the Imperial name whereunder all the Germanics had been gathered? Why had that decayed? Because the tempest of the Reformation, its after effects aided by the genius of a Cardinal—of Richelieu—had devastated the German land far more terribly than any others.

There had been a time when it seemed as though the Germans had found a remedy for religious chaos in agreed difference. The new religious conflict among them was confined to argument, and its political effects smoothed over by compromise. Even the loot of religion was condoned and a sort of pact drawn up whereby the looters should have leave to keep their loot on condition of promising to loot no more. The new pressure of the Mohammedans from the east had led to this apparent truce between the Emperor and the Reformers. Under benefit of a lull the Emperor attempted mastery everywhere. There arose an ideal of German unity with the Emperor as Monarch in full power. Against such a policy the separate German political centres, free towns and principates, rose in rebellion, using reform of religion as their pretext. The attempted usurpation of the Bohemian Kingdom by a Calvinist set fire to the heap, and there appeared the unexampled horror of Germans tearing Germans to pieces, Slavs intermingled and abetting; they ruined everything between the Polish boundaries and the Vosges.

It was apocalyptic: famine, cannibalism, pestilence—and the human race starved in Germany to half its numbers.

No decision was reached, for what would have been an imperial victory was destroyed by the genius of Richelieu. *He* hired that exceptional soldier Gustavus Adolphus to throw his Swedish sword into the balance, and, though the victories of this man were over in a year, Germany was disrupted for generations.

Time was the armies of the Emperor had pierced to the heart of France, had reached St. Quentin once, then, later, Corbie at the gates of Amiens. Now they would not appear again for 150 years, so much had German blood been drained away and the Imperial scheme shattered.

So things stood when the French trumpets sounded again in Flanders.

13

First Campaign

THE PRELIMINARIES OF WHAT WAS to be the centre of French fortunes, the business of Holland, were disconnected with Holland itself: they concerned the southern part of the Netherlands, the provinces which had remained loyal to their traditional and ancestral government and remained under the direct authority of Spain. Louis XIV, that still very young man, had no intention, nor had his advisers, of attacking the Dutch directly. There was no reason why he should do so yet.

What he had determined on in the eternal French task of strengthening the frontiers over which lay the route of invasion was the occupation of what we call today Belgium, that is the southern loyal provinces still under the Spanish Government with their capital at Brussels. His method for occupying the fully Catholic Netherlands ruled from Brussels was to claim them in right of his wife, the daughter of Philip IV of Spain. They were a Burgundian inheritance, and the old law of the Netherlands was that the children of the first marriage inherited directly from the father without concern for the children of the second marriage. This Burgundian rule, or rather this rule for the various small states of the Netherlands, was made the pretext for what followed, but it was a pretext only. The Queen of France had renounced her claims at marriage. They were revived on the plea that the stipulated dowry had not been paid.

CAMPAIGN OF FLANDERS

This first entry of Louis XIV into a national war is known as "The War of Devolution." It gets this name from the nature of the claims which Louis had made to his wife's Burgundian inheritance in the Low Countries: for the various local customs of inheritance which I have mentioned and by which the Queen of France, half-sister to the little King of Spain, claimed the Netherlands and the rest were known as "the right to inherit by Devolution."

What followed was in fact no war at all. Its effect was considerable, for it exposed the degree in which Spanish power had decayed; but its operations were insignificant and its immediate success within the modest limits set for it was certain. Castel Rodrigo, who governed the Spanish Netherlands, had barely twenty thousand men, and those of no great value, for the vital principle of the old Spanish army had disappeared. The fortresses of Flanders were in neglect and disrepair; their garrisons were what might be expected when some twenty battalions are asked to defend some fifty separate points.

Turenne was in command, the most famous soldier of his time (and, incidentally, for the purpose of future reference, the most famous Huguenot of his time). Nominally Louis was in supreme command, for that was the necessary position of a King on the field, but he was subject, through his own sense of measure, to the older captain's judgment.[1] Meanwhile, as we shall see in a moment, that military judgment fitted in exactly to aid Louis's own excellent diplomacy.

The army concentrated from its points on the Somme in three groups. As the object in view was the taking of towns and the establishment of a fortified frontier a very large number of newly-cast guns were brought forward:

---

[1] Turenne by the spring of 1667 was in his fifty-sixth year.

no less than two thousand four hundred. A main central mass of about fifty thousand men went with the King and Turenne himself straight for Charleroi; a central point separating equally Mons from Namur. Its capture would threaten both of these fortresses and give power to take them both at will if necessary. The remaining twenty-two thousand men were distributed, some of them to the north or left, to act along the sea coast, others to the right, or south-east, to act towards Luxemburg.

Nothing illustrates the campaign (if it can be called a campaign) better than the dates. They give you the rapidity of that "*promenade militaire*"—a phrase for which we have no exact English equivalent, but which means literally "taking a walk in military fashion," i.e. without serious fighting, but with bodies of troops. It partly corresponds to the English "walk-over."

Turenne had taken over command on the 10th of May of this spring, 1667. The King had left St. Germain on the 16th as we have seen and got to Amiens five days later. In less than a fortnight he had reached and captured Charleroi, a thing that could be done without effort. Young Louis (he was only half-way through his twenty-ninth year) would have gone forward at once—for indeed there was nothing to speak of against him—but Turenne advised a more methodical and slower process to season the troops. He decided for Tournai, and in a little more than three weeks Tournai was taken in its turn. The army arrived before it on the 21st of June, the town surrendered four days later, and the citadel on the morrow.

There was something symbolic about this, for Tournai (architecturally the most remarkable of the towns, with its five tall towering shafts of stone, as simple as the spirit of the earliest middle age) was the place where the little chieftain of the little Frankish contingent of the Roman army had held command when Roman local government dissolved. Tournai is the starting point of the French monarchy.[2]

After Tournai, Douai; and in Douai the French command found only seven hundred men to withstand them—nor did they attempt to withstand. The place was taken in four days. Less than a fortnight later Cambrai went the way of Douai. It was barely mid-July: six weeks had covered the whole affair.

Meanwhile the action of Louis had produced a tragi-comedy at Madrid. The widowed queen there was regent for her unfortunate little invalid son, the half-brother of the Queen of France, in whose name Louis was now marching to occupy her own inheritance in the Low Countries.[3]

The claim of the Queen of France to the Belgian plain and its towns had been only presented, as though no fighting was toward. After the French army had gathered it was solemnly discussed. Even while the troops were marching and taking towns the debate continued. The Queen Regent

---

2   I will not delay the reader by repeating the story of that little Frankish body, how the generals took over local government when the central government broke down, etc. But it is worth remembering that Clovis, being the first of the little local generals to take over local government on any large scale in Gaul and therefore reckoned as the first of the French kings, was the son and successor of the Frankish chieftain who commanded his little body of followers in Tournai. When his tomb was found in the cathedral some two hundred years ago the body carried the insignia of the Roman command. Gaul, and its first Merovingian monarchy, proceeded imperceptibly from the main body of Roman things.

3   The lingering feudal origins mentioned at the opening of this are well exemplified in the nature of the claim made. It was not a claim to the "Spanish Low Countries"—still less to one national region with regular frontiers and self-contained, such as would be made today, it was a claim to each main town and its district by the feudal title it had borne, and through which it had been united with the House of Burgundy, and thus inherited by the Hapsburgs. It was a claim to the "County of Artois," a claim to the "Lordship of Malines," a claim to the "Marquisate of Antwerp," a claim to the "Duchy of Cambrai," etc.

of Spain listened with indignation to the reading of the claim. She whisked her fan. She tapped her foot. But she did not declare war until Tournai and Douai and Charleroi had fallen: the French ambassador did not leave Madrid for weeks after that.

All Europe had seen this young man with his unexpectedly strong and numerous force walking into town after town along all that barrier between himself and the Netherlands, occupying strongholds which forbade invasion of his country and beginning to seize all the territory which he claimed in the name of the Queen. The neighbours on both sides grew alarmed, for this apparition of a strong France (though the foundations had been laid more than thirty years before), the apparition in action and in power of a strong France, one of those resurrections which the French indulge in as a pastime to counterbalance their other pastime of civil war—led to the beginnings of what was later to be a coalition against too great a power. Holland was terrified; the Empire was ill at ease; for French diplomacy had been as strong as French arms and had captured the support of the lesser princes, clerical and lay, whose lands stood on the western edge of the Empire. It is true that these also took fright at the sudden manifestation of so great a new power, but as yet that power was unhampered and the King of France could do what he willed.

The Queen of France came solemnly from Compiègne at the close of this first chapter in the operations. She was presented with these towns of hers, not as a trophy of victory but as a restitution of her own right. Then the main fruit in wealth and in population was culled, the town of Lille.

Here alone there was something like a true siege, lasting for a fortnight, from the 1st to the 17th of August; and it is here there enters for the first time on to the forefront of the stage the great presence of Vauban. Lille was taken,

Alost followed, and after Alost came the rains. Nothing more was done on the Flanders border.

But the reason for the halt was something more important than bad weather. There was a political plan corresponding to that tactical plan of the earlier wars, the interrupted charge, that cavalry tactic which had decided Rocroi and Naseby. At the King's orders the operations in Flanders were reined up and checked, while a next move was made against the distant, separate, fraction of the copious Burgundian inheritance, the Jura, the hill country of Besançon: for that also might be claimed as part of the Burgundian inheritance and, under the custom of Devolution, heritable by the wife of Louis.

The taking over of Franche Comté was even more one-sided a business than the taking over of the Flanders towns. There were perhaps one hundred and twenty armed and mounted men of the Spanish service in all the Jura, and perhaps two thousand hastily recruited men on foot. It took twenty-four hours to occupy Besançon. At Dole there were exactly sixteen troopers. Sallau, the only third town worth reckoning, was swept up as a matter of course. It cannot be called fighting, it certainly cannot be called aggression and it can hardly be called invasion. These outworks of the Alps, these profound limestone valleys and their forests, speaking French like their neighbours, thought of the Swiss Confederation as perhaps their best protectors and neighbours; they had no real bond with Madrid and no real objection to Paris. Indeed, a new bond with Paris, rather than with Madrid, would have seemed to them at such a date, their natural fortune.

Anyhow, the Franche Comté went, in quite a few winter days—early in 1668.

All this being done, the young king of France, in the consolidation of his realm upon its outer unravelled edges, offered Madrid an alternative. He would keep that fringe of

Flemish towns which he had just occupied and give back the Jura to Spain, or keep the Jura and give up Flanders. Which would Madrid choose?

That Louis should be in a position to act so had alarmed the rival powers on his borders. The Dutch merchant oligarchy, which had till lately depended upon the French as their best ally, were made anxious by the presence of such forces, conquering with such ease, immediately to the south of them. Almost within living memory Amsterdam, Utrecht, Maastricht and the rest had been all one with the Belgic towns to the south; the seventeen provinces of the Netherlands had formed one inheritance and one main polity. It was barely twenty years since the Spaniards had reluctantly agreed to recognise the independence of the Calvinist rebels and the rule of those rebels over all that half of the northern delta provinces which was Catholic, and still looked to the restoration of its religion.

During their recent war with England the merchant princes of the Dutch towns had claimed, but had not received, aid from Louis as their ally. They proposed a peace with England; Sweden made overtures, and later these three groups, the crown of Charles II, the merchants of the northern Netherlands and the political and military leaders of the Swedes, with their still high reputation, formed what history calls *The* Triple Alliance. It is odd that the term should still survive among us, who remember so close at hand, another Triple Alliance on a somewhat greater scale, when all Central Europe, Berlin, Austria, Rome, stood together against France, and the Czar as France's ally.

The formation of the Triple Alliance has been put down to the initiative of the Dutch. It may more justly be put down to the strange skill in manœuvre of Charles II, who proved thereby his power of bargaining with his cousin Louis, his value to France as a subsidised support, and the danger of losing that support. Charles II by such moves acquired and maintained the power to play that long successful game against the Money-power in England which continually threatened what was left of the English Royal Power.

But to the excellent diplomacy of Charles (who, after all, is only one lesser factor in the complication), was opposed the still better diplomacy of Lionne and of Louis himself, acquainted with every detail and working ten hours a day to master the situation.

Ostensibly Louis, shocked by the Dutch betrayal of him, by the great merchant and maritime power, turned against him, and piqued at the formation of the Triple Alliance, was willing to negotiate with Spain under the threat of that Alliance. But the reality was something very different. What was really going on behind the scenes was something of which men heard nothing for many years: "The Eventual Treaty."

The Emperor had secretly agreed with the French King to partition the Spanish Empire when the little decrepit child on the Spanish throne should die: "in the event" of that death was the treaty made, hence "eventual"—for it was thought that he might die at any moment.

By this treaty Louis made sure of the Flemish towns and of the Franche Comté or Luxemburg at choice. That was why he was willing to treat. The "Eventual Treaty" had been opened as early as October, just after the Flanders campaign had concluded. In December Lionne got the Empire to open negotiations. It was only after all this that England and Holland signed their agreement at the Hague near the end of January. The English and the Dutch governments signed four days later. The occupation of Franche Comté did not come until February.

So ended that winter: and with the spring the first of the peace treaties which were to mark the great reign was negotiated, drawn up and signed at Aix-la-Chapelle. Under this treaty of Aix-la-Chapelle Louis took over the towns which he had occupied on the Belgic frontier and for the time gave up the Jura. There was much else in the peace, but so far as the security of French soil and the consolidation of its frontiers was concerned, this was the essential first step.

It is strange how long it takes even the most thoroughly exploded myth to die. The halt called to French action we now know to have been due entirely to the Eventual Treaty. Further, anyone with a sense of proportion and some knowledge of the time and of the characters at work can be certain that the diplomatic skill of Charles Stuart had both interposed the Triple Alliance and forborne to push the threat of it too far. Yet the old legend of Louis suddenly brought up short by the formidable coalition of the three Protestant Powers lived on serenely through the greater part of the nineteenth century and reappears today in our textbooks from time to time. Even when men are ashamed to say such a thing openly, because they fear seeming too ignorant or too prejudiced, they hint at it.

The Triple Alliance had not the power and was not intended to have the power, to check Louis at that moment. What forces had the King of England to bring to bear comparable to the great armies and their reserves which had already been mobilised beyond the Channel? What could the very imperfect, ill-trained and numerically weak Dutch forces have done? What were the Swedes in 1668 compared with what they had been half a lifetime before?

No, the Triple Alliance was nothing like what has exaggeratedly been described in our official histories, but it was well worth making, because it was the first proof, and a vigorous one, of the weight Charles II could pull when he chose. It was sufficient to give pause to those in France who had thought the rivalry between Dutch maritime power and English would prevent any coalition. The Triple Alliance could not have done much of itself, but as an earnest of what might follow it was a card well worth playing. However, it was no more than a card well worth playing, it was not a trump card, it could take no tricks. The real thing at work behind it all was the Eventual Treaty.

We may pause here to consider the function of monarchy in all this. The quality and strength of monarchy as a form of government had been seen in the restraint of the King when he accepted the advice for the "interrupted charge," had followed Turenne's caution in the matter of arms and Lionne's solid planning in the matter of diplomacy. An oligarchy, a senate, a patriciate, all that is not monarchy could hardly have had the discipline or readiness to order and to effect that "interrupted charge." Aristocracy, the alternative to monarchy, has proved itself in one commercial state after another, not least in our own, eminently capable of conquest by negotiation, of expansion by penetration. But it has never proved itself capable of a set secret plan followed rapidly and in detail. That sort of thing is military, not mercantile. That sort of thing is monarchic not aristocratic.

There is another personal aspect of monarchy in all this, curiously interesting to watch. Turenne's caution was not only a military calculation, it was also a political one. The young King was with the armies. His life ran some risk, although the fighting was on so small a scale. It would have run a greater risk had he fallen before large forces were ready to meet the coalition which might await him if he advanced further into the Low Countries.

It was monarchy also, but that is a minor point, which gave to this little business of Flanders (very little as a military thing, though big with future political things) its social character. It was a war carried on under the eyes of ladies and by courtiers in the dress of the Court. It was a war of parade.

It is just like ironical Clio to have illustrated this business more thoroughly than any other. You may wander in the halls of Versailles itself from picture to picture upon the walls thereof, which give you these sieges that were hardly sieges, and capitulations which were rather facile, voluntary surrenders than defeats. There may you *see* the capture of Lille and all the rest of it, finely spread out before you, living in landscape and sky. You can enter the very skins of the cavaliers who caracole before you: Louis their chief. You can do no such thing with Wagram or with Austerlitz.

The War of Devolution, barely to be called a war, had so much leisure about it that it properly lends itself to the easel, and many a man remembers better through the eye the perfunctory cleaning up of those dilapidated defences between the Ardennes and the sea than any one of the vastly greater military actions which determined history a few years later in the Marches of the Rhine. For my part I can see clearly before me this first half-civilian advance into the Low Countries: I can visualise it through their pictures as I can never visualise "'93" or those lightning strikes in the Ligurian Range wherewith Napoleon entered glory on the Lombard plain.

How far was that brief campaign an illustration of monarchy? The rapidity of action, the sense of plan, and the restraint at the close were all of them functions of monarchy. The conditions were facile; a State otherwise organised would have proceeded perhaps in almost as brief a time, but it needed monarchy, I think, to judge the expediency of stopping short midway.

There was here a length of view and a precision that you hardly ever get except with central control. For the real motive underlying that restraint was the importance of waiting until the fruit should be ripe. It was important of course to show the very great strength of the new organisation now arisen, but with the probability that a much graver decision would have to be taken in what was then thought an immediate probability, the death of the sickly child at Madrid, the consequent vacancy of the Spanish throne and all the French claim to it through the Spanish marriage, it was better to wait. The wisdom of that delay was apparent when the secret Eventual Treaty was signed between the Empire and Louis.

14

The Main War

AFTER THE PEACE OF AIX IT WAS the business of Louis to prepare that for which Flanders had been but a rehearsal and preliminary—the main duel with Holland. In all that the King is personally at work. Louvois, now in active succession to his father, raises and organises the much larger new armies, but policy and diplomacy are the creation of Louis himself, the early well-aimed blow is his own, the responsibility for the blunder which lost him Amsterdam is his own. Lionne died before the spade work was over: he arranged the Treaty of Dover—of which later—and shortly died. Louis continued his preparations for the main war—the skilful acquirement of allies and settlement of neutrals until all was prepared.

What may be called "the main war" opens with the attack on Holland in the spring of 1672 and closes with that batch of treaties which take their general name from the particular treaty concluded at Nijmegen, and generally known by the name of that town after the particular treaty between France and Holland there concluded.

It is difficult for modern men to find any order or plan in the great series of operations. The Duke of Wellington said that one can no more describe a battle than one can describe a ballroom, and this mass of fighting was like one vast battle, all over the Marches of the French realm, the disputed ground between the King of France's admitted territory and the territory which was still nominally Spanish in the Netherlands, the territory which had successfully rebelled against Spain in the Netherlands (that is the United Provinces under the Dutch merchant oligarchy), the Empire in and beyond the Rhine Valley, the Duchy of Lorraine, as much as was nominally attached to the Empire, the Jura Hills, etc.

The political interests so far from being clear cut are one constant shifting confusion in the first fairly simple episode of Louis's attack on Holland, its failure. It is a perpetual *chassé-croisé* of alliances and counter-alliances, allies secured, abandoned, and then secured again.[1] To set down all the circumstances, even the main military interests, in their order, gives no impression of what was really happening, and the finale is always bewildering to the reader who has been given nothing but such a list.

But if we keep in mind three main threads which run continually through these five and a half years, we shall discover their character and understand the upshot.

These three threads were three driving forces and therefore three policies which those driving forces governed. The driving forces are:

1. The vision of Louis XIV: his prospect of the task before him. That task inherited by him from Richelieu through Mazarin was the consolidation of "the square enclosed field"—by which metaphor the great Cardinal and his successors described France as it came to be. They had found the French realm at the beginning of the seventeenth century surrounded by territory not only debatable but dislocated, indeed a mass of shreds under the Crown of Paris. Nearly all, but not all, of what France was solidly to become had been long organised, and it was still organised

---

1 Sweden with its remaining military prestige begins as an ally, becomes doubtful, ends as an ally again. The changes in the Dutch attitude we shall also witness. It is at first a victim, then violently hostile, at last a friend—a protective friend. The Empire is now a formidable opponent, now a supine one. Brandenburg, that is the Hohenzollerns (Prussia), beginning its career, is not consistently a foe and certainly not consistently a friend. So it is over the whole field of negotiation, military action and debate, in the years that lead up to the Peace of Niemeguen.

on a feudal tradition; the central power of which Richelieu was the main creator had not a simple basis, though it had a simple centre—the King. The King's authority worked through machinery of great complexity, varying not only with every province but with each small district. Customs of infinite variety attached even to public action. Here you would find ancient and active traditions of local representation, relics of those "parliaments" which had arisen hundreds of years before during the Middle Ages in the Pyrenean valleys and the principle of which had spread and been copied throughout Western Christendom. There you would have unchecked authority at work: certain districts were held through the inheritance of feudal bishoprics with difficulty detached from the Empire; others were held as the result of special treaties guaranteeing their constitution. Where some were in effect the radius of action of a great town the merchants and council of which were still powerful, others were purely agricultural, still in part dependent upon a mass of small local lordships.

It had been the aim of those who produced the new French monarchy under the Bourbons to make of all those highly differentiated and conflicting origins one State. But it was an aim to be only slowly achieved even in practice, and one the theory of which was not fully enunciated until more than a century after Richelieu's death and a long lifetime after that of Louis.

Not only did this French policy concern the internal consolidation of the realm, it concerned much more the simplification into final shape of the frontiers. Everywhere from the North Sea to the Mediterranean what were ultimately to be the definite frontiers of the French monarchy were a chaos of disputed ground, islands like the three bishoprics, Toul, Verdun and Metz, directly French but surrounded by territory either mainly French in spirit like Lorraine or bordering on districts of German speech and custom. On the open north-eastern side from which the very existence of the French monarchy had been imperilled time and again by invasion, there had been since the later part of the Middle Ages no fixed attachment to one House or one Government. The great mercantile towns which Spain had inherited from the House of Burgundy were taken or lost as fortresses and none could say whether the ultimate fate of any one of them would be to fall under the King of Paris or some power alien to and hostile to France. Along the left bank of the Rhine the Alsatian plain, wholly German in speech and custom, was a mass of lordships of independent cities, large and small; since the fall of Brisach before Louis was born the French power had overshadowed Alsace but had not taken root.

The character of the Jura and its vicissitudes we have already seen in the original war of devolution. All this chaos of districts it was the constant aim of the French monarchy and therefore of Louis to reduce to a simple principle with two main elements: first the frontier following the crest of the Jura, the main natural mountain frontier, then the line of the Rhine, and then from some point on the Rhine to the North Sea a special barrier which by artificial fortification could be maintained secure. On the south, though the Pyrenees formed a natural boundary, a particular local geological configuration in the north of Catalonia put Perpignan and the Roussillon under French authority through the final action of Mazarin's life and the Treaty of the Pyrenees. Even here there were a few anomalies which remain to this day, such as the upper valley of the Garonne and the isolated Catalan town of Llivia, a district in the heart of south-eastern France naturally French in character though of the Provençal sort,[2] Avi-

2   The Roussillon, with Perpignan as its capital, was and is Catalan in popular speech. Even today during the Spanish struggle which is proceeding you will find more sympathisers with the Barcelona

gnon was still legally papal territory, occasionally occupied during quarrels by French forces but not annexed to France until the Revolution. An outlier of the French territory of Metz cut right across the German-speaking plain on the left bank of the Rhine—and so on; the whole of the low frontiers were still ragged edges, hardly frontiers at all.

Louis thus saw his part in his great task, his business of kingship; the making of a completely homogeneous realm within continuous, unbroken and defensible frontiers. If we keep this in mind we understand one motive force, the main motive force of the three, and the policy ensuing upon it.

2. The second motive force was the character of the young William of Orange. He was devoured by ambition, partly family but mainly personal. Herein observe an unusual combination. This isolated character which had never really known what it was to be young and which was now in its twenty-third year (he was born in 1650), was perverted, vicious, constantly morose, detested by most of those whom he came across, disliked by the better of

---

Government in this corner of France than anywhere else. The town of Llivia is reached even now by a neutral road, is wholly surrounded by French territory, but once you are within its narrow boundaries you have the Spanish atmosphere and customs all about you. Andorra is still under dual control, or was when the Civil War broke out two years ago, the ordinary rights of the Spanish Crown being represented by the Bishop of Orgel and the French condominion by the Prefect of the French Department to the north of it. The first few miles of the Garonne, after its strange passage underground in the Pyrenean hills, is Spanish up to the point called the King's Breach. All this Pyrenean frontier is an excellent model on which men may study how the French frontiers were anomalously settled 300 years ago. To follow it is like studying a fossil in a geological formation. The curious formation alluded to in the text whereby Northern Catalonia looks towards France rather than towards Spain; the Cerdagne, the watershed, which one would think might make a natural frontier, runs here not along the crest of the Pyrenees but through an easy dimpled flattish saddle of land and then continues eastward to the Mediterranean by a well-defined spur of hills which cut off the Perpignan country, the Roussillon, from the rest of Catalonia.

his fellow-countrymen—if fellow-countrymen they can be called; for the House of Orange had no long tradition of Flemish things; it took its origin from the Germans, its title from the Rhone, and was French in speech and correspondence. But this perverse and perverted spirit, of a sort we do not usually find connected with ambition of any kind, was in the case of young William full of envious discontent against the Kings. He was devoured by that passion all his life. He always desired to be something more than he was: to redeem himself by power from his inward nervous miseries.

It was impossible even for the immense wealth which he had inherited to dominate the mercantile banking oligarchy of the United Provinces. He could not be king, he could not have undisputed command even of his own special province of the seven, Holland with its capital at the Hague. The Dutch were already organised as an aristocracy or oligarchy because they were commercial. Oligarchies or aristocracies are the natural enemies of monarchy. It would, I say, be impossible for William and the House he represented to be kings in Holland under seventeenth-century conditions, but war needed a single head for its direction, while war lasted therefore he was hereditary head and chief of the Dutch forces. The chance of continuous war lay ready to William's hand after the King of France's early determination to master the Dutch financial power which lay so dangerously beside his wife's (and therefore his own) inheritance of the Netherlands. There was no natural frontier, and Amsterdam was more than a rival to Antwerp, for the younger town had become the seat of the first great central bank of modern times. When Louis had come near to sweeping the United Provinces into a general command of all the Netherlands, William made himself the leading figure of the resistance. When, later on, Louis, having failed to capture the United Provinces, was willing to make peace and become their protector against their commercial rivals, William never wavered in his personal policy.

To the fate of his neighbours and fellows of the United Provinces he was indifferent so long as his own ambition was served. The burning flame of that ambition never slackened. It was an inward concealed thing like all about him, but it was of great intensity. Indeed William's chief quality, a quality most rare in men of the uncompanionable tainted type, was tenacity. Of that tenacity he lived to reap the reward. Before life left his little warped body he had seen the last great coalition against France formed and on a fair way to success. It is a pity he did not live on a year or two to hear of Blenheim. He would have died of satisfaction.

We must keep this second thread which runs through the political and military welter of the time as clearly in view as the first, for though the power of the United Provinces was but a financial and banking commercial power, though its military resources could not compare with those of Louis, yet it was throughout a formidable obstacle to Louis in all he did. Moreover, even when the understanding between the Dutch and the French monarchy was at its strongest, even when it seemed, after half a dozen years of general war, as though William of Orange had lost the game, even when the banking and commercial power of Amsterdam was all for peace, *he* held out. The event justified his pertinacity.

3. The third element, the third thread running through the general business and giving some sort of unity to it, is the equally tenacious motive of Charles Stuart, second of that name to be King of England.

Charles II had for the driving power of all he did the determination to maintain and even if possible to restore the English monarchy.

He was the son of a father who had been dethroned and put to death by a rebellion founded upon the mercantile power of the City of London, a rebellion supported at heart by most, in actual arms by perhaps one-half, of the landowners as well.

He had suffered in youth the bitterness of seeing his own people supine when the royal armies had been defeated and the military despotism under which they lay forbade their joining him when he made that gallant attempt to recover his father's throne. Thus abandoned he had been defeated at Worcester by Cromwell with forces double his own.

His life had been saved as though by a miracle. He had wandered as an exile whose chances fell lower and lower in the estimation of the European governments. Mazarin had deliberately allied the French Government with that of Cromwell, the man who had been the chief agent and framer of his father's death, to whom, as we have seen, Mazarin even abandoned Dunkirk. Everywhere the youth of this embarrassed, hunted young man (eight years the senior of his first cousin, the King of France) had been filled with humiliation.

When he came back to England it was to an England which had been taken over for most social and economic purposes of government by the ruling class, which was far stronger than the remaining prestige of the royal name.

Though he was king and had the disposal of lucrative places wherewith to secure the personal support of some, he was faced by the constant steady opposition of the aristocratic spirit which henceforward was to rule England.

He had no source of revenue beside whatever pittance this rich class in its two great committees, the House of Lords and the House of Commons, chose to allow him; and they took care that it should be wholly insufficient for his support. They even allowed the national fleet to fail rather than vote the money required for its upkeep. They called themselves "The People of England," and are still so called in most of our official histories.

Looking backwards and knowing how this effort failed, we are tempted to think that failure inevitable. I must confess that I think the victory of aristocracy over English kingship was inevitable, but not so sweeping a victory, not so thorough a degradation of the Crown. Charles II showed such genius in steering his craft through the rapids, he showed such supreme diplomatic ability, that if he could not have restored a living monarchy, if he could not have prevented the English polity from becoming the aristocratic thing it became, still he might have refounded a certain element of monarchy in defence of the English people against their rich masters. But for the virtues and consequent defects of his brother James there might have remained throughout the eighteenth century a considerable kingly power at work in Windsor, and even in London, reduced but alive—with such tenacity of will, with such very great skill in handling impossible situations had Charles done his work.

Even as it was, Charles did leave a certain legacy of which the nation in our lifetime has learnt to be proud. He at any rate preserved the *name* of kingship, the title "King of England," and some of our contemporaries have thought (it is but a speculation) that this nominal royal power may in future acquire substance and act as a counterbalance to the overwhelming preponderance of mere wealth in the hands of the few. However that may be, what concerns us immediately here in the story of the French wars is this third thread running through the subtle untiring action of Charles against odds that would have destroyed a less capable man and did destroy his successor.

He played against the money-power represented by the City of London and the great landlords the desire of his cousin, Louis XIV, to prevent the rising of a hostile England upon the flank of France.

Time and again he got a subsidy from the French
King, which enabled him just barely to tide over the
critical moment when his own wealthier subjects might
have starved out the Crown. He yielded at the expense
of his conscience to the murderously fanatical clamour
roused against the Catholic Minority by the best intriguer
among his enemies, Shaftesbury. At the expense not only
of his conscience but of his honour he weathered the
storm of the Popish Plot and jettisoned the lives of innocent men as one throws goods overboard from an over-
weighted ship in a storm.

To prevent dependence upon France he played the mas-
terstroke of marrying the Princess-heiress of his throne
to young William of Orange himself, a blow under which
Louis staggered. Having done that, he refused to let this
nephew and nephew-in-law[3] of his stampede him into
openly joining the coalition against France. He indeed
allowed a declaration of war when he knew that it was
too late to serve the purpose of Orange, but not too late
to make the French Government understand England's
power.

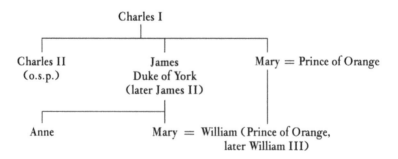

---

3   William of Orange was of course both nephew and nephew-in-law
of Charles Stuart, his mother being the eldest sister of Charles.

15

Meaning and Error of the Dutch Campaign

T HE CHIEF MATTER IN THE DUTCH War for a modern man is the comprehension of its political character.

He knows of a war with "Holland," he hears of the invasion of "Holland" by Louis XIV. It seems to him the wanton aggression of one foreign nation against another.

The Dutch War was of course nothing of the sort. It was part of the general plan for securing France from the invasions of which she had been the victim, especially on her north-eastern frontier, for three lifetimes. To secure the most open vulnerable frontier of France was in the eyes of Louis and his contemporaries what command of the sea was to Englishmen in the nineteenth century. It was also part of the duel engaged between Monarchy and the Money-power.

But the moral point is not settled by so simple an explanation; we may feel that this or that group of men are our rivals and yet have no moral right to attack them. What was the moral attitude of Louis when he had thus determined to make a main attack upon the United Provinces?

To answer that question we must remember that the United Provinces were not regarded by their contemporaries of the mid-seventeenth century as an established State. They were still, historically, rebels against their lawful sovereign, the Spanish Crown; rebels who had so far succeeded that this sovereign had consented to make peace. But those who called themselves—as Louis did by his marriage—the rightful heirs of the defeated legitimate government were not bound in honour to that humiliation. As long as the Spanish Crown continued to call the United Provinces rebels and as long as their provisional government was not recognised at Madrid, those who feared the excess of Spanish power, now the French, now the English, would ally themselves with Amsterdam against Madrid. But when a man acted as the heir to Spain he was under no such necessity.

Louis, by claiming the Spanish Netherlands in the name of his wife and at the same time bargaining for the Jura, was virtually proclaiming himself the successor to the Burgundian inheritance of Madrid, and that Burgundian inheritance included the seven rebellious provinces—"The United Provinces" as they called themselves—as well as the nine loyal provinces. It included what we call today Holland on the same footing as what we call today Belgium.

It was barely a lifetime since the rebellion had taken place, the struggle of the legitimate government against the rebels had lasted till times which men could still remember. When Louis first began his advance the final accommodation between Madrid and the rebellious provinces—which had concerned Philip of Spain alone and did not bind those who claimed earlier title—this doubtful experiment had not lasted twenty years. When the troops of the young King first entered Flanders all the eyes of Europe turned to the Calvinist mercantile plutocracy centred in the Hague and in Amsterdam, as the ultimate object of the struggle. The experiment of independence for Amsterdam and the Dutch Money-power might or might not take root; even if it ultimately succeeded it was still, for the elder statesmen of Europe, something which had arisen by flying in the face of every hereditary rule of government hitherto held sacred in Christendom.

One who would quarrel with Louis's action on moral grounds must not quarrel with it as the wanton invasion of a free and separate nation, but rather on the view that the Queen of France had no longer the rights her husband claimed: those rights had lapsed with her repudiation of them on her marriage. This Louis denied. He had given his arguments for regarding his wife as still the heir to the Burgundian inheritance. Those arguments gave their wholly juridical meaning to the recent war of devolution and held good for the northern provinces of the Netherlands as for the southern.

But all this is legal discussion, of one value to those who would establish a strict moral point, of quite another value to those who would understand the wide political struggle of the time. The motive power urging Louis so to act was not feeling for his wife's inheritance but the determination to make the north-eastern frontier secure once and for all and the invasion of France, to the very heart of that country, down the roads that led from the Netherlands towns, impossible in the future for good and all, *and* to master a growing *Money-power* hostile to the older religion and social traditions.

Louis, then, had engaged in a political adventure—definite enough—but it was a bad policy: false inheritance from Mazarin.

When Mazarin had proposed first to hold Catalonia and then to exchange it for the Netherlands—this was in his mind during his last years—he blundered badly. To have taken over the Southern Netherlands centred on Brussels which were wholly Catholic, and the upper class and general culture of which were French speaking, would indeed have been to extend and confirm the French realm. But to extend this policy to *all* the Netherlands, to include in the claim and in the political policy of reunion with France the seven rebel provinces dependent on Amsterdam, was an error of the first class.

It was bad policy for four reasons: some of which a seventeenth-century man might be excused for not grasping because their full value only became clear much later, but others of which he could already grasp in 1672 if he had a sufficient sense of reality.

These four reasons were as follows:

1. The rebel provinces were not—as some say who have argued for the military necessity of the war—"on the flank" of the French realm. Had the new Dutch group been a great Power such as the Empire or Spain it would have been another matter. But the merchants of Amsterdam and of the cities and provinces in league with them could never raise an army sufficient in quality or quantity for invading French territory. It would have been an advantage rather than otherwise to have a small *friendly* community of this kind lying immediately against the new French frontier.

2. The population was alien in speech. In those days men thought little of that but later on it would prove important as we know from the effect of a common speech in our time, since, say, 1800. We today exaggerate that effect, of course, but in Louis's day it was underestimated. It is true that Alsace, which was in process of being taken over by the French, was also alien in speech. It is true also that the most powerful family of the United Provinces, the House of Nassau—later to reign over them—were French-speaking. William the Silent had been of French culture, and most of the wealthier people around him, but the United Provinces since their rebellion against Spain had more and more insisted on the distinction of language between their territory and that ruled from the Court at Brussels.

3. Far more important than the matter of language was the matter of religion. By taking over a new great mass of Calvinists Louis could not but add to his difficulties. The Calvinists were the most dangerous dissident element in his own population at home. They had not appeared

in armed revolt for half a lifetime. They felt, as all other Frenchmen felt, the new glory of the realm. But they were still something of a state within a state and inevitably in sympathy with societies hostile to France.

It is true, of course, that a very large proportion of the population in the United Provinces was Catholic; perhaps one-half were still Catholic, perhaps even slightly more than half; but the directing forces of that new experimental commonwealth was a strongly anti-Catholic group of wealthy men who had taken their decision against the Catholic culture more than a lifetime ago, the symbol of the change being the declaration of apostasy made by William the Silent.

Even today professed Catholics are to declared Protestants as 29 to 36,[1] but even should they grow to be a majority in the near future (as they well may) it will be long indeed, if ever, before the Catholic culture gives its tone to what we call "The Kingdom of the Netherlands."

The fact that some half of the United Provinces were persecuted Catholics in 1672 was a challenge to the French King as protector of their religion and as the chief monarch therein since the decline of Spain began; but to take on the extra task of their protection was more than this situation demanded. It was unduly burdening the French.

4. By attempting to include the United Provinces—that is Amsterdam—in his claim to the Burgundian inheritance of his wife Louis was risking the addition of yet another element of the Money-power which it was his special function to withstand and tame.

Within France he had so far succeeded in doing this. But France was mainly agricultural; the United Provinces were commercial, and what was more important they were

---

[1]   Professed Jews and those who give no return account for another 25 to 26. Say: Professed Protestants 39 to 40 per cent., Professed Catholics 33 per cent., Jews and undetermined 27 per cent.

now the *chief bankers of Europe.* The principal example of that new power which Banking now began to assume.

A banking society has great advantages over an agricultural one. It uses money counted over and over again. It relies on its credit in a way to which its opponents cannot pretend. Amsterdam had become—long before 1672—the great banking centre of Europe. The Bank of Amsterdam was at this time what the Bank of Genoa had been in the past. The Dutch Money-power was now what the Lombard Money-power had been of old. Had Louis proposed or been able to destroy that banking power, well and good. But Louis did not propose to destroy that Money-power, he proposed no more than to annex the area at which it had become firmly fixed. As sovereign over Amsterdam he would have found himself saddled with another and worse burden, at issue with another and far more dangerous hostility than the burden and the hostility which Fouquet ever presented at home.

For all these reasons the effort to take over the decayed and half-forgotten Spanish claim of the Northern Netherlands which had come to be called "The United Provinces," and which we today call "Holland," was an error.

16

What is Banking?

I T IS AS WELL, AT THIS POINT, TO make quite clear the political menace (and advantage) of the new banking whereof Amsterdam was the pioneer in modern times.

I have called it in general "the Money-power," and it is true that in general the eternal duel between Monarchy and Money-power includes the special form of Money-power called Modern Banking, and lest a point not often defined should be misunderstood I will proceed to define it.

The power of a banking system lies in three things: first that it is able to create currency uncontrolled by the State, and in amounts not limited save by the bankers' own interest and convenience. It makes money "out of air" as it were.

Secondly, this "money" is not real wealth as is land or crops or cattle, and can therefore be transferred, expanded or concealed without offering any hold to the sovereign Authority which should properly govern all society. In other words a banking system is a state within the State.

Thirdly, the bank-currency thus created out of nothing is what is called "liquid." The whole of it can be used for whatever purposes the bank proposes. It comes to check industry at will, to bribe or subsidise whom it will or to penalise whom it will, to control as a money-lender the activities of the community and to drain the wealth of that community by the usury it demands.

Since the whole of this power depends upon the capacity of a banking monopoly for creating currency let us understand the trick by which it acquires this essential facility.

In the beginning a man having coin which he desired to secure from danger would leave it with a goldsmith or anyone who had a strong box and a counter for paying in and out. He left it, of course, under the condition that he might withdraw the whole of it or any part of it whenever he chose. Suppose eleven men thus leave each of them one hundred gold pieces with the man who has the strong box; he is henceforward their banker. They come to him from time to time, withdrawing each of them some portion of their money to use, or paying in some new money to be kept for them.

It was soon found that in practice the amount withdrawn in any given unit of time, say a month, would be replaced by depositors at a certain average pace: that is, while there was a certain volume or pace of withdrawal there was also a corresponding pace of deposits. But *between inflow and outflow there was always a certain large reserve on hand:* there was always a certain large sum in gold and silver which the man who held the coins in trust had by him.

In practice it was found that this permanently unused balance came to about ten times the amount required to be kept ready for meeting withdrawal demands.

The eleven men having left in trust, on the honour of the banker £1,100, a whole thousand of that eleven hundred regularly lay idle at any given time. It was enough for the banker to keep one hundred by him to meet current demands for withdrawal, for he found he could count upon new deposits coming in as freely as withdrawals were made. Jones would draw ten pounds out of his hundred to pay a bill on New Year's Day, but at Candlemas, a month later, he would pay in ten pounds which he had received and wanted to be kept safe. One-tenth of the total amount, then, was all that the banker had to keep by him to meet his obligations. He proceeded to embezzle the rest—at least, it is embezzlement when a private individual uses for his own purpose money deposited with him on trust. But custom ultimately winked at this embezzlement, so, at last, the banker felt quite secure if he had really only got one-tenth of the money which, in law and morals, he was bound to pay on demand. The other nine-tenths he could do what he liked with—and especially lend it out at usury.

But that is only the beginning of the story. It was again soon found that a banker's promise to pay would be accepted by his clients as though it were actual payment. His bit of paper would circulate from hand to hand in the sure and certain hope that when it was presented it would be cashed. *So these bits of paper became currency.* The banker had created money out of nothing, greatly to his advantage, as it would be to the advantage of any of us who should be lucky enough to bring off the same trick. You and I with eleven hundred pounds can pay eleven men to build a house for us in six months. But a banker with eleven hundred pounds can build ten houses where we build one. You and I can lend our eleven hundred out at five per cent. and get fifty-five pounds a year; but a banker can get five hundred and fifty pounds a year on the same basis.

But that was not the end of the story. There was a further development. The bank allowed a customer to draw out as much of this currency as it thought safe over and above the sum of money which he was registered as having deposited with him. It gave John Jones an instrument of credit—at usury, of course—and then another of the same sort to those who did business with John Jones. Thus a farmer with a thousand pounds' worth of stock who wanted a thousand pounds' worth of timber, but had no ready money, and the man with a thousand pounds' worth of timber who wanted a thousand pounds' worth of stock, but had no ready money, could not do a deal unless they knew each other and were in touch. They needed currency to effect the exchange. Before the trick of banking arose they would each have had to pay in coin, each receiving a thousand gold pieces and each paying out a thousand gold pieces. With banking, exchange took place unhampered by such clumsy methods. Banking therefore vastly increased facilities of exchange, that is, of trade. But the new advantage was gained at the cost of two things: (1) Interest by the timber man and the sheep owner *on the security of their own wealth* had to be paid on the sham currency.[1] (2) A trader could not get hold of that sham currency save by leave of the banks.

When a great central bank was established, such as was that of Amsterdam, and its credit firmly rooted, it could, up to a certain limit, create currency at will. It could also get into its power all those over whom its credit system extended. It could, moreover, subsidise governments, make possible vast expenditure otherwise not possible, and by withholding or extending its credit, could decide the main issues of society.

When such an institution as the Bank of Amsterdam had arisen, it was stronger than any king, or government of any kind. It conferred great benefits on the community wherein it stood, permitting a rapid expansion of all economic activity and especially of foreign trade. It could foster domestic manufacture and stimulate every other material function of society. It paid for wars in a fashion that kings could not do and repaid itself by creating what we call today a national debt, that is, by levying usury through the government's power of taxation. After the Dutch invasion of England in 1688 the way to national indebtedness was clear and the Bank of England, under the new system of bank credit, brought the same benefits and the same evils to England, as Holland had enjoyed. London and Amsterdam acquired a strength which the national

---

1 A modern American humanist put the case neatly. "The Bank builds a house with your money and then charges you rent."

monarchs had not possessed. They became the masters of their own community and in part the masters of others. The old traditional social morals of Europe were faced by a growing and vigorous force of usury.

By all this we may see why the great typical monarchy of France was at issue with the Money-power, why the Money-power everywhere worked to destroy monarchy— that which alone could control it.

Nevertheless, Louis ought never to have attacked Holland, unless he had intended to destroy its banking system: which he neither could nor would.

17

The Invasion: Amsterdam

I HAVE SAID THAT LOUIS PREPARED the way for his new venture by carefully negotiated alliances. The old alliance with the Swedes was confirmed; he had the Bishopric of Munster on his side; the German princes were neutral or indifferent or actually favourable, save the Elector of Brandenburg. He was connected by a new marriage with the Elector Palatine. He secured himself from English attack both because the rivalry between the Dutch merchants and the English was still strong and because the Treaty of Dover was to furnish him with such security at least until the peace.[1]

There was no declaration of war because it was the very core of Louis's pretension that he was not attacking a State but reclaiming legitimate rights as the heir to the old lawful government of the whole Netherlands.

As for the machinery of war, Louvois and his father had provided him with the largest force ever commanded by a French king since the French monarchy had acquired central power over the realm. There were no less than 120,000 men under arms; 80,000 to advance from Charleroi towards

---

1 The Treaty of Dover gave a secret subsidy to Charles II, King of England, to help him against his wealthier subjects, who were in permanent opposition to him. It was part of that skilful manœuvring by Charles to maintain the Crown, which we shall shortly describe. It was concluded two years before the war by the Duchess of Orleans, Charles's sister and the sister-in-law of Louis. She died suddenly just after, and, in the year of the war, her widower, Louis's brother, married the heiress of the Elector Palatine, whence the claims of Louis in her name over the Palatinate when her father died and she inherited.

Maastricht under the King himself and Turenne, 40,000 under Condé coming to converge on Maastricht from Sedan.

The junction of the two great forces—so great for those times as to seem incredible in contemporary eyes—was effected in front of Maastricht on the 22nd of May, 1672.

What followed the Dutch themselves called "a land flood." It was the overwhelming of all that flat country by this mass of French troops. All the little fortified places on the eastern fringe of the United Provinces along the line of the Rhine were taken with very little resistance, the Rhine itself was crossed where it is a diminished stream in its lower course and this operation acquired an absurdly exaggerated fame. The command of their inferior army had been given by the United Provinces to young William of Orange, who inherited the fame but not the skill of that great general, his uncle Maurice of Nassau.

But Orange had no more than 20,000 men free for active operations, and these were of no high quality as soldiers— nor was their leader. He had to fall back. Utrecht was taken by the French on the 20th of June. On the same day the French cavalry were at Muyden, and Amsterdam was at their mercy, for the bulk of the army would follow. Amsterdam, with say a quarter of a million people, counting its surroundings, with all the money-power of the north concentrated therein, with its crowded shipping, the new and triumphant rival of Antwerp, was on the point of falling into the hands of the King of France and presumably of remaining in those hands. Muyden was but seven miles from that commercial capital and there was nothing in between.

The province of Holland was panic-stricken; there was wild talk among the richer men of emigrating to the recently acquired Spice Islands of the Far East. But at that very moment Amsterdam was saved. At Muyden stood the sluices which could let in the waters of the Zuyder Zee and flood all the flat land round Amsterdam. Why the French had not provided against this, why they did not understand the critical character of that moment, has never been explained. Condé advised it, but he was absent, wounded. Turenne and Louis were too slow. The sluices were lifted by their opponents and a vast sheet of water stood between them and their prize. Beyond it a forest of masts, the spires and the roofs of the great city—and the impossible flood between. Amsterdam was saved. The 20th of June, 1672, is one of the capital moments in the history of the West.

Thenceforward all the French Army and Government could do would not be effective, though they did much.

The Feast of Corpus Christi was kept with great splendour, the Catholics showed their faces again. On the 16th of July the great church of Utrecht was opened to the ancestral worship, the Mass was said there once more and vast crowds, gathering from every side, acclaimed their liberation. But even as we watch that startling thing we must remember that the French Army as invaders was distasteful and soon to be hated for its excesses, loot and forced constitutions, even by those to whom it had restored liberty of conscience, for the war had been conducted harshly, the levies of money and goods had been excessive and brutally carried out. The mass of men and women seeing foreign armies on their territory feared ruin, besides the odious novelty of a military occupation.

Meanwhile young Orange (he was not yet twenty-two) as the suspected but necessary hereditary general of the imperilled, but not yet ruined, merchants had his way clear before him now that he had been saved from complete defeat. The war could bring *him* nothing but fame and employment, further glory to the family which he represented and which by this time was half identified with the Dutch cause: and increase of that family's already gigantic revenues; the Calvinist preachers worked the Dutch

Protestant townsmen into a frenzy—particularly those of the Hague, William's political centre.

The misfortunes of the invasion were laid at the door of the same great merchants who had made Orange the general of their armies. This body of republican men, this patriciate, this plutocracy, had already done great things for their newly-established, not fully stable, commercial and banking State. At their head the brothers de Witt had negotiated former arrangements with France and had maintained the independence of the merchant cities for nineteen years. They could boast of a commerce expanding as the commerce of no group of towns had expanded before, of colonies founded at the ends of the earth, of wealth increasing enormously. Because of that very position they held it was easy for the party of Orange and particularly for the Calvinist preachers to inflame the Hague populace against them. Already an attempt at assassination had been made. On the 20th of August, 1672, Cornelius de Witt, after torture, and his brother John de Witt, treacherously lured into a trap, were massacred by the mob of the Hague. Their hearts were torn out—and cooked. That Orange planned these horrors or rather the mob-rising that led to them has never been proved. It remains a suspicion; but certainly by the advantage he took of this happening and by his protection of the guilty afterwards, he was an accessory after the fact. Much later in life he was to be guilty of another, perhaps a more barbarous crime, the Massacre of Glencoe, and here he was an accessory not after the fact but before it.

The flooding of the flat land round Amsterdam was, if men had known it (and neither side knew it yet), a Decision. It is rarely that in military affairs a Decision is imposed not by a general action nor even by a siege but by a negative issue of this kind. But a Decision it was. Thenceforward the French realm could not hope to absorb the northern half of the Netherlands. Thenceforward a constant base was provided for the Protestant attack upon the Catholic culture, because those who controlled the government of the northern rebel provinces were Calvinists. Thenceforward was provided a base for the money attack upon Monarchy because the Bank of Amsterdam was the very type and core of the Money-power. Thenceforward it was certain that a varying but ever-recurrent coalition would be formed against Louis XIV.

The King of France had released in disdain 20,000 of the ill-equipped and poorly-fed Orange troops whom he had captured during his torrential advance. I say "in disdain." It was also a saving in money for him not to incorporate such bad material; but apart from that, to force an enemy's troops to fight against their own side was an iniquity reserved for the next century and suitable rather to one like Frederick the Great, the first man to act thus, than to a character like Louis.

Anyhow, William of Orange made use of these 20,000 as a reinforcement and somewhat improved them. Luxembourg still lay at Utrecht with the main French force. That town was large enough to give him a base. He still thought of attacking Amsterdam, first by seeking some sort of passage through the waters, then over the ice after a winter frost; but a thaw came and he had to give up the attempt. The French outposts still had to stand powerless, as they looked over something which to the eye was like the sea, with the distant buildings of Amsterdam and its spires still standing out like an island, and against them still the masts and yards of those innumerable ships.

Meanwhile the Spaniards from the south were surreptitiously helping the Dutch forces with guns and ammunition.

Not for the first nor for the last time in his life, the young William of Orange (he was now, remember, just entering his twenty-third year) conceived a strategical plan, and bungled it badly.

He thought he would march rapidly down south and cut the communications between Utrecht and France. He was in front of Charleroi ten days before Christmas in this year of 1672, and in those ten days before Christmas Eve he was badly beaten. It was the first in that long series of heavy knocks which this sour and determined but militarily incompetent young man was to receive. It was a sad thing for the Dutch that they had to rely by the hereditary custom of the day on such a Commander-in-Chief, but a good thing for their independence and political future that this chief was so dogged.

Though Louis did not yet fully appreciate the magnitude of his immediate reverse, he was filled with a very grave anxiety; the campaign had got into a blind alley. Turenne, the greatest of his commanders, marched into Germany and forced the Prussian Hohenzollerns to make peace—for the moment. Condé—the next greatest and in certain circumstances equally great—old Condé, from Maastricht made a new plan; but the floods extended and still it rained. By sea the Dutch Fleet more than held its own. In June of that year, 1673, the second year of the main Dutch War, Maastricht fell: the King himself in command, with Condé far to the left or west, while Turenne was on his right, or east. The event gave cause for a fine piece of meiosis such as the French love, and such as the laconic Louis, though neither himself achieving wit nor greatly admiring wit in others, was capable of framing. He wrote to Colbert on the 1st of July: "You will not be displeased to hear that the town is taken."

Coincidently with this success a congress to negotiate peace was opened at Cologne. It came to nothing, but the terms proposed are worth noting. Charles II of England, as the ally of France, demanded from over half a million to a million pounds indemnity, the salute to the English flag as supreme in the Narrow Seas, *and hereditary rule over the Dutch for young William of Orange.* The French wanted to take the Netherlands up to the Scheldt, but their second point was even more important. They insisted upon freedom of worship for the Catholic half of the population in the United Provinces. We must never forget this cardinal point, that the struggle between the French Crown and the United Provinces contained at its heart the old religious conflict of Europe awakened at the Reformation a century and a half before, and still at work.

Meanwhile, the check Louis had received led to the formation of a coalition against him. The Empire would support the Dutch on promise of a subsidy from the Dutch banking-power.

With the beginnings of that coalition the war, though essentially the Dutch War, is no longer the Dutch War alone, nor even mainly so. Louis himself went off to the Rhine, to Alsace, and held Colmar, dismantling it. Meanwhile Luxembourg began to retreat from the hopeless adventure which was at one moment to have decided the war in one campaign. He painfully but successfully withdrew from Holland. Orange tried to cut across his right and bar the retreat, bungled, and failed as usual.

All the next year, 1674, the wrestling marked time. But the tide seemed to be setting against Louis. The anti-Catholic feeling was rising in England and supporting the City of London and the great landowners against Charles. As early as February of that year, 1674, England made a separate peace with Holland. By the spring the Empire had sent such reinforcement to the Dutch that William of Orange found himself at the head of 40,000 men north of Charleroi. With this really large though motley force, he proposed to strike into France itself along the line of the Scheldt. Condé had dug himself into a very strongly entrenched position north of Valenciennes. William of Orange attacked him not far off at Seneffe and achieved nothing. There were very heavy losses on both sides; each called it a victory, but the word is an empty one. The only military effect of that day at Seneffe was that it rendered the proposed invasion of France by the allies impossible.

Once more Louis offered peace and once more William of Orange, as Commander-in-Chief of the Dutch Army and their allies, was the obstacle to peace. He could not have put his motives more clearly than they were put by his own agent, who privately affirmed that "with the war over, the Prince of Orange would be at a loose end for the rest of his life."

This second effort to make peace on the part of Louis was genuine enough. The taxes needed for the prolonged campaign had already provoked riots at home: he did not hope to gain much more by going on. The event proved him wrong. The continuance of the war brought France further advantage, but that Louis should so have urged peace, and so early, throws a strong light upon his general attitude. Sir William Temple, narrow but no fool, thought France exhausted and perhaps sincerely anxious to lay down arms. If many agreed with him among those hostile to Louis (and many did), such a belief was enough of an incentive to continue the pressure on the French King.

The war lasted four years more than it need have done. To begin with, in the summer of '75 the Great Elector, the Hohenzollern, badly defeated Louis's ally, Sweden, at Fehrdellin. This was in June, 1675.

Towards the end of the next month, on the 27th of July, the great Turenne fell suddenly, killed by a cannon shot as he was inspecting a battery near Salzbach in his duel with the Imperial general (the only one in the coalition worthy to stand up to Condé or Turenne himself) Montecuculli. It is difficult for us today to appreciate how in this war which was largely a war of sieges the loss of an individual could be accounted so grave a matter, but indeed the talents of individual commanders weighed very heavily in these wars.

Some have imagined (wrongly, I think) that with the loss of Turenne French arms were never the same in the wars again. He was a man of the highest interest to posterity. Inheriting through his mother the Orange blood, much more moulded by that inheritance than by any other, it gave him caution and decision combined. It also gave him an unfortunate pride, justified by his great feats of arms and the veneration with which he was regarded—a singularly honest man, and drawing his traditions from a time before the rise of such absolute kingship as Louis now enjoyed. He had been bred a Calvinist, of course, with such a mother. His conversion to Catholicism after years in the French service was none the less genuine; it was part of the general movement whereby but for the error of the Revocation of the Edict of Nantes ten years later, Calvinism in France would probably have withered away.

In the same year, 1675, Charles Stuart, King of England, had played yet another of those masterly moves which he played successfully his whole life long to maintain the throne he had inherited. That move covered two years— nearly three. It began with checkmating the Money-power for the moment by getting from Louis just so much subsidy as would help him to tide over. The wealthy men whose committees, the House of Commons and the House of Lords, proposed to ruin what was left of kingship in England had to postpone their plans, and it was worth Louis's while to pay the money at that price. Parliament was prorogued for over a year. In the next year, 1676, Louis, for the moment free from anxiety on the side of England, found and refused the great but doubtful opportunity of the whole war: this was the opportunity of Heurtebise.

HEURTEBISE

Heurtebise! Cense of Heurtebise! If I were writing this book as a study of wars or as a Chronicle of Louis the Great, what could not be made of your name!

In these fields called the "Cense of Heurtebise," close to Denain, lay pitched the French camp covering the siege of Bouchain. Over against that camp and its army lay William of Orange and all his men, attempting the relief of the beleaguered fortress.

Should Louis attack? The opportunity was unique. William's incompetence was now notorious, the French personnel superior. A decision would not only end the war but give the French King at one blow all that he had sought: the destruction of the Dutch forces and their General. All the future. Defeat, with Louis present in person at the head of his forces, would have shaken, might have overthrown, the whole structure of that Monarchy which had been made so single and so splendid in that one name.

Had the dice been thrown and had the victory been won Heurtebise would sound today, as sound Bouvines or Hastings: immortal. Had the day been lost Heurtebise would sound today as sound Sedan or Waterloo, immortal also.

The Marshals grouped on their horses round the King gave advice, each in turn. One only was certain in his advice to attack. The others uncertain or strongly opposed. Among them Louvois, the only civilian, but the maker of the armies and he who had most power with Louis from long companionship and proved achievement, spoke most strongly of all. With his violent insistence and authority he swayed the decision of the King. There should be no battle. Bouchain was theirs for the taking; a gamble, staking all the future, was not war or policy. Leave Orange alone and complete the capture of Bouchain. Louis accepted the verdict and rode silently away. But to the end of his life that mortification inhabited his spirit, and, years afterwards he spoke of it in words that are remembered: blaming himself for yielding to other men and especially to Louvois, the most imperious of them. He might have reached the height both of glory and of gain, of permanent security for the realm as well, in one great hour! That he might have lost all he would not remember, and it is commonly so with vital decisions: we regret the unknown, we prize too little the certain results.

The end also was the beginning. There at Bouchain next to Heurtebise, Marlborough found the last of his triumphs. There at Denain, next beyond Heurtebise, was fought and won—half a lifetime later, the action which in the very article of death saved France, nearly forty years on. Heurtebise is Bouchain, Heurtebise is Denain; but who now murmurs the name of Heurtebise? "Storm-break?"

And who knows that name today, which might have been in the foremost of names? Even if you seek the place today you will hardly find it.

18

The End of the Campaigns

WHILE THE WAR BY LAND LAY thus undecided French power at sea increased. It looked for a moment as though in the Mediterranean the French fleet might, after the indecisive battle of Stromboli, get the mastery.

All 1677 was filled with negotiations for the peace that should have been made long ago. The plenipotentiaries had met at Nijmegen at the end of the year 1676. Charles King of England was acting as mediator; the Dutch patriciate was willing. Fargel, the Grand Pensionary, confessed to Temple that he thought it better to compromise lest the continued power of Louis should wear out the United Provinces. It was again William of Orange that stood in the way and determined on the continuance of the war and thereby the continuance of his own occupation, position and power. At the moment the odds were against him, but he had everything to lose personally by the pacification of Europe, and to William personal things were alone considerable: a more self-centred being never lived. He was a prisoner of self all his wizened life. Nothing personally to gain.

So early as March the French stormed Valenciennes under the eyes of the King and threatened to take Cambrai and St. Omer. When Orange marched against them to relieve these towns he suffered yet another of his interminable discomfitures and Cambrai and St. Omer capitulated.

It is worth while pausing a moment to consider the way in which this young man (he was now in his twenty-seventh year) alone of the commanders clung to the idea

of action in the open and a war of movement. It was silly
and brought him no luck, but that he should have so clung
to it in spite of continuous disaster testifies to that tenacity
of his, the "second factor" spoken of a few pages back.

Before the year was out Charles Stuart, King of
England, played that masterly move which he had begun,
by checkmating his Parliament—for the time. He continued, so long as the war lasted, to take subsidies from
Louis, to keep the Money-power of the City of London
and its allies, the squires and lawyers in Parliament, at
arm's length. But just when this situation might have
made him independent and have made the Bourbon think
himself the permanent protector of the Stuart, Charles
did something enormous. He sent for his nephew, young
William of Orange, and married him to Mary, heiress to
the throne of England. (Charles, of course, had no heir
of his own. Catherine of Braganza had suffered miscarriage
after miscarriage.)

This shock affected Louis profoundly. He had planned
to marry Mary to his own heir the Dauphin. In the face
of such a thing, an action of such magnitude, we cannot
but ask ourselves a question, although that question is
unanswerable. Was the move, though a masterly one, worth
while? In the light of what later happened we know that
it was a disastrous move. Within a dozen years it made an
end of all that for which Charles himself had laboured
without ceasing. It destroyed the English throne, gave full
victory to the wealthy opposition who took up aristocratic
and commercial rule on the last ruins of the Monarchy.
But how could Charles have foreseen all that?

Charles, remember, had one determined policy—the
rehabilitation of the English monarchy. But though he gave
all his attention, all his remarkable power of manœuvre,
he could not succeed, he could not reach his goal in sheer
opposition to the most powerful element in England, the

wealthy landowners and the new wealthy moneylenders, the wealthiest men in the City of London. He could not reach his goal in direct antagonism to the always latent and often violent anti-Catholic feeling and consequently anti-French feeling, most active in the better organised of his subjects. He certainly would not reach his goal if he were to reach it as a mere client of Versailles.

Any man judging things with full knowledge of the time but having the future veiled from him, as it is veiled from us all, would have applauded Charles. Anyone sympathising with his design to set the monarchy again upon its feet in England would have praised all this manœuvre unreservedly—the checkmating of the Money-power, the checkmating of Louis's complacency, the escape from French domination, the whole careful balance maintained.

But as continually happens with the best moves, things beyond calculation destroy their value. That marriage proved in the end the destruction of English kingship. The first of the puppet kings called in by the Money-power was this very William (now the husband since November, 1677, of the woman who was heiress to England). She was a poor-witted creature—some would have said half-witted—which may be an excuse for her early oddities (as in her letters to her governess), but those very defects in her made the marriage a further element in the failure of the Crown.

Following on that move, Charles the next year himself joined the Dutch, for the moment, against the French: he sent them supplies and troops.

Louis countered successfully. The negotiations were proceeding at Nijmegen: peace was slow to come—the slower for the last move from England. Louis gave up his efforts in the Mediterranean, and effected a strategic surprise. Going round by Louvain, he swerved to the left, fell suddenly on Ghent and took it in a week, holding it on the 12th of March, 1678.

The manœuvre was quite unexpected and achieved its object. After Ghent Antwerp might go—and Antwerp, the formidable rival to Amsterdam, in the hands of the French King would become more formidable still.

THE PEACE OF NIJMEGEN

It was certain after this blow struck by Louis that the war would be wound up, but hardly so certain that it would be wound up so very much in Louis's favour. An ultimatum had fixed the 10th of August for the last day on which the Dutch must make up their minds whether they would accept Louis's terms. Close on midnight of that day they signed.

The French King gave back Maastricht, but on condition that Mass should be freely said there. He restored to young William of Orange what was essential to him—whose position depended on wealth—the great revenue received by the House of Orange from its estates in the Jura country and in Flanders.

The Dutch having made peace, the coalition crumbled. A month later Spain accepted the French terms. Louis kept the towns of Valenciennes and Maubeuge which he had taken and fortified, and which, with long line from Bouchain through Bavay, made a wall against invasion. He gave back to the Spanish Crown the parallel line of fortresses to the north-east, Oudenarde, Charleroi, Ath, etc., including Cambrai. *He retained the Franche Comté.* It has been French ever since.

In the first days of the next February, 1679, the Empire surrendered. Its nominal vassal, Lorraine, indignant at the French terms, refused to accept them, but only with the result that it became more actually dependent on Louis than ever. The French kept Freiberg just beyond the Rhine, with a road to give them access thereto. At last, just at the end of June in that year 1679, the Great Elector himself gave way. The French arms could now do what they willed with Brandenburg; the Hohenzollern gave up Pomerania— not without a piteous appeal to Louis to be generous; and Louis sent him a tidy sum of money for which he gave grateful thanks.

So ended, surprisingly to the advantage of the Bourbon kings, the long struggle for the eastern marches. So ended it for the moment, but only for the moment. The struggle was to be renewed before Louis should be dead, and it was to be renewed in the next century, and again a lifetime ago, under the genius of Bismarck. It was to be renewed in our own day. But the names which appear in the Peace of Nijmegen are names which stand on the map of France, now, in the third century after that peace. Alsace was virtually held as a whole, Lorraine actually. The Jura was French, and the frontier fortresses to the northeast made in general the same line that they make now.[1]

It is a long and confused story, is this central war of Louis's maturity, but in the upshot he emerged not only more powerful than he had been before but ready for a further extension of power. For during the peace that followed he consolidated that victory strongly.

THE TREACHERY OF ST. DENIS

The moment is famous for something other than the treaty: something, a crime, and a crime that should never be forgotten.

After the peace was concluded—four days after—William of Orange played a dastardly trick to further his own ambition. This was the occasion:

---

1   The main exception is Ypres. Ypres was French under the Treaty with Spain but was Belgian again in the final settlement when the Spanish Netherlands went to Austria.

The French army under Luxembourg lay outside Mons, containing that fortress which was hard pressed for food and cut off from Brussels. It would have fallen if the peace had been delayed by but a few days. The French stood upon land somewhat higher than the town and to the north of it on the plateau called that of St. Denis. They, knowing that peace had been signed, stood unprepared for any attack. William, who had recently been working to relieve Mons, took advantage of the situation and treacherously attacked. Happily he was beaten back, but only with great difficulty and after a violent action, where Luxemburg had been taken quite unawares. It was a form of "tactical surprise" happily rare in the history of war.

William of Orange tried to escape the odium of this crime by lying. He pretended he had not heard the news of the peace, and then said rather more shiftily that he "had not heard it officially." No one believed him, and the falsehood was but one more of half a dozen major falsehoods that were to distinguish his career. Now falsehood is not so rare a thing in public men as to need special comment here. What was rare, what was exceptional in this bloody and useless fighting outside Mons, was that five thousand men died by treachery, many of them in agony, to serve the personal ambition of one man.

19

The Fixing of the Frontiers

1. "The Reunions" and Strasburg

FTER THE LAST OF THESE GROUPS of treaties which we call in general the Peace of Nijmegen, that is, after the summer of 1679, the business of completing the political work of the reign was vigorously carried forward.

That business had two departments: the unifying of the new frontiers and the fortification of them. As to the fortification, that was, as always, Vauban's department, and before 1683, that is, within the space of five years, all the work had been done. The unifying of the frontiers, the tracing of that political wall behind which France was in future to lie, has for its main political interest what are called the "reunions."

The "reunions" meant the establishment of record and title to territories included with the towns or centres which Louis had acquired by treaty. A phrase generally used in the treaties was—after mentioning a town or other centre—"and the dependencies thereof." On the meaning of this word "dependencies" turns the criticism and counter criticism of what the King did. Naturally he strained the definition of that term to the utmost limit. Had he not done so, he might as well not have reigned or carried on war or have pursued his lifelong task of securing the country against invasion for the future.

There is no statesman who, establishing a title to this or that, does not make it as full as possible. It is for his opponents to counter that effort, to reduce its effect.

The innumerable critics, contemporary and modern, of the King's whole policy have argued, justly enough, that the terms of the treaties were inherited from an older, half-feudal, time and should by rights have been interpreted in the archaic spirit of the days from which they inherited. But had this been done, the whole purpose of Louis's action would have been frustrated. His whole purpose was to make a homogeneous realm and to consolidate those ragged edges, especially along the Rhine. This could only be done by interpreting the word "dependencies" as widely as possible and joining up as much as could be the dependencies of one ceded town or district to the dependencies of its neighbour. The whole task of Louis here and throughout the realm was the "liquidating" of the relics of feudalism. The crown of this work, not exactly a "reunion" but in the line of the "reunions," was the occupation of Strasburg.

Oceans of ink and tempests of rhetoric have been expended on that capital step. In the nineteenth century, men who wrote history backwards with donnish perversity talked of it as "a rape of German soil and of a German city." Those who have known Strasburg, as I have known it between the seventies of the last century and the Great War, could never have passed such a judgment.

Strasburg was not in 1678-81 a part of any unity called "Germany"—for there was no such unity. No one thought in terms of such a thing at the time. What it was, and what all its more vocal and established citizens took pride in, was an imperial city of the Rhine: it was not actually on the great river but it counted with the chain of cities which live by the traffic of the waterway.

Strasburg would have preferred independence. Its bond with the Empire had been very loose; its bond with the French Crown was to be, though nothing comparable to connection with a modern government, at any rate tighter than anything the city had known in the past.

The authorities and the owners of property, the discordant religious bodies—for the town was divided in religion, as it still is—had in effect no choice. They could not live henceforward in the air and surroundings of territory increasingly connected with France without accepting the new position. Yet they accepted it and it was not galling, for there was in those days no such tyranny of State rules—above all, of universal enforced official schools for all children—as there is today; the native language of Alsace went on its common course, and the free local government of the old régime worked in Alsace as it did everywhere. A considerable military force was gathered over against the walls, but there was no need to use it. The daily life of Strasburg continued to be as German as it had ever been, the political status alone had changed, and that in no fashion which the ordinary man would feel.

Nevertheless the event was what I have called it, "capital." For it locked and bolted the main door of invasion. The Rhine was the physical obstacle to invasion, and Strasburg was the door in the Rhine-wall. With Strasburg in other hands Alsace, the gift of Turenne to the Crown, would never have formed a province—and if there is one thing the Alsatians demand more than another it is the unity of their highly defined separate wealthy and unusual little country—a thing the Third Republic has never sufficiently understood, though today the French understand it better than they did. All French districts would be the better today for a larger local autonomy, but Alsace most of all.

In some degree this has been begun though not achieved. Religion is secure from the odious anti-Clericalism of the French Radical tradition, public education has respect for the two main religions of the parents, and the language of course is completely free—for that is the French tradition—but there is room for a great deal more.

With the rounding off of the realm by the putting of Strasburg under the French Crown, the main political work of these years of maturity is accomplished. The date was the 30th of September, 1681. It was upon this day that the French received the town. And if I were dealing only with the political effort of Louis, that date might be taken as the terminal limit of this period.

2. THE FORTRESSES

So much for the political consolidation of the frontier by the Reunions. Now for its physical consolidation, the chain of fortresses.

First, let us note how, apart from acting as a wall, fortresses were the main matter of all that war. Fortified towns play the chief part in this conflict just as castles played the chief part in the earlier wars before the full development of artillery.

Now why were fortified towns of such high importance at this moment? What part does a fortress play and why was that part essential at the moment when Louis was thrusting back the old pressure and irruption from which had suffered so long the realm he had inherited? It is a question a modern man must answer to himself clearly, because conditions of war changed so much from one hundred to one hundred and fifty years later, and have changed so much more since, that the answer is not easy for us moderns to grasp.

To begin with, fortification in every time and place since human conflict began has one prime military object: to gain time.

It has been said, truly enough, that no war was ever won by fortification; which is another way of saying that there is no such thing as a merely defensive war. But many a war has been won through the exhaustion of an enemy whom fortification baulked. Some say that if Hannibal had

had a siege train and had thus been able to batter the walls of Rome, victory in the second Punic war would have fallen to the Carthaginians. That judgment is probable enough.

Anyhow, fighting men from the beginning of time have used fortification, not because a mere defence could ever be in itself victorious, but because defence multiplies the factor of time. When the defence is at its strongest—as during the castle warfare of the Middle Ages, and especially the early Middle Ages—fortification may gain the defending force a vast extension of time for the exhaustion of the enemy. A large mediæval castle, such as the great works of the Crusades, could last out indefinitely. It could easily defy, if it were sufficiently garrisoned, all the efforts of a besieging army for many months, and sometimes for years. Even a few hundred men in a place like Kerak could hold up an army of thousands.

But a fortress does not only exist in order to gain time, it exists also in order to threaten a hostile line of advance. A hostile army cannot afford to leave a fortress behind it untaken, because every fortress thus neglected can shelter men who will then issue to cut the communications of that army. An army is not a moving island. It is a peninsula at the end of a long isthmus, that isthmus being the communications whereby it receives its munitionment of all kinds, including recruitment, and by which it evacuates, when that is necessary, its sick and wounded and receives government orders and sends home dispatches. An army lives by its communications. A chain of fortresses, therefore, so disposed that there is no gap between any two of them wide enough to let an enemy through unmolested, acts as a continuous wall.

Now fortresses in this last part of the seventeenth century were of such importance for two reasons. First because armies being voluntary in recruitment were necessarily limited. Secondly because the resources of warring states were also more limited than they had been in the past or were to be in the future.

Both these conditions sprang from the same root, which was the liberty the mass of men then enjoyed. There was no conscription, or at any rate none except some fitful experiment on a small scale. Men had to be hired to fight, and the imposing of the strain upon the whole population would have been thought intolerable.

As of man-power, so of money. The resources of the late seventeenth century government were limited in money as no modern one is. The State could not levy money any more than it could levy men on the huge scale which came later.

Fortification, therefore, whose function it is to gain time, advantaged those who possessed many fortified places on the critical field of operations in two ways: it drained the man-power of the offensive, often to exhaustion; and it drained the money-power also often to exhaustion.

In the period of the Dutch wars (as they were called, the main operations of Louis XIV) there were two kinds of strongholds. The first, which was the most effective (because it gave you just enough civilian support to lodge or garrison, provide workmen for it and the rest, without needing heavy subsidy in money or much strength in men to preserve it when it was under siege), was the small fortified town, such as Rocroi, Bouchain, Brisach and a hundred others. A little market town, surrounded by a very wide belt of scientifically constructed works, was the ideal. And that is why all up and down Europe you find these little towns with enormous fortifications which astonish us today by the contrast between their scale and that of the habitations which they seem to defend. As a fact, of course, the fortifications were not built primarily to defend the houses of the town and the people in them, but to check the advance of the enemy; the little town being only subsidiary to that main purpose.

The other kind of fortress was a large town such as Lille or Brussels or Strasburg which *had* been fortified for that very purpose of protecting a civilian population: a purpose not contemplated in the first type. The large town had been fortified in order to protect its population and buildings against the shock of invasion. It was useful, of course, because all fortification was useful, but it was expensive in its use compared with the small town. There was this further weakness about the large town, that the population, in days when there was no strong police and no tyrannical organisation of government, as there is today, would riot if it were put under too great a strain and demand capitulation. A large fortress could much more easily be starved out than a small one.

Now in these main campaigns of Louis XIV, and especially in that effort to close for good and all the open frontier of the north-east, whence invasion has perpetually threatened France, history and geography have provided a mass of points suitable for fortresses. These plains were fertile, filled with market towns and with larger provincial capitals. The seaboard of these plains and their navigable rivers nourished towns of their own. Inland you have a crowd of them, familiar to English readers because so much of English military history has passed under their walls: Ghent, Oudenarde, Bouchain, Tournai, Valenciennes, Namur; and on the sea coasts and on the navigable rivers, Calais, Boulogne, Dunkirk, Montreuil, Nieuport, etc. This debatable land of the north-east plains, the gates of invasion, lent itself singularly to the development of fortification at that moment, first because their open character made fortification necessary everywhere, secondly because the materials for it were everywhere present. Nowhere could earthworks be more rapidly thrown up, nowhere was brick-clay more plentiful for the support of earth.

2 0

Vauban

SINCE THE STORY OF THESE WARS is the story of fortification, it is fitting that the greatest name connected with them should be the name of Vauban. For Vauban was to fortification what Napoleon was to artillery. Vauban is the master, and in a sense the origin, of all those forces which are called in modern armies the "Engineers." Vauban was the great engineer; the sapper; as Bonaparte was the great gunner.

Yet the name of Vauban has never taken the full place it should.

For this there are many reasons. The reign is famous for monuments. Vauban left more monuments by far than all the architects put together. They are that splendid girdle of fortification which still stands all along the frontiers, from the Mediterranean to the North Sea, at every gate of the Pyrenees.

He was among the best balanced and the strongest. Travelled more and worked more than any. Yet is he today less remembered than Louvois, than Turenne, even than Villars.

In his time the conception of the engineer as a soldier was still unfamiliar. The men who counted socially (and that is always very important) were the officers of mounted forces. Not only the picturesque, but the decision of battle was mainly with the cavalry still. In the work of the engineer there was nothing so flamboyant, nor, indeed, does the engineer ever win a battle directly. The engineer leads no armies. I am afraid he does not even as a rule get his statue. I can remember no military ode addressed to a sapper. Yet Vauban is, take it all in all, the most important soldier of them all. He lay behind everything between 1667 and 1695.

Vauban is also the most interesting character, as a personality, of all that lifetime except the saints like Vincent de Paul. He was a man of a special sort, different from his time, more like our time; indeed more like the solid man of all ages than were the brilliant captains his contemporaries.

He was born, as were more than half the useful men of the time, from a bourgeois family, local in origin (country solicitors), people who, as they gradually enriched themselves—on a very modest scale—rose somewhat socially, but never to any great height. Le Prat was the family name. It was not a lifetime before Vauban's own birth that the Le Prat of the day bought a little land in feudal tenure, which gave him the technical status of a noble. These had but a few hundreds a year, and no standing to count. It was difficult to say whether they thought of themselves, or were thought of, as townsmen or as very small squires. They were of the Morvan, the old country of the Aedui, as interesting a patch of land as there is in Europe, and I am glad to say not very much known, though the famous house of Vezelay stands on its hill in the midst of it. It is a land of woods and many meres, of hills rather high, but not marked or abrupt. It is not starved land, but it is not rich, and the people live still somewhat apart from their neighbours.

Vauban in boyhood lived thus nourished by a countryside, and finding for equals and playmates sons of the small farmers and the peasantry. All the formative years of his life in boyhood were steeped in the populace. Short of a provincial accent—that he never had—he might have been any husbandmen from those hills. Of such an origin we are reminded throughout his strong life by his humility, his tenacity and his profound common sense. All through that life he retained close sympathy with the men of the soil; he pleaded their cause. He was in sympathy with, and always near, the populace; but that word "populace" did not mean what it does today—unfortunate dispossessed serfs of industry, crowded sullenly in towns—it meant yeomen.

Such schooling as he got, he got from the village priest, who evidently knew something of geometry. His intimate life was strange enough; picked up as a recruit during the civil wars of the Fronde, following Condé's army with just enough birth to count as an officer, but not enough for what we should call today a full commission. He showed great courage and resource in skirmishes, and attracted notice as a young prisoner. Mazarin became acquainted with his name. The first efforts of his genius had some obscure connection with the strengthening of Ste. Menehoulde, but he takes no place until, with the opening of the wars, being already fairly well known to connoisseurs in armament, Louis takes to him at once by that mixture of recommendation and personal choice which you find in nearly all the great king did, whether with poets or engineers. Before the main siege operation of the opening Dutch campaign, the great business of Maastricht, the name of Vauban was already the name which men had seized upon for the symbol or title of repeated success in sieges. The formula was made of him, "Whatever he defended, held; whatever he invested, fell."

It was characteristic of Louis that he followed with curiosity almost minute the development of fortification. His common sense seized all its continually growing importance and he and Vauban are in this department what he and Colbert were in defence and in the navy, what he and Louvois were in the raising and organisation of armies, and what he and Lionne were in the making of foreign policy.

The King associated with him much. It is a pity they were not together yet more. He would have counterbalanced Louvois, who was indispensable but too harsh and therefore often risky. Also he lived so long that he could advise Louis almost till the end when all the other great names had gone down the wind.

The traveller today in France still sees in its magnificence everywhere the work of Vauban. He can follow it up from the Alps to the North Sea. In Besançon, Strasburg, Metz, Mézières, Maubeuge, Valenciennes; and against the south, where, a generation before, invasion had menaced, there is Perpignan and Mont Louis. The principle was everywhere the same and is the flower of that long process which began in the Italy of the Renaissance when first walls were defended from the fire of artillery by slopes of earth thrown up on their outward side. At first this cushion of earth was subsidiary to the main purpose of the wall. The wall remained the strong and high thing it had been in the days before heavy cannon had gradually acquired precision.[1]

Then, as the power of heavy artillery increased, it was clear that the less the angle of slope in the earthwork the less violent the impact. What had been the main part of the defence, the wall, became no more than a support for the earthwork at the back, and its height was successively reduced.

1   It is an interesting point, which is sometimes forgotten, that what destroyed the mediæval system and its forerunners of Roman and pre-Roman times—the wall as a fortification—was not artillery in itself but the increase in precision of heavy artillery. Pounding away at a very thick and solid piece of masonry with round stone or iron missiles did not shake the defence appreciably until one could be certain that the impact of the missile would fall over and over again on a small area; that was how heavy artillery took the place of and did the work of the old battering ram. The point of the battering ram was that it struck the same place over and over again until it loosened one group of stones and everything above them fell. Cannon was not accurate enough, especially cannon of large calibre, to do that thoroughly until quite late in the sixteenth century. The earlier gun founders had to strengthen their piece with hoops. They found it difficult to have a large piece accurately bored. Nor do we get high precision until the introduction of rifling, almost within living memory.

Vauban, like all masters of any trade, combined a very few clear principles, which anyone could understand, with an infinity of applied detail.

The clear first principle which any man can understand in connection with siege work is so tracing the defensive lines that fire from one part of them shall be supported by fire from another part—that is the whole principle of the star fortress. The next is that in tracing offensive lines or trenches we should extend them as far as possible in order to give the opportunity for surprise.

The third is that works being designed to economise men, siege work on the defensive should be as unwasteful as possible—one should never run the risk of a chance on siege work as a man may well do in open warfare. Last and essential principle, "Fortification is designed to keep the enemies fire at as long range as possible from its objective."

All those principles are self-evident. Vauban's greatness consisted in his completely thinking out their application. His plans for his star fortresses, especially his later ones, have reached perfection, under the conditions of his day. They are, to the story of earthworks, defended and attacked by artillery, what the late thirteenth century castles were to stone walls before artillery had made them obsolete.

It is a delight to go over such a place as New Brisach, for instance, after having studied its plan at home, and see every principle illustrated and developed. But, indeed, the two Brisachs, old and new, are the most striking contrast between the necessities of a fortress before the development of artillery and after that development.

Being an engineer, Vauban was a calculator of mechanical things, not a calculator of the imponderables, and therefore not too serviceable as a statesman.

His splendid character—strength, industry, integrity and sanity in all he did—made men, including the King, turn to him for advice. His experience of unparalleled success in his own sphere made him confident in tendering such advice in other spheres. But the advice was not always good. It is a pity because it was always clear and based on sound reasoning. It was not always good because he had not sufficient knowledge of the obstacles before him, and often not sufficient knowledge of the general political circumstances on which he had to advise.

He has been praised, of course, especially by moderns, for the strong line he took against the revocation of the Edict of Nantes. There his advice was right, but was given for the wrong reasons. France, as we shall see, was weakened by the Revocation because the full policy either could not be, or would not be, carried out. We shall see later in this book how the whole point of the Revocation was political and how its whole story is the story of a failure in practical politics. Vauban emphasised the loss of wealth it entailed through the emigration of a considerable body of merchants, the loss of technical skill through the emigration of artisans, and especially the loss of some hundreds of first-rate professional officers, who gave their service to foreign crowns and were led, for the sake of their religion, to fight against their country. All these objections are obvious. But the answer of any man who is in favour of the Revocation is equally so. "The price is worth paying if we can obtain religious unity." But religious unity was not obtained. That was the whole point. A heavy price was paid and the goods were not delivered.

In the case of the Irish expedition Vauban's advice was excellent. He said that the attack on William III was really the decisive point in the whole European struggle, and, had Louis understood that as well as Vauban did, history would have been different.

The most famous of his advices, the proposal for a reform of taxation, failed altogether. It did not fail, as too many critics have taken for granted, from the obstinacy or folly, or the routine of the government, but from the impossibility of effecting so vast a revolution "under fire," as it were; that is, during the increasing strain of the French defensive against the coalition.

What Vauban proposed in what he called "A Royal Tithe" was what will always be an ideal common-sense taxation, a simple tax on income. By this he proposed to replace the highly complicated irregular taxation based on lists of assessment and farmed out to the profit of corrupt and unpopular officers.

The system of taxation inherited by Louis XIV from an older and much simpler time had become unjust in its application also. The privileged classes, not subject to direct taxation, were no longer what they had been in former years to the community. It is not true to say they did not take a share of the burden, the wealthier of the nobility made great sacrifices for the Crown and the nation, in blood and often in money, and though the Church revenues did not pull their weight, grants were made from them. But what is true to say is that the old revenue obtained on the land assessment of the non-noble—and therefore falling primarily on the peasant, who had now long been a free man—was an anomaly. When, during a long war, the economic strain was severe, the pressure on the peasant was intolerable. But the reform could only have been carried through in a time of retrenchment, started by a vigorous and new system of government. The reform was impossible under a personal monarchy caught in the toils of increasingly difficult war.

Another example of his advice missing fire was his approach to the King in favour of peace during the middle of those last wars of the Spanish Succession. Vauban's advice was for compromise, and compromise would have been reasonable if the enemy had been willing to treat. He said, in effect: "Let Spain and the Empire arrange their quarrels between themselves." That is as much as to say, even if not put in so many words: "Let the Bourbons give up the claim to the Spanish Succession, and concentrate upon home affairs." But what Vauban left out of account was the determination of the coalition to go much further. The King was ready for compromise, but the coalition said, "Give up Alsace and dismantle your maritime fortresses." It would take nothing but the breaking of French power.

It was not so extravagant a claim. They were in the full tide of victory, even more than they knew, for this moment is the eve of Ramillies, the capital importance of which we shall see later on before the close of this volume.[2]

Vauban was without vanity, but he felt, towards the end of a long life filled with unceasing public work, that he might have had more titular recognition.

He had the King's friendship and admiration. He was undoubtedly recognised as the first in his trade and as an architect of victory and siege work, let alone the drawing of plans. But this trade was not yet fully considered, either socially or in the military world. "The tumbling about of earth" was not glorious as the cavalry charges were glorious.

There is many a passage from his own pen which illustrates this mixture of fatigue and disappointment. Let me quote one, the pathos of which is, I think, appealing:

"Now that I have spoken of the King's affairs, I make so bold as to speak of my own for the first time in my life. I am now in the seventy-third year of my age, with the burden upon me of fifty-two years under arms, and the work of fifty main sieges and of nearly forty years of ceaseless travel and inspection. All this has drawn upon me such weariness of body and of soul, for winter and summer are

---

2   Vauban's lengthy proposition was February, 1706. Marlborough's victory at Ramillies was gained on the 23rd of May of the same spring.

all the same to me. The life of a man who has held up all that weight cannot but be worn threadbare.... I feel that I have fallen lower than I was and I am greatly weakened.... I can no longer undertake enterprises in which strength and skill might fail me so that I should be dishonoured: that I should be dishonoured [as a soldier he means] God forbid. Rather death an hundredfold."

Good for a sapper.

Nevertheless he was still set to work. The old man growing deaf, uncertain of his sight and with these regrets in his soul, was sent off, after the disaster of Ramillies, to look after that Flanders frontier, to inspect Dunkirk, which he had made, and to renew the works at Lille.

A last blow was the refusal to print, or at any rate to publish, his recommendation on the reform of the taxes. He was already suffering from his lungs—a cough had troubled him for years. He sent for his confessor, a Dominican; he talked to him of this fiscal proposal as though it were a case of conscience, lest he should have been disloyal in acting too energetically against the King's will, or in appealing so strongly for the common people of whom he himself almost came, and for whom he had felt fraternal affection all his life.

The phrase of his servant, who loved him well, may in its simplicity serve for his epitaph. "On Wednesday, the 30th of March, at about three-quarters of an hour after nine in the morning, the Marshal died."

The King, who had sent the best of the royal doctors in haste to that contemporary and forerunner of his on the road to the end of the road, said: "I have lost a man devoted to me and to the State." For Louis excelled in restraint of expression.

V
Maturity and the Wars (*Within*)

1667–1693

21

Montespan

T HERE FELL UPON KING LOUIS
during his thirtieth year one of those major disasters which lie in wait for the fortunate and the
strong: his body enslaved him.

The process was slow and came through various
approaches; but the forces which captured him converged
within a year; after their conquest they held him fast for
twelve. By a singular grace (the reward of what was permanently good in his life) he escaped: a violent experience
freed him; but only through a storm which might have
made shipwreck of his spirit, that is, of his very self—
which is, in every man, his soul.

Among the young women of the court, maids-in-waiting
to the Queen, was one of very great lineage and splendid
youth, the wife of a young nobleman, her equal, from the
Pyrenees: Montespan. His name taken from a fief so called:
that Castle whose ruins you may see overlooking the young
Garonne from the south bank, a little below St. Gaudens,
at the foot of the mountains.[1] When Louis was preparing

---

1   He was the son of the Marquis d'Antin, whose title and name
his son inherited. This man, the son of Madame de Montespan,
was raised later to the title of Duke of Antin, through his mother's former connections at court. The family name was Pardaillan
de Gondrin. French titles are difficult to follow because all the
sons—and often daughters also—are given a title and name from
some family land even while the father is still alive; also they are
very numerous. But a title in France was, and is, of little account
compared with blood. It was and is a man's family that counts and
counted. I have called the young husband the "equal" of his wife,
but she came of a more distinguished house. She was a daughter of
the Duke of Mortemart, of the family of Rochechouart.

to invade Flanders she was twenty-six and the more radiant for her four years of marriage and the little son at her side. It was the moment when La Vallière was fading—or at least, had begun to fade. Louis was still in the habit of her commerce; six years of the affair had as yet but in part reduced its charm for him, though the frequent birth of children had borne heavily upon her gentle body. As for her, she loved him with a love still increasing in its simple intensity.

It has been thought that there was an overlap between the closing episode of the La Vallière and this opening misfortune of his Montespan years. If that were true, it would be shameful indeed: a confusion. But the assertion may be doubted. Such confusion would not be consonant with the King's character, nor with the nature of his new obsession; for that as I have said came gradually by various approaches: her vigour, her wit, an initial persistency about her (it was her doing) and the appeal of the Flesh: also continued presence.

Louise de Vallière permitted herself a last appeal. That was an error in her and a weakness—but, then, she was despairing.

It happened at Avesnes, near the Front, whither he had summoned the Queen and the Montespan who waited on her. Though Louise de La Vallière started later she bade her coachman press forward that she might be the first of these women to see the King. She arrived and stood in his presence, unrepaired from the long and rough progress. He received her—but reproached her coldly, saying: "What! Before the Queen?" It had been a breach of a ritual and completed her discomfiture. When she returned to Paris from the armies it was to retire again to those secluded rooms over the Palais Royal and to await another birth— the last. That was the end of the six years, of her youth and his: of their morning: and a bad end. Thenceforward the Montespan possessed him more and more. Her lodging while she was with the army stood next his own. Within a year their first child was born.

You must see this woman at that moment, holding as it were, a stage, pressing forward, occupying, like a troop that invades and conquers. All about her proclaimed this: her carriage, firm and entrancing, her confident gaiety, her now resplendent and still ascending beauty—clear as her laughter was and her colour: regal with abundance of hair to crown a face which mastered as well as shone: hair like a plentiful burden of ripe wheat at harvest, answering in its strong colour the rest of her strength. Her eyes, which were now so certain and over-rode all she looked upon, had the same strength. Blue, as had been her rival's: but the blue of those younger eyes had been the blue of heaven; the blue which hardened in the eyes of Athenaïs[2] de Montespan was the blue of the darker flowers, so dark that sometimes they seemed almost black to those who watched her when her gaze was turned aside from the light, and even at their lightest, still a porcelain blue.

She was not tall—yet she gave an effect of dominating presence which all who have spoken of her remembered and which was enhanced by the proud curve of the nose, the fullness of the lips and the slight arch of those nourished brows: and Louis knew that he had in his possession the outstanding, the imperial, loveliness of his realm and day.

He was held also, in some degree, by an element which was again shameful. I will not call it rank for it was not so crude a thing, but rather that effect of reputation among one's peers and the habit formed by unquestioned parity with all that must esteem itself for superiority in social things and is so esteemed by all others around. The La Vallière was noble of course, and where these distinctions

2   She is commonly called "Athénaïs." But she was not christened Athénaïs.

are real all nobility of status is equal. But the La Val-
lières were of the lesser, lesser noblesse. That little country
house of theirs in Touraine exactly defined their station.
The Mortemarts were among the supreme—for those whom
such things affect. Louis the King should have regarded
all such differences as a mountain regards the hills at its
feet, but this social difference between the La Vallière and
the Montespan did tell. It was but a minor strand in the
web that now held him—but it was there.

As for the young husband he rebelled, and his rebellion
was met by sheer force—a brutality. True, he had provoked
it, but that provocation is to his honour. We all know how
he put his household into deep mourning and paraded such
mourning on his coach, his arms and his harness for all
to see. Imprisonment and exile followed. There ran (and
runs) a calumny—that he emphasised his proud retaliation
in order to be bought off. It was not so, it was indignation
at white heat that moved him.

It is true that the young household in its brief married
life had been more and more embarrassed. The Duke was
harassed by that constant plague of high birth, called "out-
running the constable." He had never paid his daughter's
dowry and there was probably a project at one time that
Montespan and his wife should leave the court and retire to
the country to retrench—in connection with which project,
presumably, stands the story of her having asked him to
take her away from the temptations of Versailles. But it is
one thing to be embarrassed and another to sell your honour. Look around you and you will see men selling their
honour on all sides—but very few, or none, from penury.
On the contrary, it is the perpetually embarrassed who are
the greatest sticklers for the *Pun d'Onor*. No; Montespan's
violent advertisement of his anger was genuine and, in spite
of its extravagance, it was to his credit. He went off to
his distant place in the Pyrenees and never saw her again.

When, years after, she being then of middle age, fallen from her great place and penitent, she submitted, as a matter of religion, to ask his forgiveness and to return to him; he let her know that in his eyes she was dead. Since he had not received his due from her father he allowed his debts to be paid out of her wealth. It has been reproached against him. But in his own eyes he thought he was doing no more than receiving part of his own property which had been withheld from him.

As for her, she, in that first flush of triumph, jeered at him and sought to make him ridiculous in the eyes of others. It was a thing characteristic of her and not to be pardoned by posterity. But indeed most of what this woman did was base, and she presented that common contrast, easily understood by her own sex and always a bewilderment to the other: the contrast of Beauty (not only of beauty, but of grace and charm and the externals even of sympathy, of active taste and creative use thereof), with a complete contempt for honour: a complete lack of magnanimity.

Other defects she had, and a leading one was greed. Not avarice—on the contrary, she was a spendthrift and a mad gambler of thousands upon thousands (well knowing that all she lost at cards would be met from an inexhaustible purse)—but greed. She advanced her sisters and brothers, but without affection for them, nor even for her children. Long after she had left court she still watched her dependants lest they should pilfer from her; and though she gave much in charity toward the end, it was never spontaneously, but always as a sort of mortification.

She was grasping, insatiably so; and when the man she had captured strove to please her with unexpected gifts, she was not content but persistently complaining. The little palace which he built for her leisure she sneered at, saying "It might just do for a dancing girl," and she would not rest till he had swollen it from a gem into a show.

A good side she had to her: her religion was real. Even when she could not practise it, she retained it, and all through the end, after her retirement, returned to it. Even in the height of her false glory and her enjoyment of its fruits in luxury and splendour and vast wealth she is to be praised for remembering death and for the terrors with which that prospect afflicted her: for all are to be praised who remember death, even with affright, as all are to be praised who face reality. They are, in so far, free from the Lie in the Soul. It was religion in her as well as in Louis that led to those occasional gaps in their intercourse of double adultery. They were genuine moments of repentance and attempted reparation, though they did not last.

Also she was not without kindness to those in distress and she honoured talent, a grace commoner in the rich world of those days than in our own. Such appreciation of gifts other than wealth has its reward; for when the rich despise or ignore excellencies other than their own wealth, they lose magnificence and leave no record: when they recognise the painter, the poet, the architect, they are remembered by the pictures of their day, its verse, its monuments.

The Montespan was, then, a good patroness. We must always remember that *she* presided in the days when Versailles was rising. The beginning of the New Palace corresponds with her entry into favour and the completion of its main features with her ambiguous reign. The Great Gallery is hers.

But when that has been said for her, all has been said; and there remains against her the worst charge that can be made against a woman, unfortunately the charge most usually and most justly deserved: hardness: hardness especially to the man who did all for her.

Man is monogamous. That is a truth surprising only to those who do not see things as they are, but live in print and fiction.

Man is monogamous: even men as individuals are normally monogamous. It is of their nature, especially in and after maturity. The life of all the world, its social terms and institutions prove the thing. This does not mean that men are necessarily rigid in morals or unexceptional in their commerce with one mate, but it does mean that the nature and general course of life lead men to this condition of monogamy and maintain them in it. A man's mate is his wife: the man, his wife and the child are the cell and unit of human affairs. The departure from such a norm may be rare or frequent, but norm it remains. Custom at the least, and at the most some obscure deep-seated instinct creates that social thing, monogamy, and roots so and nourishes a bond that all permanent rupture of it is disastrous. All but a very few, very imperfect men, take monogamy for granted even when they least profess it, even when they least know it. A few very wise women know how to take advantage of that constant set of the tide in men's souls.

Louis was a man, vigorous and very normal: he was a man for one mate. His destined mate had been denied him, and therefore the heart of the whole affair—which is love—had been plucked out of him; yet did he in each of the three associations he formed seek unity, and in the last he found it.

After 1660—that is for a whole lifetime after his twenty-second year—he never loved. But he sought, and returned to, one companionship. By what I have called a major disaster something not much higher than concupiscence caught him as he entered maturity. There was brilliance and a sort of glory about the Montespan alliance, but at heart it was no exalted union as that with the La Vallière might have been: for with the La Vallière Louis was a god, but with the Montespan a victim.

Yet even in that new carnality he sought peace.

She was fruitful, exceptionally so, having that of Ceres about her also like her hair. *Almæ fecunditas alma*; but the benignity which should accompany fruitfulness, *that* she wholly lacked. When she felt sure of him she began to make scenes. His forbearance with her vile temper is good proof of that continuity in him which forbade him to abandon a habit strongly formed. He broke away twice—but each time for a reason quite alien to her intolerable tantrums. In each case it was with him, as with her, I repeat, the motive of religion that moved them.

Their double adultery was glaring. Bossuet, for all his adoration of kingship, reproved Louis continually; on two great occasions—perhaps on many lesser ones—with effect. But he returned; and from the association in Flanders on till after Nijmegen, that is for over eleven years, perhaps, first and last, for twelve—the relations between him and her intermittently endured. How, with such a foundation, he degenerated into promiscuity we shall see; but for all that span, the thirties of his life, he was bound. He was forty-one when the bond abruptly snapped under a shattering blow.

Here consider how kingship stood in all this business.

It is manifestly a product of kingship, and an evil one, that the sort of idolatry which it provokes permitted a king to act as though he were not a man and were absolved from the responsibilities of a man. It did not only permit Louis to do so because he had power, it actually persuaded him, the man himself, that he was so much different clay from his fellows that the Commandments did not apply to him as to them. This grave lesion of the soul is a standing moral menace to monarchy.

Such insane pride is a menace indeed to all power. It menaces a rich man or a man possessed of arms in a primitive society or a man gifted with the power of persuasion. But in all these cases pride is on sufferance, as it were, and not part and parcel of thought and conduct. With kingship it becomes exactly that; part and parcel of thought and conduct. Power, which is always perilous to, and may easily damn, a human soul, becomes, when it is pushed to this extreme, inhuman. And as with power, so with flattery, not only the conscious flattery of all self-seekers, but the far more dangerous, unconscious, instinctive flattery of those who approach superiors as though they were divine.

It is because kingship does this harm that nearly all men, reading of episodes like that of La Vallière in her innocence, or that of the Montespan in her brazenness, have—the most part of them—a feeling that treating the matter as one of common morals is unjust. We feel, most of us, that there is for kings a licence which others cannot claim. The best of the ecclesiastics, and notably that great Bossuet, overcame that tendency. They denounced the evil and in the end they corrected it, though only with the help of disaster working for the correction of the wrongdoer, and only with the help of a new woman at his side, who could see reality more clearly than he.

But if this were true of the effect of kingship upon the king, it is true also of the effect of kingship upon the associates of the King. One may say of the pure and good La Vallière that her love was profound indeed and spontaneous indeed. It was that. But had the young god not been a king she would not have fallen, nor have needed expiation.

As for the Montespan, she would not have so cynically destroyed her young home and her honour save for kingship. It was not merely yielding to temptation, like the temptation of serving a rich man and obtaining the material advantages of such service. It was the feeling that here there was a sort of supernatural alliance at hand, a piece of sublime fortune of an exalted kind offered to no other woman.

When Louis first noticed her, when she first tempted him (for she was the tempter), she was filled with an ambition of a transcendental sort, something with the supernatural about it: therefore with something of the diabolic.

It is at this point that there comes in one of those mysteries which perplex history. Did Athenaïs de Montespan procure the King by unlawful dealing with Evil Spirits? Or (if the reader be one of the old-fashioned sort who is still confident there is no devil), did she at any rate so debase herself as to play with Black Magic for the purpose of achieving that toppling place which she was to hold intermittently for so many years?

22

When Louis XIV Broke with de Montespan

HERE IT IS ESSENTIAL TO ESTAB-
lish a date. When exactly did Louis first hear
of his mistress's commerce with the Diabol-
ists? The fixing of an approximate historical date in matters
which, of their nature, cannot provide direct evidence is
of the first importance, and in nothing more important
than in this matter of the sudden break between Louis
and Athenaïs de Montespan.

It is the chief event of his spiritual life, and therefore
the chief event of his temporal existence. It stands at the
origin of his conversion, the stabilisation of his life, the
saving of his character and the preparation of him for that
heroic resistance against a world of enemies, that ultimate
sufficient victory which so dramatically concludes his long
achievement—on the edge of death.

The data we have whereon to base our judgement are,
as in all such cases, inferior and superior limits. Even the
worst and dullest of historians, even the most provincial
of academic men steeped in ignorance of what Versailles
meant and was, must appreciate that all commerce between
Louis and this woman had ceased before he returned to
living regularly with the queen. We may certainly fix as
an inferior limit, therefore—as a latest date—the return
from the Rhineland in 1681. We have an equally certain
superior limit indicated by the birth of Toulouse, the date
of which is proof that Louis and the Montespan were still,

in early '78, the sort of husband and wife which they had long been. The King's loose and increasing vagaries of 1680-81 are not germane to the matter. The affair with one unfortunate and doomed secondary mistress would by no means of itself necessarily mean that de Montespan's command was abandoned.

Common sense or moral certitude will give one a fairly narrow limit on another line of conjecture. Louis was shown the depositions of the witnesses before the court of enquiry into the sorceries, etc., in the late autumn of 1679. It was during the summer of '80 that there took place that dreadful scene in which the disappointed and angry woman so offensively insulted him. That interview had been procured with some difficulty by Louvois and obviously only after a complete breach of relations between Louis and her.

We may be morally certain therefore that the end came sometime in that winter of 1679-80, and probably at the earlier end of that season.

How much must we believe of the stories which Louis then heard for the first time? How much even of the recorded evidence connected with all that affair?

It is important to answer this question. On it depends the degree in which we condemn this physically splendid and morally despicable woman.

Some of the most careful historians dealing with the episode, have believed pretty well all that was said against her: that the black masses were said upon her naked body,[1] that she was prepared not only to make the King devoted to her by philtres, but even to poison him. On the other hand, base and criminal men and women, under threat of

---

[1] The very place is recorded in the false or true evidence of the wretches who denounced her: the Château of Villebousin on the southern road out of Paris, near Montlhéry: a place of remote dignity till recent years: a fine house of high roofs, moats, fountains, silence and great trees.

torture, or to escape the fire, will say anything. We cannot even examine the evidence properly, because the essentials of the evidence, in so far as they concern the incriminated woman, were sent for, kept secret, and later destroyed by the King's own hand.

We have to judge here, as in so many major historical mysteries, by our knowledge of the characters involved, and by our general knowledge of mankind.

It is quite certain that this woman had fallen to be without honour, and even without scruple. It is quite certain that her ambition and her determination were enough to make her go to any length; but it is not certain at all—contrarywise, it is most improbable—that she would have done the degrading things which these very dubious accounts describe.

She certainly asked for magic aid. She certainly visited the magicians. She certainly used her dependants to discover all that could be discovered of such affairs; but there was no need for her to debase herself so abominably as the stories told of her affirm. She had a sufficient hold upon her lover (if we are to use such a term) to be fairly sure of recovering him. In spite of her grave defects as a companion, she presumably—as do all termagants, women with such vices of temper and hardness—took it for granted till too late that she was necessary to him.

It seems more probable that she was innocent of the excesses ascribed to her, although in common with the rest of the world she knew that such practices existed, and she was indifferent to their vileness in others. It is only a guess, but this would seem the safest guess. On the other hand we must not dismiss the whole business because it seems to us today incredible. The spiritual attitude of any past generation is always difficult for later generations to grasp. The credulity on magic of men and women in the late seventeenth century, seems to us amazing. But then, the brute materialism and incredulity of our own times would have seemed to *them* incredible.

Any one of my own generation, now ageing, can bear witness to the revolution which has taken place in the mind of the average Englishman during the last fifty or sixty years, upon what may, and what may not, be believed. Some sixty years ago a mass of English men and women— or at any rate, a large majority of them, especially those who had, in their childhood, lived as villagers—were in practice "Bible Christians." That is, they accepted the literal truth of all that Hebrew folklore, poetry, legend and record which the Catholic Church had bequeathed to their fathers as "Holy Writ."[2] We who are now reaching the term of human life—"The three score years and ten" as the age of seventy is termed in the quaint hieratic language of the Jacobean English Bible—can remember the generation which took as plain history all that was told them in that Book. By such an example we may judge how a credence in astrology and black magic survived to the last third of the seventeenth century.

Moreover we have but to wait a little while for the return of some new credulity. Our generation swung to the other extreme: it could believe nothing. Soon it will again believe too much. The pendulum is never at rest.

The evidence for the Montespan's disgusting sorceries against Louis is not to be rejected because of its enormity, since from what we know of the woman, of her ambition and of her brazen assurance, anything is possible. Rather is it to be rejected because there was hardly need for such extravagance.

---

2   It is perhaps the most astonishing paradox in European history that tales on the face of them incredible but accepted on the statement of the Church that their moral teaching at least was inspired and their prophetic character assured, were treated as unquestioned historical truth when the Church was declared the enemy of truth.

Whatever be the truth, the essential thing in the whole business is the shock which the story told by the poisoners and the diabolists made upon Louis even if he believed but one-tenth of it. She had first approached the sorcerers *before* her cohabitation with the King began, when he had but begun to remark her: that is in 1667-68. The examination of the criminals is of 1678-79. It was not till *then*—after ten years!—that this crushing blow fell upon the King's head and saved him.

This woman, who had been so thoroughly his mate he found, in one dreadful hour, had all the while regarded him contemptuously, making of him a dupe. He had known her to be, in any case, treacherous, indifferent, insulting to him in private, but he thought she had always respected his supreme station. He now found that she had made the Crown of France a matter of traffic with the gutter.

From the effects of that salutary shock Louis never returned. He had been cleansed. Let all those who have seen such things bear witness to the truth. A shock so strong *can* renew a man.

For be it remembered that violence had been done to that Medicean pride which was impressed upon his features from birth, and had been nourished and enhanced by the whole experience of his life. His superhuman function of Kingship had been derided at its very core. He, the Divine King, had been thus mocked by that one being who knew him best. After that wound of scorn he could never go back to what had been.

Some little while later Louvois arranged a meeting between him and her—her to whom now he refused to speak a word save of public ceremony.

She had hoped, unwisely, that from this meeting there might spring a reconciliation. She found it was impossible. It seems that for this very reason, because, and at the moment when, she saw all hope must be abandoned, she went deeper in her insolence (filled with spite of despair) than ever she had gone before. She is said to have told this intimate companion of eleven and twelve years' standing, that *she* was to be pitied—not he. That *she* had borne with him as others would not have borne. She taunted him with his offensive breath, or what she, for her own purpose, said to be such.

That was a last Parthian arrow shot from the bow in full retreat. Perhaps she lied, but such words were not words any man could forget. They were intended to poison and to fester till the end of life. It is high testimony to his self-mastery, that, after such a day he was content to forego any vengeance, though he treated her henceforward as though she were not. She stayed on at Court for years, determined not to be publicly degraded. Nor would *he* publicly degrade *her*. She was half-royal now. She was the mother of Princes and Princesses legitimised and treated as being of the blood. Her apartments at Versailles were changed to the second storey, her court had dissolved. But she was still of the Palace. Her great income was still counted out to her regularly. Louis had paid the price, and the business was over. After all, she had served him.

In truth she had served him, but without intention to do so, and much more than he himself knew—the true knowledge of her had snapped the tie, and thereby making of all the last half of his life, a quite different, an honourable, satisfaction.

Louis had broken with a whole past. We need not know much of men to be sure that there was no transition. There was a climax and an earthquake, after which much in him disappeared—whereupon came a renewal.

It was high time! That central episode of the Montespan had been all that I have called it; an enslavement to the Body: the bonds were not bonds in which a man could rest at all. Towards the end of the Montespan years he was beginning to show the fruits which commonly follow an extravagance in appetite. He was beginning to show something of that promiscuity wherein such characters often dissolve. He might have ended—he would have ended—as his successor ended, bitten into and corroded by the things of the flesh.

He was saved, I say, as by a special providence. The road was clear, the beginnings of a new repose, and the return to religion. Not that he had ever lost religion, but the long lapses had become so necessary to him and so much a habit after two abortive efforts at reseizing himself, that never would he have become again fixed, regular, and practising in his worship, but for that storm, that hurricane, of his forty-second year.

It is strange that a happening of this kind, to which in so many lives so many men and women can bear witness, should have been so utterly misunderstood. It is represented as a mere gradual substitution of one woman's influence for another: the Maintenon replacing the Montespan—a commonplace change-over. His conversion is sneered at by fools as a lapse into senility—senility in this man who, to the edge of the grave, remained of marble and of bronze, completely master of himself, of his function, of his subjects, of all! It was in truth a sort of Resurrection: a Resurrection of the *Will*. The man's whole life to this moment in 1679 had been a continuous function of the right of the *Will*, that is of duty, save in the one perilous article of the flesh. Therein, first indifferent, then more fixed he came nearer and nearer to self-abandonment, to a decay of control. He had come in those critical forties to the edge of a steep, in slipping down which slope he would have ended by losing his public as well as his private dignity and function. From that edge he was snatched back just before catastrophe to himself within and therefore (later) to the State without.

It is true that side by side with that revulsion—but *not* the agent of it—went the growing appreciation of Frances de Maintenon who was to support and nourish him henceforward to the end. It is true that during those years of the 1670's there had come more and more into his view the character of the woman to whom he was to owe so much over all the long remainder of his life.

Athenaïs de Montespan choosing for her children some discreet woman whose necessity would leave her open to a wage, but whose repute and character guarantees of virtue and steadfastness, had chosen the widow of Scarron. It is also true that this woman, whose life had been so barred and so completely oppressed with poverty, though deriving from one of the great names of the past—for she was a d'Aubigné,[3] a name great in letters and, for that matters, in arms and in greatness of birth—had refused the office from the hands of the King's mistress. She would accept it only at the command of the King. Having accepted it, she played her part with zeal, with discretion, but still more with industry. Of these bastards, the least amenable respected her, and the best of them, the little crippled Duc du Maine, loved her like a mother; for, indeed, a mother he had not known. He it was who, at the end of all that business, was given the duty of telling his own mother from the King that she must leave the court. He discharged that duty without too much affliction. He would not have borne such a message to his foster mother.

But here we are talking of things long after. We have seen how Louis retained the Montespan at Versailles for the sake of her children, for the sake also of his own dignity and his honour. He would call formally at her rooms.

3   People always talk of the d'Aubignés as of lesser nobility. She certainly was *lesser* nobility for she had been staringly poor in her youth and straitened throughout her mature years until this piece of good fortune came to her. But nobles such as the fighting d'Aubignés of the Huguenot armies were lesser in no ordinary sense.

As there had been some eleven years before the violent change came, so there were now nearly a dozen before the Montespan left Versailles. It was not until 1691 that she disappeared to take up her retreat at a convent of her own founding in Paris.

So ended the last echo of what might have wrecked the Monarch and the realm. But to know how and why the peril had been so acute one must see the deeps.

VI
The Defensive
1684-1715

23
Madame de Maintenon

THE FIRST EFFECT OF THE KING'S conversion was his return to the Queen. It was duty, and justly performed. She had not that which would suffice even for tolerable conversation. She was of his own age, well past forty, of that pitifully small stature mentioned at her marriage: meaningless. But he returned to her sole association as a husband. Moreover he remembered in this the dignity of the Throne which she shared.

She, poor thing, was overjoyed, rejoicing too openly. Her last two years were happy and in them she seemed to forget the long neglect and mortal isolation of grandeur uncompanioned. In the summer of 1683, prematurely, she died.

For now years past Louis had been more and more attracted by the speech and manner, the advice and judgment of that woman whom he had seen more and more frequently as the guardian of his children. She was with him when the Montespan discoveries had appalled him; she had seen all. Her influence had attended his spiritual change. Her welcome of it was sincere, her tending of it assiduous. With *that* about him he could at last live content. At some decent interval after the Queen's death on a date not certain, but probably as early as January, '84, they were very privately married. Thenceforward they are together through the growing gloom of the great defence, through the dereliction of the last defeats, through the rally of Denain, to the end: thirty-one years of unseparated companionship.

What was this woman, the last, and the only sufficient, woman of his life?

Frances d'Aubigné, widow of Scarron, now titular Marchioness of Maintenon, had been formed and annealed under the following chain of circumstance:

Her grandfather had been most remarkable among those fighting nobles who had surrounded Henry IV, the grandfather of Louis, in his civil war for Calvinism and for his claim to the Throne of France. He was of good birth, a noble like all his colleagues, but has survived with an especial lustre because he added to his conspicuous courage in battle, his loyalty and his energy, a rare quality of learning and even a vigorous literary talent. He was the chronicler poet and satirist of the fighting reformers in that first generation when the Counter Church of Calvin was still enthusiastic and confident of victory. The pedantry of a time steeped in the classics gave him the name of "Agrippa."

Agrippa d'Aubigné reaped no material reward for his virtues of military daring and religious sincerity. His son lived impoverished and, being a wastrel as well, sank into penury. That son's child, Frances, the granddaughter of Agrippa, was born in the precincts of a debtors' prison, grew up dependent on relatives (one of whom had her converted to Catholicism in her 'teens), lived in desperate genteel poverty with her mother, and emerged from it to make a singular marriage, a marriage with the very well known wit Scarron, to whose house would come the fine gentleman of the day. It is the habit of such to frequent and despise as buffoons those whose wit they find entertaining.

It was but a nominal marriage, but he was good to her, he brought her into a wide company, and when he died she had just the wherewithal to live. She had known the various forms of trial whereof the sharpest is the humiliation always suffered by the impoverished gentry, for Cervantes said: "There is nothing so miserable as gentlefolk in poverty." Such experiences break or confirm the will: they made of her will a secret steel spring which gave life to her reticence, her power of plan, her excellent conversation, a certain wit, and thorough accomplishment of whatever fell to her hand.

The friends of Scarron had pressed on the Crown the claim of his widow. Louis is even said to have found their repeated efforts importunate—for he then had little knowledge of her though she already moved in the great world. When she became the governess of his children by the Montespan he bought for her the land, and confirmed her in the title, of Maintenon, on the Chartres road, a long day from Versailles. The scenes between her quiet order, her known moral protest, and the violent temper of her employer, the reigning mistress, were frequent; yet the relationship between herself and the Montespan endured. Through it the King met her more and more frequently, felt more and more and more the contrast between his disorder of emotions and that firm mind. He heard and even listened to her judgments on right living. Not that she effected the great change in him—the upheaval of the Voisin relations did that—but she accompanied the conversion and her words were a permanent feature of it in his memory.

What was she at this moment of her private marriage to the King, he in his forty-sixth, she in her forty-ninth, year?

We may say of her that she combined what is rarely combined: the attractive and the admirable with the unsympathetic. The conversation, the due measure of wit, the liveliness, though sober liveliness, of attention, the continued personal devotion to such human characters as she set out to serve; all this was attractive. Her rooted and practised religion was admirable, as were her sense of measure, her good sense and good temper, her spiritual strength and the even process of her mind. Her strength of will was admirable, too, and still more admirable the use to which she put it. For, like Louis himself, she devoted her will to a task: she harnessed it.

The common accusations against her are silly enough. They were made, and are still made, by minds of such a calibre that they cannot apprehend the greatness of virtue: of virtue displayed as loyalty, as consistent right-doing and as equally consistent observance of strict rule in worship. It is more picturesque to break, than to obey, the commandments of God: and therefore this fine mind and well-directed balanced soul appeals not to the chroniclers of scandal or brilliant things—still less to the novelists. I say that in all things which the wise admire in women, in all the *general* things which they admire, she was admirable; but I have also said that she was not sympathetic. It is by combining this positive with that negative that you may best apprehend her.

I mean by "sympathetic," having those qualities of fellowship—often superficial, sometimes profound, always pleasing—which bind a man or woman to their fellows almost on first acquaintance.

She had a quick perception, she was commonly a little too enthusiastic for a new experience of acquaintance—and would have had enough of such in a day or two; but there was in this no reciprocity: she made few permanent friendships.

One may not affirm a universal negative, but so far as I know there was not one occasion in that long life when anyone, coming upon Frances d'Aubigné, lit up at an encounter with her. It was by gradual effect that she made her impression. She was remembered by not a few with affection, by scores with respect, and with devotion by those to whom she devoted herself; in particular, as I have said, by the Duc du Maine, he who had been her foster-son, her little boy, her darling. But more than that you find not.

It has been said about her that the barrier between herself and those about her came from her formation as pedagogue: "Too much of the governess." That, again, is an ignorant judgement. It was just those whom she had brought up who loved her most deeply and most profoundly. In that relation she was perfect. Those early years of poverty which had so strengthened her will had left it well tempered indeed, but supple, never crude. I have told how she used that will of hers, persistent and retentive. That way of using the will always ultimately affects society but is no passport to immediate and general reception by one's fellow beings. She never cringed and she never gave way. The strength in her was the more apparent from such continuous unbroken control of her purpose.

She was not herself of the sort that desired the more considerable advantages of human conversation. She did not even desire praise. She loved to order and to arrange, because she had very high talents for organisation, and to exercise one's special gifts is a natural bent. On this account it has been said that she loved to dominate. I should have thought the word ill-chosen. She loved to be in command, but she was not of the sort that usurps command.

We must further remember this about her: that not only her anomalous position, her astonishing progress from one status to another, her very restraint and exterior coldness, the more repelled those who were originally prejudiced against her, but also the very fact of her position made far more enemies than friends.

It needs a high degree of intelligence to distinguish between possession of power by another and their exercise of it. It is one thing for a man or a woman to have the opportunity for deciding events; it is quite another thing for them to use that opportunity or even care to use it.

It requires also not only intelligence but judgment to distinguish between those who are in a position to move events and those who actually move them. One is perpetually told, "You can never get anything out of so-and-so until you get on the right side of such and such a one." One commonly finds, if one reaches intimate knowledge of the matter, that the situation is quite other. That though the second *might* influence the first (being intimate, trusted, and always at hand), yet the second is either indifferent to the opportunity or carefully selects but rare occasions for employing it, and for the most part treats it as though it were not there.

So it was with Frances de Maintenon. She knew very well what manner of mate she had now. She attentively and thoroughly disassociated herself from great public affairs. She used influence in certain departments which concerned her, as, for instance, now and then in ecclesiastical promotions and nominations. But to call her the authoress of any main decision of State is nonsense. It is a contradiction of all that we know of her, especially of her excellently central and subtle judgment. Her whole position depended on detachment from politics.

Now before we conclude this appreciation we must remember one last thing, which, in a secret fashion, underlies all her legitimate and powerful relations with the great king. She could be tender.

You will not find it written down in tittle-tattle, nor even apparent in any letter or memoir. You will discover it by going over in your own mind what you have known of the influence of women over men—a matter wherein academic history is deaf, dumb and blind. She was of that very sort (at their best and most fruitful in middle age) who know how to proffer true tenderness in privacy, and it is that which does not so much conquer the strong as bind them firmly, while jealous of their independence, to the giver of so great a gift: unfailing kindness.

No wonder that Louis was grateful to her and for her! There is an affection which, if not autumnal in its origins, is at least Septembral; it arises between those who certainly will not feel again—have not felt for a lifetime—the earlier thrill. Such communion of later years is as full of content as a clear, deep, woodland lake apart and undisturbed. It assuages the thirst of the soul.

Nor let this be forgotten. That the eyes of the Maintenon were the eyes of the Mancini: very dark, marble dark, but of a living dark, tardy in glance, receptive and responsive too, having about them something of permanence and of home; but having still more for Louis—after so many years—something of reminiscence.

The eyes of the Maintenon meeting in calm communion, not seeking, the eyes of the King at forty-five—and she at forty-eight—were the eyes that had looked into his as he lay between life and death in his twentieth year.

We must not leave this great figure—for she was great in the sufficiency of her attributes to her position—without deciding on what contemporaries meant by "her desire to be queen." It is a matter on which mere denial would be folly. It is a matter upon which the common affirmation is a greater folly still.

In such a day she, being a woman, and a woman conscious of such capacities, and being moreover one who had risen, as though under a miraculous fate, to the height she had reached, certainly felt that to be called "Queen" before she died would have been a culminating satisfaction. But to say that she worked for it, that she awaited it, is false. It is a misunderstanding of her whole position. If there was one mind had worked in such a direction it was not the mind of the woman but of the man—as might have been expected. It was Louis who wondered whether he ought not to give his wife her full position. She made no scheme to attain it, nor regretted its loss.

Saint Simon writes wildly melodramatic nonsense, as we have seen, about Louvois's protestations to the King, but there is probably something behind the exaggerated story. It does look as if Louis had once or twice hesitated on the verge of publicly proclaiming the marriage, which would have been equivalent to putting his wife upon the throne. It would not have been unnatural. The complete sovereignty which he had reached made him think everything possible. To call his wife by her full name publicly would have been a far less thing than that proposal for his bastards to inherit the crown of France, which so shocked the mind of the time. Also there was something in the King's character, apart from his love of proving himself supreme, which recoiled from a false position. And what could be more false than the position of himself and Frances de Maintenon. He had found, and daily discovered with increasing satisfaction, a companion in a life wherein spiritual isolation had only been supported at all by strength of will. Once more "He was grateful *to* her and *for* her." Grateful to God that he had been granted true companionship and repose unexpected, gradually discovered and exactly suited to his needs. Grateful to the woman herself for her support and constant solicitude, her solace, her active speech, her choice and distinction of spiritual wisdom expressed. Why should he not manifest his gratitude by proclaiming her Queen?

But he did not do so. The word was never pronounced. She stood on the steps of the throne at his side till the end, but no higher. And the degree in which others may have worked for her recognition, the degree in which she herself desired it or aimed at it, even the degree in which Louis, who did certainly consider it, did so consider it, we cannot tell. For that goal was never reached and it came no nearer as time proceeded.

He knew in his heart, though perhaps he did not formulate the knowledge, that he was at an age when men of his too vigorous kind, being isolated, can make fools of themselves. Men make fools of themselves at all ages, but in youth fate and friends forgive them; in age such folly damns them irretrievably. It is much worse than folly; it is corruption; it is deliquescence. Had *that* come upon Louis XIV as it came upon Louis XV, how would the realm— which was the Monarchy, that is, the King himself—have stood against the coming storm?

He knew, I say, perhaps confusedly, and without fully formulating the truth to himself, what his coming to her had been to him, and gradually he discovered, in his companionship with her, that she played her part unbrokenly, continuously. He found there right to his hand a sense of understanding without assiduity: bodily habit, comfort and habitation; home.[1]

---

1   It was true of Madame de Maintenon, as of all other public figures; the further from actual knowledge the worse the misapprehension. Thus go-betweens, obscure spies, and still more the superficial of a remote posterity (such as Macaulay) made her out an intriguer and a suggester of policy, and misunderstood her in proportion to their ignorance. The Revocation is the test, and it is certain that she stood aloof in that major crisis.

24
Saint Simon

THE TRUE PORTRAIT OF MADAME
de Maintenon has been both blurred and warped
by many separate influences: by the tireless opposition of the anti-Catholic to the Catholic; by the irritation
of high acknowledged birth with the newcomer of lesser
station; by the misjudgement of what is serene by what is
emotional; by the impatience of the young with the elderly;
by, most of all by, the combined malice, talent and limited
unwisdom of Saint Simon.

Here, then, let us pause a moment to consider the effect
which the publication of Saint Simon's Memoirs, more
than one hundred years ago, has had upon the popular
view of the King's years.

What that enormous but lively compilation has to say
about the time beyond which its author's memory could not
reach[1] has little actual value, though he had met scores of
people who had known earlier times. It was not first-hand
and it dealt with a world that was already old-fashioned by
the time Saint Simon began to look about him.

He stood to the last years of the reign, to the epoch of
Madame de Maintenon, as men of my generation, who am
writing this, stand to the time between the first Jubilee of
Queen Victoria (1887) and the Boer War (1900). What
he had to say about previous things stretches right away
back to the early days of the reign. It is like what anyone

---

[1] He is only a contemporary adult witness after 1695: nearly a
dozen years after the King's private marriage: only a couple of years
before the Peace of Ryswick.

of my generation might have to say about the Crimea, the American Civil War, the Second Empire, the literary world of Tennyson in his prime and of Browning or (in the ecclesiastical world) of Kingsley, Newman, Maurice and Manning. I have met any number of people who survived into my own youth and were contemporaries and intimates of all that time. I have heard what they had to say. But I know my judgment of things before the eighties of the last century to be something very different from my judgment of the things of my own youth. Anyone will agree, I think, with the justice of this example and parallel.

Saint Simon has, as an authority, a worse defect by far than lack of contemporary knowledge. It is a defect that one feels even more when he is talking of what he knows and has seen himself than when he is talking of the past at second hand. It is a defect in judgment so radical, so all-pervading, that his immense labour is but one prolonged example of it.

We must remember that he was a very vain man, and vain men are always weak in the article of judgment, for indeed vanity itself is nothing more than a misunderstanding of the relative importance of different qualities in oneself. Most men who think themselves great statesmen, for instance, today, are in that position. We know they are wrong the moment they open their mouths. It is Parliaments that do this to our poor politicians. So did the Court to Frenchmen of high rank in the earlier eighteenth century.

Saint Simon is not only out of focus, he is actually grotesque when he considers matters of etiquette and of rank and of caste in the society to which he was born. Those things have their importance. So has money, so has good looks, so much more has health, and so, still more, has intelligence. But in some particular circumstances where rank should be given, let us say, five marks out of one hundred, he gives it ninety-five. His judgement is also (as is now, I think, commonly recognised) hopelessly warped where his personal pique was concerned. He had resigned a Commission on the very threshold of life because he thought he had not been treated with sufficient deference by the King. He could not bear to see anyone of the "lesser nobility" (Madame de Maintenon herself he thought a glaring example) moving amid the "greater nobility"—of whom he was himself one.

He was especially and wildly wrong about his patron, the Regent, the man who ruined the monarchy. The Regent was exalted by Saint Simon because he was Saint Simon's crony and actually gave him high political opportunities which the favoured recipient was quite incapable of using. The National disaster (as we shall see) in connection with the Regent was that he should have been appointed Regent at all. How and why Louis must be excused in the matter is clear to anyone who understands the claims of the Blood Royal. But at any rate the Regent *was* Regent and that is the thing lying at the root of the final breakdown at the Revolution. He has been called the "Gravedigger of the French Royal House," and the judgment is just.

But in Saint Simon's eyes the Regent was half a god because the Regent had (as he thought) appreciated Saint Simon.

They err most thoroughly about Saint Simon who say he was a relic from feudal times. They err as thoroughly as people who, complaining of police tyranny today, call it "mediæval."

The feudals from whom most of the high nobility descended were formed by riding and the open air: by frank brutality and the perpetual physical exercise of war. Saint Simon was the exact opposite of this. He was of the drawing-room. He was petty. He was one of those men who secretly revel in advantage. Rank and wealth are two incontestable advantages among the many a man may have. On wealth he fixed little attention, for he lived in it. He noted it in so much as it made him dislike those who were richer than himself. But rank he wallowed in. This imaginary excellence had, in his mind, real existence.

Lastly there is this to remember about Saint Simon while we are drawing up a category of his deficiencies. Nowhere was he more at issue with reality than in the matter of religion.

His mind was of that sort to which organised religion is repellent. This is not a defect in judgment; it is merely a temperament, often to be discovered in men of very excellent judgment; but in Saint Simon's case he takes his own temperament so much for granted as being that of the whole human race and, one might say, of the Creator Himself, that he is quite blind to the majesty of the Faith and even to its magnitude. It is significant that Saint Simon was also at odds with the Military spirit. He disliked officers. He disliked armies.

The Jesuits are a supreme example of organisation: a strictly-disciplined army levied and disciplined to save what could be saved of Europe in the earthquake of the Reformation. They set out to save what could be saved of Catholic Europe and they succeeded. One may regret their success or approve of it. But Saint Simon talks of them as might any anti-clerical provincial newspaper today. He even believes in the secret Jesuit: "The Jesuit in disguise." To read him one might think that the members of the Society were compounded at once of devilish cunning, fatuity and a thin absence of human stuff: a set of stage Jesuits. There is nothing brands a man with the mark of bad judgment more than thus reducing complicated effects to one cause. Saint Simon on the Jesuits (indeed, I suspect, on the whole Catholic scheme at heart) is as deficient as the anti-Semite upon the Jewish problem or the Orangeman on the Irish.

Why, then, has Saint Simon been of such effect? Why must he be called, in spite of those prodigiously lengthy volumes, a master in his way? Because he presents a very unusual combination indeed, *a combination of vivid observation (wherein is included vivid portrayal) with a living style and with the rarest extreme of industry.* He noted everything down, whether what he himself witnessed or what he heard: having done so there arose a picture in his mind as sharp as a vision. And that picture he sets down on paper after a fashion which makes it rise in all its original poignancy before the reader's eyes.

To put it briefly, Saint Simon is a first-rate example of the Power of the Word. He is also a first-rate example of the deception against which the historian desiring truth chiefly arms himself. One never tires of reading him. On this account he has received the greatest reward that he could have desired. He has helped to mould the judgment of posterity and to mould it askew.

It is worth noting that Saint Simon is not as a rule consciously unjust. This truth is not to be regarded as a tribute to his moral character, which is not very well worthy of praise, but as a factor in estimating the value of his testimony. How far conscious of injustice a thoroughly prejudiced and petty and peevish man can be is a doubtful point, but I think in the case of Saint Simon his vast interest in mere observation, in seeing *things*, and noting them down, often overcame his desire to malign, and this is conspicuous in his developed notes upon certain aspects of the characters which least pleased him. He bears full tribute to Vauban.

Again his testimony to the King's fortitude, especially in the last years of his life, is remarkable. So is his testimony to the liveliness of Madame de Maintenon's well-restrained wit. I fancy most people would not have extolled this excellence in her intellect as Saint Simon does. There is one field, however, where he makes no effort at justice at all, but simply gives full rein to his animosity, and that is the field of religion. Here let us recall how and why he felt so strongly on the Society of Jesus.

I cannot remember an instance (though it is a bold thing to say of any book which challenges the *Encyclopædia Britannica* for length) in which he has a good word to say for the Society of Jesus or for any one of its members. Moreover there is in all his anti-Jesuit attitude the special mark of unjust judgment, which is fatuity. He tries to say (as so many other people have said before and since) that Jesuits are filled with diabolical cunning and at the same time a lack of general appreciation. They misunderstand every position, and yet they deal with each in detail and with unbroken tenacity—if anything *too* thoroughly.

Now such a combination of vivid observation with lack of judgment has often been predicated of devils by those interested in the natural history of devils: but it certainly never applies to human beings. If you have an opponent who studies the whole field and gets up every aspect of it and is unremittingly secret in his plots against you, you will not at the same time suffer from his dullness of comprehension. The enemies of the Society cannot have it both ways.

As with the Jesuits, so with the Church as a whole. And I repeat here in conclusion what I said above: the unorganised hates and fears the organised. The organised religion of the Faith was hated and feared by this man, not because he preferred unorganised religion, but because at heart the very spirit of Catholicism itself offended him.

For such a man the King's wife was odious in every way: as an interloper, as one born in poverty, as a balanced and firm mind which attained its ends. Therefore has he not originated but confirmed the wrong conclusions upon this woman's real self. In this as in so much else the belated "releasing" of Saint Simon's memoirs were a godsend to all those at home and abroad who, in their various degrees, are enemies to the achievement of Louis XIV and to his character; to the national tradition of the French and to its unfailing expression in arms and ideas.

THE TURN OF THE TIDE

With this new phase—the conversion of the King to right-living, the Maintenon marriage, the settling of the court—coincides what was certainly not produced by any of these things but was coincident with them. It may be called "The Turn of the Tide."

Hitherto all had been, on the political and material side, a continuous ascension of France and of the King for over twenty years. There had been checks—especially the failure to seize Amsterdam; but the progress was continued, in strength, glory and the project of the future, from the young man's grasp of power in 1661, to the climax of Nijmegen, of Alsace and Strasburg, of the "reunions," of the accomplished frontiers, of the reputation attaching to Louis, his name and power.

Now—in 1684-85—it is slack water. The tide is about to turn, and the remaining half-lifetime of the King is an ill ease as to unity within the State, a grievous, at last intolerable financial strain, and in the field a defensive ending in the approach to catastrophe.

There now appear the disadvantages of Monarchy, side by side with those qualities in it which had engendered such triumph. Just as in a Monarchy the Monarch is the State Incarnate, so the Monarch's ageing ages the State also. The State being one man, his youth and vigour go to the strengthening of the Nation's personality and initiative. But then also, as the man decays, the State decays. It is not so with class government which is always of its time, and, if it must grow old, grows old imperceptibly and very slowly. Monarchy fails from the failure of the Monarch, and therefore, inevitably, from his age. Louis had begun to exist and think, as the ageing cannot but do, in terms of the past; the State itself suffered from that illusion.

He made a better fight for it, physically and morally, than any ruler of whom we have record. He won his last and decisive victory not very far from his eightieth year. He continued to the end to do all that had to be done: but the summit was past.

Those thirty years and more, then, have a various aspect to be considered if we would see them justly: the high social achievement accomplished, that is the splendour of the arts and of letters harvested and bequeathed to posterity; the religious policy, never more detailed than at this time and filled with consequence; the two great wars, assaults the first of which was repelled, the second of which all but destroyed the realm; the tragedy of the succession. These must be taken separately in order to comprehend the general effect. I will take them in this order:

First the three main religious debates, the Jansenist, the Gallican and the Huguenot, with the Revocation of the Edict of Nantes and its fruits. Next the splendours in building, sculpture, verse and prose which, arising in the first years of the reign, shed to the end (and beyond) so steadfast a glory. Then the last wars, with their final moment of deathly grapple and ultimate partial but sufficient victory. He stopped the landslide. He restored France.

After this it remained for him to die.

25
The First Effort at Moral Unity

THE ATTACK ON JANSENISM

JANSENISM UNDERLIES ALL THE RELIgion of the great reign. It explains, or illuminates, or holds commentary upon all the other religious developments of that lifetime. It therefore illuminates the mind of the time, for everything human must ultimately be interpreted in the moods of men, and the mood of a generation is expressed by its religion: by its conflicts on religion—whether in such conflicts it uses the word "religion" or not.

Jansenism was born long before Louis and it far outlasted him. It was threatening birth, it was stirring in the mind of the French people, before ever its name was used. It affected all the directive part of French society even when, seventy years after the King's death, that society seemed about to abandon Christian discussion altogether. It may fairly be pretended that even in the modern whirlpool strong elements of Jansenism run like streaks through the foam.

Moreover, Jansenism has its value in history. It attaches to something permanently Gallic: something that made Gaul the focus of the early Manichæan brooding, the Albigensian thing; something that produced that eminently Gallic product, John Calvin.

Now what is this thing, for which Jansenism is only one name applicable to a particular moment, the seventeenth century?

It was one phase of the unending dread man has of his environment, and his doom.

In his environment man rejoices. His spring into life is through a morning sunlight and he savours his landscapes, his wine, his loves, his glories, his beauties, his laughter, even his repose.

All these are of joy and for joy was man made. Happiness is the end of man.

Therefore is man's delight in the universe, in himself and his Creator the normal and healthy mood. Therefore that other contradictory mood of dread is always in peril of descending into disease. But it has a vigorous root, founded also in religion and therefore in truth. Who that has much rejoiced has not also known despair? Who that has much enjoyed has not also known satiety? The Christian philosophers well put it when they say that there is no lasting satisfaction save in everlasting things. The things that pass not only cloy; in due time they breed repugnance. More than that, they lead us too often netherwards, and we smell the pit.

As to what is called nowadays "reaction" against joy, something of the sort would have arisen anyhow. Anyhow there would have come the influence even on a Catholic society of the tendency which, in societies cut off from Catholic unity, had produced the vile fruit of puritanism. Life in the Renaissance had been so exuberant that it was bound to grow fatigued. So it had been in the highest moment of the pagan time, more than 1,000 years before, and that is why you find the Manichæan so lively in the moment when Europe and her barbarian fringe was being conquered by the Faith. Even the very great Pope Gregory blasphemed in this matter, attacking holy marriage itself as *sordes*.

I say that this reaction against beauty, against joy, against repose, against the satisfaction of the body and the soul of man, tends to evil: it is always in peril of evil and, when it gets its head, gallops straight to evil.

Thus none can doubt that the savour of Jansenism was Calvinist. They were wise who smelt that wrong scent at once and set their time on guard against it.

But they are not wise who on that account misjudge the Jansenists of the earlier and better time or underrate the holy souls which clasped it still so desperately at the end. Not only did the actual movement stop far short of Calvinism but it essentially differed from it; not only did it sheer off from Calvinism but it would never have ended in Calvinism, though it might indeed have ended in some fatal schism.

For remember that Jansenism honestly proclaimed its devotion to *Unity*—the informing idea of Catholicism. Also Jansenism was not only honestly but passionately devoted to the real Presence—the Sacrament of the Altar, the very touch-stone of the Catholic soul.

There was, then, nothing of the pit about Jansenism; but things must be judged in their potentiality, not only as they are in their present moments but as they will be if these moments develop on their initial lines. Thus much Jansenism led to the pit. It isolated the soul, not in some exceptional case as an ascetic or anchorite may be isolated, but in principle. It isolated all souls from everything but the ultimate end of souls. It isolated from fellowship all whom it touched. Now *that* is anti-Catholic—and it is mortal. Moreover *that*—such isolation of the soul—is quite out of tune with the mission and the character of the French people who are inflamed by common action, by mob courage, by marching, by massacre, by martyrdom, and by vineyard song.

The moment in which this new fervour later called Jansenism was still young enough to be confident yet sufficiently matured to advance and conquer, was also the very moment of the Fronde. Its press manifestos were beginning to appear before the civil war. But it was also a moment in which was at work a fervour peculiar to the place and the time, which fervour opposed the substance, value and meaning of Jansenism; that fervour was the already established spiritual power of the Jesuits.

Now let us understand what the Jesuits meant in this early spiritual crisis of the seventeenth century.

The Society of Jesus was that which had saved the Church. Its father, St. Ignatius, by far the greatest of the Basques, had arisen contemporary with that explosion against the tradition of Christendom which we call the Reformation.

The zeal, the vision, but much more, I think, the military character of St. Ignatius, forged the weapon whereby the Reformation should be halted.

Like all those who achieve, Ignatius achieved much more than he had intended or knew. Like all those who do, he was led on. He had intended at first, in the solitude of his burning soul, to frame, perhaps to lay down for others, a guide for the object he had first conceived, an object generally missionary: in particular, work for the Holy Land—for which the time was past.

Like a torrent which runs too violently to be checked yet is canalised by the rocky banks around it, the strength of the Ignatian soul poured out at last into the salvation not of heathendom or Islam but of Christendom and of the Christian culture. They became, did the sons of Ignatius, the soldiers of Christendom. But for them, the central thing by which our civilisation lives would have disappeared from the Slavs and from the Germans. It was *they* who counter-attacked. It was they who covered the ground, aided of course by the Capuchins. This direct impulse they retained on into the seventeenth century.

It might be imagined, then, that the Society of Jesus in its intensity and power would have become the opponent of the anti-Catholic thing alone and that, within the

Catholic body, it should be recognised everywhere as a spearhead and a leader of re-conquest; of re-establishment; of rebuilding after ruin.

But the Jesuits were not only strong in spirit, they were also a highly disciplined body; now an organisation highly disciplined and filled with an interior flame which inspires it and actively maintains that discipline, provokes a violent reaction against itself; not only against the cause which its members defend but against themselves personally.

Therefore within the general Catholic body, within the general body of that which had withstood the hurricane of the Reformation and had set up Catholic things again and the right tradition of our culture, there spread (increasingly) enmity against the Society; an enmity which spread in circles wider and wider. Such enmity within the Catholic body was the better nourished through the fashion in which the Jesuit Colleges had captured the education of the cultivated classes, and the spiritual direction of the courtiers and of their kings. The Jesuits had made themselves the champions of our common civilisation against those forces which would have dissolved it. But when they had come, through this feat, to hold the levers of the colleges and the political groups they became, primarily on account of their power, still more on account of their solidarity and the hardness of their armour, detested.

A strong contradiction of them arose on every side. It was established among the Jansenists because Jansenism savoured of heresy, but the highest intelligences of the day who were not Jansenists at all in spirit, joined the attack; became the associates of the Jansenists, mixed with them and were thus unavoidably touched with the Jansenist spirit. Consider Corneille and consider Racine. That great poet, that very great poet, was above all the poet of Eros. Profoundly did he understand the passion of human love. Yet for him a *passion* love was; that is, a thing *suffered* by

mankind; a thing imposed upon mankind from without—
and ultimately an ill. Corneille is *Will*, Racine is *Doom*.

To understand the meaning of Jansenism in the story
of the seventeenth century, I say, contrast Racine and
Corneille.

Corneille, the elder, and we may justly say the greater,
poet, a very great poet indeed, drew the life of his verse
from older things, the severe, the Roman note. The
æsthetic of the Renaissance had after two generations bred
Corneille. Heroism is his theme, dignity the necessary
idol of his admiration; and there runs all through him
a strong, overwhelming tide of spirit which inspired the
phrase "*Il suffit de vouloir*"—the Will can conquer fate. He it
was also who wrote in that matter of Eros "*L'amour est un
plaisir, l'honneur est un devoir*": a blasphemy to the romantics,
a prime and profound truth to another and a stronger kind
of man than the romantics are.

That was Corneille. But Racine knew Eros too well and
was filled with dread—especially (as is the custom with
such men) did he fear more and more with the advance
of years. Fate was his faith. Fate conquers us (thinks he)
especially through the affections and the appetites.

But the Jesuits were on the side of happier human
nature and also of that by which human nature, led away
through desire, recovers again through the Will.

The Jesuits, intent on conversion and on leading men
back to the Church gave scope to beauty, to pleasure and
to joy. Therein was there a violent contrast, a necessary
antagonism, between themselves and the Jansenist, or Puritan spirit. Therefore it was that the Puritan spirit accused
them unjustly of laxity.

Wherever there is authority and law, case law arises.
Special circumstances must be interpreted and general principles must be suited to particular conjunctions. In morals
case law is called casuistry.

For instance, "Thou shalt not kill." What about the execution of a murderer or a traitor? "Thou shalt not steal." What about recovery of what is one's own? May one, if there is no other way, recover it by guile? The ritual of religion must observed if religion is to survive. What exceptions may be made in the rigour of ritual practice? The Sabbatarian must observe his odd taboo or deny the very principle of his creed; but even he must make exceptions and allow beds to be made on Sunday, perhaps even cooking.

In the interpretation of special cases there is laxity at one extreme or rigour at the other. "Thou shalt not bear false witness." But in a particular case—for instance if a murderer should ask you the way to his victim—may you not use ambiguous language? The more you allow this the more lax you are in your casuistry, the less you allow it the more rigorous.

Well, the Jesuits in their passion for conversion and for bringing back all possible souls to the one fold were accused, not justly, of laxity. No doubt some of their casuists erred on that side, others, it is certain, erred on the other, but they all bore the public name of Casuists and of men lax in moral interpretation in the eyes of the Jansenists.

Take it all in all, the great Jansenist quarrel was in practice a duel between the Jesuits in France and all those who reacted against the Jesuit influence and power.

The Jansenist movement may roughly be tabulated thus:

At the very opening of the seventeenth century, more than thirty years before Louis was born, a young theologian from the Netherlands, Cornelius Jansen (a very common Flemish name) came to Bayonne in the south of France at the call of a rich young man slightly older than himself who was acquainted with his talents. Jansen was wholly absorbed in theology, though only twenty-one to twenty-two years old. He had tried himself to be a Jesuit and had not been received, but one may doubt if that had much to do with what happened later. Till he was thirty years old he absorbed himself in the study of doctrine, for it must be remembered that of the Flemish population the great bulk was, and is, Catholic and that even in the north Netherlands, which broke away and was led by Calvinist multi-millionaires, the House of Orange at their head, Catholicism still made up at least one-half of the community. Jansen was so Catholic that he attacked the policy of Richelieu in supporting Protestant Europe in order to weaken Austria. All his earlier writings are without doubt orthodox. By the power of the crown at Madrid he was given the chair of Exegesis at the University of Louvain. His name in the Latin form, Jansenius, was already famous when in the year 1636 he was made Bishop of Ypres by the King of Spain.

He was strong on the infallibility of the papal See, defining it in a doctorate treatise. The only thing apparently savouring of the heresiarch about him while he still lived was his contention that his theological status would revolutionise thought. He had a certain pride about him, it is said, which may have been no worse than the vanity of a scholar. He wrote to that early friend of his, Duvergier (who had become the Abbot of St. Cyran) that in his work "things unexpected would astonish the world."

They did; but Jansenius had no intention of upsetting the world, and he left it on solemn record that he was a loyal son of the Faith, that he had so lived to his dying hour. He proclaimed in his will that to maintain such loyalty was his final wish. He died on the 6th of May, 1638, four months before Louis was born, and himself fifty-two and a half years of age.

Some few months after his death there was printed and appeared his work on St. Augustine of Hippo, that great father of the Latin Church.

Now anyone who dabbles in St. Augustine, still more anyone who will be profound in reading St. Augustine, steers along the boundary between predestination and free will, along the boundary which theology, the queen of sciences, has with such difficulty attempted to trace.

For us who are laymen in every sense of the word, neither scholars nor disputants, it is happier to leave the thing alone. But the thing will not let us alone: no, not even us. The matter of predestination and free will will only leave untouched those who are far below it or far above it. With most of us it is too near the knuckle. At any rate there is no doubt that Jansenius (God rest his soul!) slipped over the edge—on the Doom-side. The year after his book was published he was condemned by the Holy Office and thenceforward all through those years (which were in England the years of the Civil War) the quarrel rose and began to rage.

The friend in youth of Jansenius, St. Cyran, worked for and supported and was supported by a family which had great effect in giving growth to the movement, the family of Arnauld. The Jansenists held their ground stoutly. "If we have exceeded," they said, "on the side of rigour, if we smell of the puritan heresy" (which they undoubtedly did), "let some clear thesis be put forward. Let some statement of ours be analysed, and defined, and condemned. Until such a thesis is condemned none can call us unorthodox."

It was in 1649 (the year in which the King of England had been put to death, the year in which the German Civil War ended, the year in which, by the peace there concluded, French domination in Europe began) that the Syndic of Sorbonne, that is, the theological faculty of the University of Paris, extracted from the Jansenist writings five propositions which could be blamed as heretical, particularly the doctrine that the Saviour did not die for all mankind but only for the elect.

After four years Rome spoke clearly in a Bull con-
demning the five propositions. Arnauld and his following,
including the most powerful person in his family, his sister
(the Nun Mother Angelica of Port Royal) protested that
the Pope's condemnation did not affect them, for (said
they) the doctrines read into the Jansenist writings were
not really there. A doctrine the Pope could decide, but
whether a doctrine were really present in such and such a
body of writing he could not decide: the Arnaulds, shocked
by casuistry were becoming now far too subtle themselves.

Let it be remarked that even in the Sorbonne itself
one-third of those who voted—sixty-eight out of about
two hundred—were on the Jansenist side. The Jansenists
refused to abjure. Port Royal was refused communion by
the Archbishop of Paris, but no less than four bishops
supported them in one way or another. This outbreak of
the quarrel in its original violence corresponded, then, with
the early years of Louis as active King, his early glories just
before the early wars, the years of the La Vallière. In 1667
the Pope of the day, Alexander VII, who was a supporter
of Louis, ordered a formal trial of the four recalcitrant
bishops, but in May of that same year this Pope died—and
the new Pope hesitated to act.

For more than ten years there had been fermenting in
the intellectual life of France the effect of those famous
pamphlets, the Provinciales. The great Pascal was their
author, originally hidden under a false name.

Here you may see once more of what effect is The Word
in the story of mankind. Pascal set out to attack the Jesuits. It was the whole motive of his work. He proposed to
expose the laxity of their moral theology, of their casuistry.
He was briefed by the Arnaulds—but he never read the
documents he proposed to condemn. He made, one may
say, modern French prose, and the power of his diction
triumphed—but not that of his scholarship nor, it is fair

to say, that of his reasoning; for not only had he not read the casuistry he proposed to expose, but half of it he had not even understood at second hand. Nevertheless (as might be expected, for it is always so) the false interpretation outlasted the truth. Anyone who will take the trouble to read Escobar (I pride myself on having done so) will see that Pascal had *not* read him; but men still go on believing that Pascal destroyed the Jesuit position: at least they will go on believing it until perhaps in the long run truth catches up. But truth is lame.

Anyhow the Provinciales had been fermenting in the French mind for over ten years when the trial of the recalcitrant bishops were ordered and when the Pope who had ordered the trial of them died.

The new Pope, I say, hesitated to proceed. The reason was this: a turning point had been arrived at in the reign of the French King. The foundation of his greatness in war was being laid, the fruit of the splendid opening of that reign was being felt; what was later to be the strength of Gallicanism—that is, a national feeling opposed to the full papal power, had appeared—though it was to be many years before it came into full flower. More important than anything, perhaps, was the attitude of Lionne. The expert in foreign policy is always of the greatest weight with a government occupied in conquest and expansion. What followed, therefore, was a truce if you will, or rather a running fight. Louis did not want the Pope to show too much power within the kingdom of France. His mind was also set on unity. He felt, as did the populace, that the Jansenists were budding heretics and anyhow not anti-national—not in the stream of French tradition—"Un-French."

One may fairly say that by the time of Louis's conversion, of his final and profound spiritual change, the battle was won and the Jansenists were bound to lose. They still stood out and long after their dispersion their influence remained. The refusal of the more determined to abjure and what was certainly rebellion against the King led at last to the destruction of their walls. A few years before the end of the reign (in 1709) Port Royal was razed to the ground, its inhabitants dispersed. It was seven years later, in the year after Louis's death, that Mother Angelica died at Blois without the Sacraments.

All those events of the final catastrophe are the romantic things which stand out in most memories in the story of the Jansenists, but the combat had really been decided long before. There was a moment when they might, not have triumphed indeed, but have formed a permanent organised body within the French people. That moment passed and their possible action failed through the instinct of Louis and of his people for national unity. But as I have said the cause survived above the doom and a story of austere restraint was inherited from them, transmitted to some who are still among the nobler though the more arid of French minds.

They still influence. They will not revive but they will be remembered.

26

The Second Effort at Domestic Unity:

GALLICANISM

THE SECOND MAJOR RELIGIOUS issue of the reign in connection with the effort at Monarchic Unity is Gallicanism.

The word and the thing remained closely associated with the name of Louis XIV. It is subject to misinterpretation, as is most of what he did, and especially what he did on the religious side of policy, but it is perhaps better understood than the matter we shall deal with next, the revocation of the Edict of Nantes.

The first thing we have to do in understanding the Gallican quarrel is to appreciate that it was the final act in one of those "triangles" which perpetually recur in the story of any country. Some issue divides men into two camps. The mind, being simple in its action and a single thing, likes to deal with that situation as a contrast between a yes and a no: black and white. But there perpetually arises a cross section. White is opposed to black, but black has within it opposing forms. There are two lines of cleavage, the line between white and black and the line between the two forms of black. Now right judgment, and therefore good history, consists in discovering and emphasising the *main* line of cleavage; that done, the rest is a question of degree, as indeed all judgment must be.

Here you have a white block of marble, opposed to which you have a black heap, but the black heap is not made of black marble only, it is made of black marble and coal. Have the two marbles more in common than either of them have with the coal, or is the colour the true distinguishing mark? That is the kind of problem which arises in our judgment of Gallicanism.

Englishmen are well acquainted with a similar "triangle" in the matter of Church, Chapel and Rome. It is a triangle which arose a hundred years before the religious troubles of Louis XIV, but it continued into his time. To many Puritans of Charles I's reign it seemed that the Episcopal party was virtually Roman. They were wrong. From our distance of time we can establish the true line of cleavage, which was not between the Nonconformist and the Churchman, but between both on the one hand and the Church of Rome on the other. So it is in the French quarrel.

France, after the storm of the Reformation, had settled down on the traditional side. It preserved the continuity of Europe. Louis XIV's crown was the chief power—the chief ostensible, temporal, obvious power—in the Catholic culture of Europe. It was as the head of the Catholic culture that he was hated in his own time by that culture's opponents, and is maligned by them today.

But within that Catholic culture of France there had arisen, among many other lesser lines of cleavage, a marked line of cleavage between what is called "the Gallican attitude" and, opposed to it, "the Ultramontane."

The main line of cleavage was not between the Gallican and the Ultramontane, it was between the Catholic and the anti-Catholic culture of the West; yet it is true that if the Gallican contention had enjoyed sufficient vitality and had produced a schism, then the French people would have been gradually pushed, as they have been over and over again nearly pushed, into the anti-Catholic group.

The quarrel between the Gallican and the Ultramontane was this: the Gallican favoured Episcopal power as against Papal power, but especially favoured national power as against the international power of the Catholic Church. The feeling for Episcopacy, the rights of the individual bishop in his see, the claim to authority of a council made up of bishops, all these were not negligible. Often these claims of local churches and their customs against the central see had been a chief issue, but at this moment, the latter part of the seventeenth century, the chief issue was national. The Episcopal claim was but a function of the national claim. At that moment also the word "national" meant "royal"; at any rate that is what it meant to the people who were fighting the battle. Whether it meant that to the mass of the faithful in France is something we will consider separately. One party were for the Papal monarchy, which had been growing throughout the centuries, and to which the reaction after the Reformation had given peculiar strength. The other party were for the ultimate supremacy corporate of the Church Universal, as expressed in General Councils.

The Gallican idea had its roots, of course, as had all these religious ideas, in a remote past. The struggle between the temporal and the spiritual powers had begun with the foundation of the Church, and had continued throughout the centuries. The conflict was of long preparation. The Church was older than the nation, but the nation, and the kingly power which stood for the nation, had become conscious and active as soon as the nation appeared. When, in the twelfth century, still more in the early thirteenth, national feeling grew conscious, the challenge it threw down to the international power of the Church strengthened with it. If some claim St. Louis himself on the Gallican side, because he would not admit the temporal consequences of excommunication, they exaggerate. But their exaggeration is an example of the spirit that was afoot even so early.

Nearly three hundred years later the concordat between Francis I and Leo X (of which a wit has said with false exaggeration that "each party gave to the other something which was not his to give") played a great part in preventing the loss of the French Church to the Roman communion in the whirlpool of the sixteenth century. That concordat left to the King chief powers in appointing the Ecclesiastical revenues, to the Pope the King's spiritual allegiance and support. Such an arrangement in contemporary England *might* have saved the English people from their breach with Europe. The concordat of Francis I prevented the wealthier classes in France from looting the Church as they did in England, and thereby prevented a vested interest in schism and heresy; but it also emphasised the power of the King to deal with the affairs of the Church in Gaul. It gave to the King nomination to the bishoprics and the great abbeys, and many another ecclesiastical right. Then came the religious wars in which the main issue of life and death was so glaring that lesser issues were forgotten: one sees, none the less, in the early seventeenth century the Gallican thesis obstinately reappearing: the thesis that Rome should not have power over a National Church, nor the Papacy priority over a Council.

Even two years before the death of Henry IV, the parliament, the great determining body of lawyers, had affirmed the King's right to the "régale."

Now with that word "régale" we touch, not the heart of the question, but the thing which started ultimate quarrel.

The word "régale" meant the right of the Crown to administer a vacant bishopric, to receive its revenues and even to appoint to spiritual offices within the empty diocese until a new bishop should be appointed.

The "régale" had worked in practice over half the bishoprics of France, because, as the power of the French Crown extended over more and more territory, bringing district after district under its direct control, changing the authority over each from feudal to immediate and monarchic, the new territories thus absorbed had not known the old practice. By 1673, more than sixty years after the parliamentary decision just quoted, fifty-nine dioceses—half the total number of bishoprics of the then France, one may say—were still in the anomalous condition of not being subject to the "régale." A bishop died; his see was vacant; its revenues went to Rome until a new bishop should be appointed and the spiritual offices within the bishopric were not in the gift of the King.

There is an infinity of complex detail and exception, but that is the general picture.

Let me emphasise that word "anomaly." People had come to think of the "régale" as a regular right because it had been exercised for so long over so much of French soil. The fifty-nine dioceses to which it did not yet apply seemed exceptional. When the King, therefore, in 1673, decided to put them all under the same rule he was doing something that seemed obvious and natural, though it is true that this "obvious and natural" thing gravely diminished the revenues of Rome and its patronage. To act thus, without the consent of the other party, the Papacy, seemed to that other party outrageous. Therein lies the origin of the quarrel.

But the quarrel came to a head three years later with the advent to the Papal throne of that marked character, worthy of a close appreciation and judgment, Innocent XI. It would be an error to say that the personality of this great Pope decided the affair. The clash was approaching. Things were coming to a head. But it is certainly true that the personality of Innocent XI gave both strength, character and rapidity to the development of the next few years. Let us consider him.

Benedetto Odescalchi was of a wealthy banker's family from Como. He had always taken his exalted duties as a priest, a bishop and an administrator of church things with the awful seriousness such things demanded. He was also holy, in his humility, in his integrity, in his boundless compassion for the poor. He had, in his earlier years, been favoured by the ruling Popes of the day. He had been himself, on the death of Clement IX in December, 1669 (when he was already fifty-eight years old) a candidate for the Chair of Peter. Note that the French government, as the chief Catholic political power, had objected to his election on account of his feelings for the Hapsburgs, that is, for Austria. It is bad history to say that the memory of this rankled—Benedetto Odescalchi was not built upon those lines—but it is good history to remark that already so early the French royal power had noted a potential enemy. Less than seven years later, when Pope Clement X died, there arose again the question, or rather the demand, for the election of a man whom the Romans, and (one may fairly say, I think) the mass of the Church, demanded. His character inspired everywhere intense respect—the greater because it was, in its way, simple.

Louis XIV opposed the candidature again, and by this time the opposition was full of meaning, for the business of the "régale" was afoot. But in the face of the really strong movement of opinion everywhere, and especially in Rome, the French King gave way and bade his French cardinals vote for Cardinal Odescalchi.

After an interval of two months Benedetto was on the papal throne as Innocent XI.

Now Pope, the character which all had noted became famous throughout Europe and, if one may use the word, "dominant." No man was less assertive, but no man was more convinced of the Divine function attached to his office or more inflexible in maintaining it.

From the day of his election, the 21st of December, 1676, he set out to reform and correct everything. He "balanced his budget," wiping out the heavy debt left him by his predecessors. He set his face against undue patronage, and especially nepotism, which had been the curse of the Reformation Papacy. He set out to improve out of all knowledge the direct government of the Roman city. His complete lack of personal vanity, pique or resentment aided him; so, much more, did his positive virtue of exalted devotion. That devotion showed itself particularly in obstinate adherence to principle.

And that brings us back to the "régale." When the French monarchy, true to its vital principle of unity, had extended the "régale" to the whole realm, applying it to the hitherto exempt fifty-nine dioceses, there were among the numerous French bishops two who had protested. Of these, particularly note Caulet, the Bishop of Pamiers in the south. His colleague in protestation was Pavillon, Bishop of Alet. Both these men had refused to accept the King's officers in their sees and to pay on demand the arrears of the old "régale" which had fallen due upon their appointment. In 1677, the year after Innocent's succession, Pavillon died. Caulet survived. Louis was determined to be rid of his opposition. His revenues were seized. He appealed to Rome.

Now note that both these protesting bishops were Jansenists. Therefore, if mere sympathies were at work, the Pope would not have considered them. But Innocent was a man not moved by sentiment but by principles. Having received Caulet's appeal he wrote, in March, 1678, to the French King protesting against the seizure of the temporalities and in the following January took the Bishop of Pamiers under his protection. The national assembly of the French clergy was summoned by Louis XIV for the next year, 1680. He expressed his "displeasure" at the Pope's attitude, for indeed Innocent XI had expressed himself in terms which offended the Majesty of the Throne.

Here arises a question of very great importance, not easily to be solved. Where stood the French people in the quarrel? Religious conflicts were of high importance at the moment; they were discussed in every class of society. How ran the bulk of French opinion? It is a point very difficult to decide, but on the whole I think it ran with the Pope. The populace—all of whom were still practising Catholics outside the Huguenot country districts and urban groups—saw things simply, as the populace always does. The Pope was head of the Church, and had a right to protest in the name of the Church about Church affairs.

The wealthier classes, especially the high nobility, were always glad enough of an opportunity for showing opposition, even now, so late in Louis's reign. They went about saying that the clergy had merely obeyed orders in following the King, and the incomparable Madame de Sévigné wrote that the assembly of the clergy was like a woman who likes to be beaten and falls upon anyone who interferes with her domestic misfortunes.

Meanwhile the Bishop of Pamiers had died, and the Pope did not make the quarrel any less by appealing to the suffrages of that sainted Jansenist in heaven. Caulet would pray for the Holy See in the security of Paradise. Let us remember also that Innocent the Pope had threatened the King. He had said that if necessary he would have recourse to the powers of his office. But let it also be remembered that neither party, King nor Pope, was going to push things to the limit. The Pope feared schism; the King, who, *now as always*, was absorbed in the political task, the kingly business of governing, of reinforcing order everywhere by the doctrine of unity, was certainly not going to break with the Papacy, but was determined to affirm what seemed to his common sense rights, the additional rights of the Crown, and to emphasise the special rights of his nation, and came very near to talking of a national church as something distinct from the Church Universal.

Here let us again remember certain points in Innocent's character. He was now (1680) a man just on seventy. He was tortured with the stone. He had always had vivacious fits of temper, sometimes of anger, but God knows he was as humble as he was inflexible in his sense of duty. He was a man very nervous, with jerky gesticulations from time to time, and shifting in his seat after a fashion which onlookers thought undignified—as though that mattered! He slept abominably.

All this is said not in extenuation of his attitude, for his attitude was due to nothing so little as temperament, on the contrary his attitude was due to a noble constancy, but to know how he showed and what he was makes it easier to understand what he did. The King was ready to give up some part of the spiritual side of the "régale" the appointment to benefices, etc. But he was somewhat wearily determined to hold what seemed to him the obvious political point, the sensible administration of the royal power.

Such bishops as were in Paris met in a sort of little assembly—there were fifty-two of them, which showed, says a contemporary, that fifty-two bishops were not "men in residence." Then the general assembly of the French clergy was summoned to meet in June, 1681. The opening sermon was preached in the glorious eloquence of Bossuet, and that greatest of orators, a man who also was great through common sense, attempted to reconcile as best he might the opposing claims while supporting the King. It is a singular lesson in perhaps necessary compromise to read those famous words.

He had to say, and not to say, at the same time. It was the very height both of the King's power in Europe and of Bossuet's own towering genius, yet nothing could properly be said because nothing is properly said unless it is said clearly, and in this juncture Bossuet himself could not be clear—the great Burgundian!

Behind all the quarrel was that other quarrel, giving tone to it throughout, the conflict between the Jesuits and the Jansenists. Europe looked on at the paradox of the Pope supporting the Jansenists and appealing to the prayers of a Jansenist safely in heaven, of the Jesuits in Rome supporting the Pope, and in France the King—or at least the enemies of the Jesuits ascribed to them this double role. But really it is difficult to see how a double role could be avoided, for it was the business of that military company, the Society of Jesus, to defeat Jansenists and at the same time to be a bodyguard for the Apostolic See. Let it also be remembered that all the while the enemies of Innocent were emphasising his intensity, calling it his extravagant humour, saying it was something native in him to be an extremist because he was a visionary. Was it not he who had been perpetually preaching a new crusade against the Turk, dreaming dreams of the King of France recovering Constantinople and becoming an emperor of the East, of the Mohammedan driven backward and Christendom freed? Yes, he had had such visions, for he had seen further than any of the grosser men around him. The reunion of Christendom, and its common front against external enemies, was the business of the Father of Christendom.

He was not unpractical—such active visionaries in office rarely are. He had always said that nothing could be done without the King of France. But there he was, in principle, inflexible—and who would not be glad to have been so when in the hour of death he considers his actions in the days of his life. The other side was not without a visionary character either, though Louis himself never fell into it. There were plenty of people to talk of the old tradition, of the anointed king who was in his way a priest, of sacerdotal royalty.

On the 19th of March, 1682, the great assembly of
the French clergy solemnly passed the four unforgettable
decrees or articles.

Briefly they may be summarised thus:

1. The Pope's power is spiritual; he has no dominion in
temporal affairs, he cannot even indirectly oppose kings.
There is no absolving a king's subjects from their Oath
of Allegiance.

2. The plenitude of the Holy See's authority in no way
diminishes the permanence and absolute character ("irre-
movable power") of the decrees embodied in the decisions
of the Council of Constance, which in their turn may be
summarised in the phrase "the Council of the Church is
the ultimate authority."

3. The usages of Gaul in matters of religion are inviolable. Indeed, that principle is necessary for the dignity
and authority of the Papacy itself, which reposes on the
force of such traditions.

4. The Papacy has the chief part in defence of doctrine,
but these are open to reform until the consent of the whole
Church is arrived at.

Anyone who will read the original articles (or will be
content with this brief summary) will, I think, agree that
nothing can be made of them. They are deliberately ambiguous, but their tone is clearly for the limiting of the Papal
power, and in particular they had opposed infallibility.

Innocent himself was in no doubt about them. They were
passed on the 19th of March, 1682. Within a month, by
the 11th of April (and even in conditions of haste it took
something like a fortnight to reach Rome and another to
come back, so perhaps one might say that the answer came
post-haste) Innocent had issued his brief, in which there
was no ambiguity whatever. He simply said, "We disap-
prove, we break, we tear up everything that has been done

in the matter of the régale" by the assembly of the French clergy. And that, if I may so express myself, was that.

We must see the thing in the light of its time, the moment of its appearance. The episode of the Montespan had ended, Louis was forty-three, his fixed maturity had come, his examination of conscience had begun, his entry, that is, into himself; at the same time he was reaping the full harvest of his power. It is the moment of Strasburg and the lull before the reaction against French supremacy in Europe. It was, as I have called it: "High water before the turn of the tide."

The uncertain struggle continued so far as this issue of Gallicanism and its special definitions was concerned. It was determined by that the full meaning of which Louis himself never appreciated in time: the event which determined his future: the fall of the Stuarts. While the Stuarts were still upon the throne of England Louis could feel secure. In 1688 all was changing. In 1691 all had changed. Innocent XI died in 1689, not without the consolation of having seen something that was far dearer to him than any other matter, the driving back of the Turk—he had already been the chief artificer in the saving of Vienna by the great Polish hero, at the moment when the Turk was hammering at the gates of the West.

His successors continued the conflict with more urbanity but with no less attachment to the principles involved.

It was eleven years before Louis, the clouds already beginning to gather round him, yielded. The assembled clergy of France were bidden at long last to express their regret for the extreme to which they had advanced (after all, it had been an ambiguous extreme) and on paper at least the Papacy had won. It was under Innocent XII, the second in succession after his namesake, that the four articles were recalled: but they were not recalled until the eve of that last fight for life in which the French Monarchy was involved during the last years of the King.

But was Louis wholly defeated? Was Gallicanism wholly defeated? It was not. The national feeling which lay behind it strengthened. When, a hundred years later, the French Revolution and its Parliament framed the constitution of the clergy (by that time religion had reached its lowest ebb among educated men) their arguments were drawn entirely from Gallicanism. The destruction of thrones by the revolutionary armies and the subsequent splendour of Napoleon emphasising, but centralising still further, the Papal power, the chief evil attached to Gallicanism, a lack of discipline in the French higher clergy, was blown away in the violence of the tempest. But the suspicion of a necessary antagonism between the Papal power and the French nation remained.

The chaotic changes of our own time will perhaps at last dissipate this long-lived conception, but it still has force in the most detached, and least anti-clerical, of French diplomatic agents.

27
The Third and Far the Greatest Effort at Unity

THE REVOCATION

IN OCTOBER, 1685, LOUIS THE KING completed by a decisive act what had long been a progressive advance towards the complete absorption by the general body of the remaining fully dissident and alien minority, the Huguenots, or native French Calvinists.

This act was his signing of "The Revocation"—the Revocation of the Edict of Nantes. To understand why this was done, how it was done and the reason it failed is, after understanding the Monarchy itself, the chief business of all who would appreciate the great reign and its effects upon our civilisation.

The Edict of Nantes was a public document issued by King Henry IV at the end of the religious wars which had so nearly destroyed France a century earlier. It guaranteed to the French Calvinists, called "Huguenots" (who had warred incessantly against Throne and people for half a lifetime in their desire to maintain a separate society and morals) the conditions under which they could achieve that end. They were granted freedom of worship and therefore freedom of proclaiming the new doctrines and morals and of supporting that new counter-Church which the genius of their compatriot John Calvin had created. Certain strong cities were handed over to them. They were to administrate their own affairs as a State within the State, and to be free of access to public office and its emoluments. Some had, from the beginning, thought of this as a truce, some as a final, solemn and sacred peace. Some held that it was a settlement achieving for good and all the internal security of the realm by an enduring compromise, others a temporary necessity of exhaustion.

Such an instrument was the very negation of Monarchy.

With Monarchy it could not co-exist. When therefore Richelieu took over the task of remaking the Monarchy in the generation before Louis XIV, his principal care, after counter-balancing the Hapsburg power abroad, was to deprive the Huguenots of such anomalous powers as the Edict had given them. He reduced their main refuge and port, La Rochelle, but he left them all their domestic and religious privileges.

They stood thus in the realm a body still exceptional and still quasi-hostile, but shorn of physical strength at any rate for the moment. Their sympathies were with the anti-Catholic side of Europe and therefore opposed to the national character and genius of their fellow citizens, just as the large remaining Catholic body in the three Stuart kingdoms of the day, England, Scotland and Ireland, was inevitably opposed to the Protestant Government and people about it. But the French Huguenots entered into no open rebellion.

Let me repeat what I said on a former page, for it illuminates at once the attempt and the failure of the Revocation, showing why the Huguenots were ceasing to be formidable. "They did not budge during the whole of the Fronde. The Edict of Nantes was reissued just before the end of that civil fighting, and Mazarin himself congratulated the Protestants on their loyalty. The reason of this Huguenot support lay in the nature of the Fronde itself. The Fronde had been a by-product of the very thing it was attacking: the Monarchy. The Huguenots had no standing in the monarchical tradition. It was not of their nature to be either monarchist supporters as courtiers or to be helping rival claimants for the guardianship of the young King. They had obtained, as a result of the religious wars, a great deal more than their numbers or even their wealth could have led them to expect. To enjoy what they had and to maintain it was their obvious policy." Their preponderance in commerce and finance continued to grow, but at the same time their original acrid hatred of Catholicism was softened by time, as men entered the third generation after the religious wars. The Huguenots of 1661-78 were the now elderly sons or younger grandsons of the men who had torn France asunder before the Edict appeared.

Nevertheless, as the Great Reign proceeded the presence of the Huguenot body in the services of the State grew less and less consonant with the State's character under the new high Monarchy of Louis. The Huguenot nobles furnished numerous and excellent officers to the Navy and the Armies of the King: Schomberg, whose foreign sword and strong talent of generalship was of them; but they were in spirit, and could not but be in spirit, of the same stuff as had produced William of Orange, the Dutch Patriciate, the power of Amsterdam and of commercial London. Between their attitude to contemporary Europe and the King's aim of a strictly united and defensible realm, immune from outside influence or attack, direct or indirect, rose increasing strain.

Would time resolve this strain and absorb the Huguenots in the general spirit of their fellow citizens? If so, the best policy was a tolerance of their remaining power. Conversions increased: the great Turenne was among them. To disturb the existing arrangement would be perhaps to stir up resistance and renew the old divisions. On the other hand, as it became more and more evident after the Dutch War that the Protestant side of Europe would menace the

King's achievement, might it not be better policy to has-
ten what seemed to be a rapid process of conversion and
to have done, while there was yet time, with this alien
influence incompatible with National Unity? Might it not
be well—as the storm increasingly menaced—to put all
straight aboard before it broke? In England the Catholic
opposition had been successfully ousted from power though
far more numerous, in proportion, than was the Protestant
opposition in France. Could not the converse be effected
by Louis and unity finally affirmed by a consistent policy of
reducing Huguenot employment, of favouring converts, of
harassing the more stubborn remnant and, as a conclusion,
of ending the privileges of the Edict altogether?

To the first policy Vauban inclined, to the second Louvois. It was the second which was adopted. But before
we decide whether that decision were wise or not, let us
understand how the situation had reached the point it had
in the early eighties of the seventeenth century, the years
of the King's change of heart. To comprehend the scene
we must return to the general picture of the time.

The problem which lay before the various governments
of the later seventeenth century, when the open religious
conflict had died of exhaustion in the double peace of
Westphalia, 1648-49, was how to use that peace for the
consolidation of the State.

A lifetime earlier men had been still concerned with the
religious revolution; the most eager minds and the bravest
combatants were set upon the confirmation of that revolution or on its final defeat. The most sincere and therefore the most powerful protagonists had till nearly the
year 1600 fixed their eyes upon a religious remedy; the
one would destroy that ancient united traditional Church
in which he saw the enemy of God and of mankind; the
other would defend it and attempt to achieve its triumph
over all opponents. The one looked forward to a Europe

from which Catholicism should have been driven forth altogether; the other to a Europe in which Catholicism should have returned in its plenitude and majesty and the last broken fragments of what he still held to be a temporary anarchic revolt should have been crushed forever.

All this was overlaid with an increasing mass of temporal considerations; the financial interests of the new commerce and the new banking were already becoming more to the merchants of Amsterdam than the interests of religion; the new English landed fortunes built upon the ruins of the Catholic Church were fully consolidated; the dynastic ambitions of the Hapsburgs as of the Bourbons were at least as strong or perhaps stronger than the devotion of either family to the old civilisation, that is, to the Catholic Church. By the mid-seventeenth century temporal concerns had come definitely to outweigh on the surface of men's minds the eternal. The battle was a draw, neither party had achieved a decision, and each turned its attention from 1648-49 onwards to the strengthening of that new idol the Nation, the State, the Prince, the Polity to which each belonged. The main problem now was to achieve unity piecemeal, throne by throne, government by government, since the general unity of Christendom was now thoroughly despaired of.

Among the Germans an effort had been made to produce a united state under the Emperor; it had failed altogether. The diplomatic genius of Richelieu, hiring for money and using as his arm the military genius of Gustavus Adolphus, had been too much for Vienna. It is perhaps also true that the German people cannot of their nature make a permanently united state; they attempt to do so on the model of more ancient and more deeply-rooted, more lively, societies, but the effort is not native to them and its object is never reached. They are at it again today and will fail as they have failed before; for by so much as the Germans excel at imposing a general air of their own, a tone which is German wherever Germans colonise or govern (and they have even succeeded in thus absorbing many of the Slavs), by so much also have they hitherto failed properly to conceive, let alone execute, the *moral* structure of an organic nation. No mechanical union can replace that organic unity. Germans of the sixteenth and seventeenth centuries had met the problem—if that can be called meeting a problem at all—by giving it up. The ancient religion and the various forms of revolt against it lay among the Germans in intermingled or huddled heaps side by side.

In some German districts, notably in Alsace, it was not even a mosaic of towns and petty states, it was a mosaic of villages and petty lordships, Protestant and Catholic elbowing the one the other.

The Spaniards had solved *their* problem by a universal stamp of orthodoxy; they had driven out not so much the heretic (for heresy had never taken root among them) but the Jew through whom the disintegration of the country and its religion was threatened.

These, Spain and the Germanies, were the two extremes; the full Catholicism of the Spanish Hapsburgs and the abandonment of the effort at unity by the Hapsburgs of Germany.

But the Crowns of France and England were not in such a case; neither could abandon the struggle, neither—it was to be discovered after bitter experience—would be able to impose unity either.

The problem of destroying Catholicism in the British Isles and of making it universal beyond the Channel was in reality insoluble, though it appeared capable of solution, and even easy of solution, to many men of the time. So it does in another form appear soluble to the men of our time. Indeed the men of our time take its solution for granted, while the less instructed or more stupid actually think it has already been solved by the disappearance of religion. Obviously it would be solved if the religious interest were to disappear from men's minds. The more intelligent of our fathers in the mid-eighteenth century thought that the dissolution of religion was at hand in *their* time. They erred as their less intelligent descendants err today. The Catholic Church will endure and therefore the effort to destroy her will also endure.

The men of the later seventeenth century accepted and even accepted with violence the reality of the religious struggle, but they believed that the will of the Sovereign was strong enough to prevail in the end.

Thus in the United Provinces that Sovereign was the Patriciate of the great Dutch merchants and bankers; their Calvinism, they were certain, would get the better in time of that half of the Flemish population which still clung to Catholic traditions. In England the Sovereign was already a governing class made up of the big landlords wedded through vested interests to the Reformation, while their allies, the merchants and bankers of the City of London, were equally determined on Protestantism. They were certain that their will would prevail; the Catholic minority in Great Britain and Ireland was large but increasingly impoverished, and would ultimately, they believed, be eliminated.

The French Crown had begun with a truce which had left not only a large but an armed and very wealthy minority of dissidents in the midst of the State; yet the French Crown also thought that these would be eliminated.

Both failed. Within Great Britain Catholicism was indeed completely crushed, and to its destruction we owe the marvellous moral unity of England today; but the anomaly of Ireland not only remained but ultimately flourished. In France the revocation of the Edict equally failed.

Indeed, this double failure at unity north and south of the Channel is the characteristic of the later seventeenth century in the west of Europe, and particularly in the most active centres of the west, the Governments of Westminster and Versailles. The original effort of the Reformation to change the whole of our civilisation, to remove it from its ancient Catholic basis and to re-erect a new Europe in which the Catholic tradition should be destroyed, had failed. But the Catholic reaction against that revolution had also failed. Western Europe had fallen into those two camps, the one based upon the Catholic culture, re-established, centralised and made in its structure more mechanical by the counter-Reformation. The other inspired with various forms of Protestantism, but having some sort of loose unity from a common detestation of the whole Catholic tradition.

But while Western Europe had fallen thus into two camps, the division was not a simple geographical division. The Germanies had fallen into a chaos of various states and cities, in part retaining the old tradition, in part support-ing the new movement. But in France and England, where, unlike the Germanies, the Roman idea of "The State" was vigorous, the effort to impose religious unity on that State was vigorously pursued. If the two western Governments, the Government of Westminster and the Government of Versailles failed in their efforts at unity in their subjects they failed in two different ways. In France the disunion of Catholic and Protestant remained present within the inti-mate formation of society, it was not a territorial division; in the British Islands the division became in the long run territorial, and was summed up in the two historical facts which mark the whole of our history after the end of the seventeenth century: first, the complete victory of the anti-Catholic forces in Great Britain south of the Grampians; second, their ultimate failure in Ireland.

To say that Louis XIV failed in his effort to impose religious unity in France while the new English governing classes succeeded in imposing it is the common way of stating the case, but it is a thorough misapprehension. Both failed, only they failed in separate fashion.

The difference may be made clear by a simile. Two owners of estates in marshy land desire each to reclaim his land and make it one dry block. Neither succeed. But the one owner ends by getting the surplus water drained into a large pond or lake, the other owner gets the water drained into a large number of small isolated ponds, several of them no larger than puddles. Indeed, this second owner can claim no area of complete drainage, many patches of the original marsh remain where the watery soil and the hard soil merge continually and can hardly be distinguished one from the other. If by dry land we mean that proportion of the population which adhered to the general religion of the State and by watery we mean the dissidents from that religion, the parallel of those two estates is accurate enough. The English Government had drained England and South Scotland of Catholicism; but at the expense of creating a large hostile area, that of Ireland, in which the dissident religion, though persecuted to the death and deprived of nearly all its economic basis, survived; while in France the dissident portion (in this case Protestant) equally survived in very numerous separate patches, large and small, and the two religions were left in many areas closely intermixed.

The ultimate political effect of these two failures, the English and the French, we cannot yet affirm. There is a further development to come. But by the nineteenth century this much had appeared: the failure of the attempt to eliminate Catholic Ireland—an attempt upon which such great energy had been expended and which had seemed at one moment (that of the Irish famine in the mid-nineteenth century) triumphant—left England highly homogeneous, with a moral unity the like of which no other State in Europe could display, yet still faced with a problem which the victors affected to despise but which has continued to harass them heavily, and presumably will harass them still more: the problem of a world-wide Irish race and tradition permanently hostile to the English. In France the failure to establish religious unity had political effects equally grave but of quite a different sort. As nearly always happens when two opposing ideas fight it out, a third, a new mood, appeared.

Through the failure of the Revocation the French mind, in its divided allegiance, fell more and more into religious indifference, coloured by hostility towards organised religion and therefore especially towards Catholicism. At long range, it was the failure of the Revocation which bred French anti-clericalism and the momentous, still uncompleted, struggle between the Church in France and her opponents.

For, though the Huguenots were not a tenth of the nation in, say, 1675, and perhaps not much more than a twentieth after the Revocation had done its work, they were much more than a tenth of French financial power. They were of the urban upper and upper middle-classes for the most part, they had great effect on the towns, especially on the seaports and on the wealthy sub-capitals of the south, Nîmes, Montpellier, Toulouse.

Let us be clear on the moral issue, for confusion on it has darkened the whole affair. The Revocation was in no way a moral fault; but it was a political blunder.

No blame attaches to the repression or even the destruction of a hostile body within the State; and nothing is more hostile to the general life of the State than a sect fixed in a spiritual attitude to life opposed to that of their fellow citizens. All men approve of eliminating what they feel to be a poison. All men approve the fruits of such action after it has been fully successful. Ask any average English patriot today what he thinks of the force used to carry out the Reformation in England. You will find he approves the process. Nor need you consult the extremist in order to get such a reply. There are few indeed of those who approve what happened here in the sixteenth and seventeenth centuries who are not glad that Catholicism, which they now regard as a force hostile to the development of English national power, was crushed.

Ask a Mohammedan of high culture what he feels on seeing, in the countries which his creed has transformed, the ruins of Greece and Rome. *We* regret; *he* approves.

So it was with the Revocation of the Edict of Nantes. The whole point of that episode in history is *not* that the French Government's action was unjustified but that it failed of its purpose. Things of themselves were making gradually for national unity when this sharp experiment in policy ruined that prospect.

The King could not foresee the future, he could not foresee the way in which the new spring of the Protestant culture should surpass the old traditional world of the Catholic culture; he could not see that this Protestant culture in Europe would increasingly dominate for two centuries after his time. But what he might have seen—had he been sufficiently well served—was the strength of the Protestant body in his own country.

There is no more illuminating phrase in the years following on the Revocation than the cry of Schomberg at the head of his troops, leading them against the Irish at the Boyne. He pointed with his sword towards the ranks commanded by James and cried, turning to his own officers and men, "There you see your persecutors!" The cry agreed with the mood of his French Huguenot officers who formed the solid framework of the Orange command. Whether it agreed with the mood of rank and file is another matter. Schomberg having said this was shot in the neck from behind, presumably by some one on his own side and so died: for troops in those days were recruited at random from the poorest classes without regard to their private feelings. This was true of the bulk of private soldiers in every war of the seventeenth century, and even, so far as the foot were concerned, in the Civil Wars of England.

How came Louis to be misled into false judgments, into misunderstanding the remaining strength of that Huguenot society of which he proposed to destroy the last remnant (as he conceived it to be) at one blow?

His error was due in part to the fact that long habit of unquestioned command had cut him off from full opportunities for information.

Men of every profession—especially the King's civil servants and also the military men as well—felt their advancement to depend upon pleasing the master. Those who were immediately around Louis were certain of success, and the two Le Telliers in particular were absolutely confident. The old Chancellor was "glad to have seen this day" and was content "that the Lord should now dismiss his servant in peace." Which indeed the Lord did, for he died eight days after the Revocation was signed. Everything had hitherto favoured the Le Telliers in their private fortune and in their public policy; they felt not only the natural and intense antagonism which the mass of their countrymen felt towards the Huguenots, but they felt also with special intensity the anomaly of a dissident, sullen, at heart rebellious, body in the midst of this new strong union between their Prince and his people. "They presume," said Louvois speaking of these dissidents, "to set themselves up against the command of their King!"

There was another factor stronger than all the rest, and urging Louis on to the expected elimination of Huguenotry from the State.

It is one we can judge by our own experience in contemporary matters: the factor of an overwhelming public opinion. The nation in bulk detested the Huguenot faction. It has been well said that had universal suffrage been the custom of those days, the popular vote in favour of the Revocation would have been a blizzard in which all opposition would have been snowed under. The mass of the clergy supported the Revocation as a matter of course, but still more the mass of the laity: of the Trade Corporations, of the Town Governments and chiefly of the peasantry, who were the bulk of the French people. These, as I have said, outside a few remote hilly districts where certain Huguenot herdsmen, etc., could be found, were enthusiastically for the policy of repression. The Huguenot was the enemy of the peasant, of the peasant habit of mind, the peasant tradition, the peasant soul. He stood in their eyes for the Money-power of the townsman. The peasant had often known the Huguenot in the past as a hard creditor, but apart from that the peasant instinctively felt that the new Protestant forces in Europe stood for rising urban and mercantile power, at daggers drawn with his own.

Of all the group of political effects following on the Revocation, by far the most serious was its warping of the French monarch's relations with England.

It was getting more and more difficult for a man of French training to understand the new England which Protestantism had made. As England abandoned the last spiritual supports of her ancient national monarchy, and adopted aristocratic class government; as she undertook the destruction of her own peasantry and the erection of an urban proletariat upon their ruins, and, in the place of her old yeomanry, wage earners; as her capital city, her great port and mart swelled out of all measure and became more and more the only effective centre of England's strength; as the Money-power in London allied with the great landowners rose to supremacy and eliminated English kingship; as trade and banking began to form the foundations of

English society—as all this great change proceeded England became increasingly incomprehensible to the French and therefore to Louis, the typical figure of his nation.

The converse was not true. The leading Englishmen of those days were not as ill-informed about France as were the leading Frenchmen about England. The new governing class of England travelled widely, observed intelligently and framed a foreign policy which was to increase the power of their country immensely, and to maintain it for two centuries still expanding. The judgments on foreign policy passed by the Englishmen who framed it between the Restoration and Waterloo, resembled those of Venice in the older time; for Venice was the forerunner of the new aristocratic England.

Today all this has changed. Today England has a governing class far more strongly organised and mature than that of 1685. The fruits of aristocratic government—unity and order—flourish in England today as they never flourished before. But one essential product of such a system is lacking: England no longer understands the outside world. No one of England's rivals has committed such enormous blunders in its foreign policy as have those responsible for the direction of England today, especially since the Great War. The Bank of England, the Civil Servants, the Millionaire Press, have in the twenty years since the Armistice accumulated more errors than might have been thought possible! They have restored Prussia; they have worked as though France were their danger—that is why France grew increasingly weak; they have wholly misunderstood and underestimated the new Italy. They have even miscalculated so simple a problem as the pace of rearmament (and still more the quality of it!) in the countries hostile to our own. The consequences of such inefficiency are perhaps already upon us, at any rate they will be increasingly manifest.

But in that distant day of Louis XIV's reign when the French Monarchy still overshadowed Europe, and when the vigorous English oligarchy was still young, the blunders were not on this side of the Channel but on the other.

In nothing did Louis XIV miscalculate worse than in his failure to grasp the ways in which that Stuart support might be lost to him and the Stuarts themselves ruined.

The England of 1685 was still largely monarchic. Though the process of class government (which is the opposite of kingship, and its death) had gone far, the idea of active rule by a real king was still vigorous and carried out in practice. But such kingship can only work when it is in tune with the nation. Now the English nation had begun to go anti-Catholic between 1605 and 1625, that is, sixty to eighty years before the Revocation. There was still, in 1685, a very large minority which favoured the Catholic traditions of an older England, but that body was divided, increasingly impoverished, diminishing (though slowly) in numbers, and torn between religious and national leanings.

Again, London alone had an organised opinion. London directed England and London was in the main anti-Catholic, in large measure intensely so, and its wealthy money-dealers were the natural opponents of Rome. On London in alliance with the great landed families, based on the spoils of religion, English affairs turned. The Revolution was a hostile challenge to that combination and therefore to the Stuart throne which could only survive by compromise.

The Popish plot was barely ten years past, the panic into which the mass of Londoners had then fallen from their dread of the large Catholic minority in their midst—which still sympathised with the old religion—the intense emotion aroused by the connection between the Catholic culture and the very great power of France close at hand, should have been sufficient to have warned Louis of the effect his action would have in London.

He did indeed appreciate the outstanding elements of the affair; he privately urged James to abandon his policy of toleration, wrongly estimating the strength of Catholic sympathisers at no more than a tenth of the English people.

More and more careful estimates of the Catholic strength in those last days of the Stuarts have appeared from scholars in recent years, and with every new estimate we get closer to reality. We can be certain within a narrow margin what the proportion of the active Catholic English minority was in the days of the Revocation. About one-eighth of Englishmen were openly and professedly Catholic. The only doubt is as to the size of the "penumbra" which in varying degrees sympathised in the ancestral religion. It ran down the scale, from those whose family traditions were strong but insufficiently strong to make them sacrifice wealth and prospects, to those who had half-lost such traditions; for many though still sympathising, sympathised only vaguely, and less and less as time passed, feeling it to be a lost cause. In what I have written elsewhere on this very important problem of English history I have suggested—without certitude but with I think sufficient probability—that the margin of sympathisers for the persecuted cause which they dared not openly follow was at least as large as the body of those who were prepared to suffer heavily for openly avowing their adherence to the ancestral religion. An eighth of the English were still professedly Catholic in 1685, and counting even the vague sympathisers with the spirit of their ancestors, probably a quarter of England all told.

The tendency to read the present into the past is so strong that the real remaining numerical strength of Catholic tradition in England at that day is difficult to appreciate in ours. But let my readers recall the proportions of majority and minority in any much-debated issue of our own time, and they will admit the large number that remain dissident or wavering until the victory is won. Moreover, nothing but a large remaining body of sympathisers with the old national religion can explain the recurrent panic of the anti-Catholic majority, especially in London, or the hopes of their opponents. Our official history with its myth of a mere handful plotting against a whole nation is quite unable to fit in either the Popish plot or the expectations of such men as Colman or the continual and prominent conversions of the seventeenth century.

But that Louis also failed to understand the character of James II is manifest; he was not the only one to be confused and repelled by James's integrity, obstinacy and ill-judgment combined, virtues and defects which between them destroyed the last of the reigning Stuarts. Where, on a later page, I shall deal with the decisive moment when Louis turned aside from the Dutch, marched on the Rhine, and so gave William of Orange the chance to invade England, I will estimate the extent of the consequences following on that final error.

Let me repeat the obvious truth that religious toleration is not of itself a politically good or evil thing. It may or may not strengthen the State according to circumstances. It may or may not appeal to the general conscience and so make for internal peace. When there are considerable groups who violently dissent from the philosophy of their fellows, political disunity must inevitably follow: for a difference in philosophy involves a difference in conduct. Our fathers were right when they insisted that the political unity of the State involved unity of religion. Today those States are most solid in which such moral unity is apparent. When men plead for what is still called religious toleration they only mean a toleration of something which is purely speculative, or at any rate has no disruptive effect. To read such phrases as "the man of the time did not *understand* toleration" or "progress had not advanced sufficiently to make men see the value of toleration" is to make one despair of common sense in history. No State has ever been tolerant, or could be tolerant, of something hostile to its principle of life, unless such toleration were judged a lesser evil than the friction or conflict between citizens of opposing schools, or unless (as is more often the case) the dissident minority half conforms to the mind and social habits of the majority.

The real interest of the Revocation, then, lies in the answer to this question. "Was it probable that the goal aimed at in 1685 could be reached? Was the gamble justified?" And the right answer to that fundamental question is "No; it was not justified as a piece of politics." The crushing out of Catholics in England, which the Cecils began and which was successfully concluded shortly after the Revocation, *was* politically justified, because the end envisaged was reached. The disturbing body of the old religion, which had come, by the later seventeenth century, to be an alien religion, had not the power to survive after 1688. It thenceforward rapidly sank to insignificance and left England a nation today more absolutely united in moral character than any other in Europe. In Ireland, by way of contrast, the policy of intolerance completely failed. The end aimed at, the unity of all Irishmen as Protestant subjects of the British crown, was rendered impossible by the policy of persecution. In other words, the task was beyond achievement with the methods of the day, and the effort was an error in policy.

In the case of the French effort the miscalculation lay in two very different things. First of all Huguenotry was dying of itself. They had only to leave it alone and it would have been no significant effect in another lifetime. Its strength had lain in the great families rebelling against the crown, and when these were reconciled the faction was doomed. In the second place the Revocation came just at the moment when that other major attack against Catholicism was just beginning to show above ground: that modern attack, the outstanding name in which is Voltaire. In a country strongly Catholic and of a religion which promised to become more intense, the destruction of the Protestant action might have been accomplished and a final Catholic unity might have made the quarrels of the seventeenth century no more than an ill-remembered memory. But the event was far otherwise. Those who resisted the Revocation soon found themselves faced, not by an enthusiastic Catholic people, but by a society the younger members of which were already sceptical with a scepticism which was to spread throughout the cultivated classes most rapidly during the next lifetime.

The Huguenots survived—and in half a lifetime they were in alliance with new anti-Catholic forces which were rapidly developing in the French State.

In our own day the work of the Republic has been essentially the capture of French public life by anti-Catholic elements in the body corporate of the French State. These elements comprise a very wealthy Huguenot body, only one-twentieth of the population, but controlling much of French Finance, a large minority organised by a small active nucleus and calling itself "anti-clerical," and a very small but still more active and powerful Jewish body. It is the combination of these which has captured the French official machine and which makes laws for the nation today.

The Revocation of the Edict of Nantes was based as a policy upon the idea of a population permanently Catholic in overwhelming numbers, and officered by a cultivated class who identified Catholicism, even in Gallican form, with the nation itself. That idea proved to be an illusion. The factors it took for granted were not to be the deciding factors of the future, and one reason that the enemies of Catholicism were ultimately to cleave the French State asunder was the reaction caused by the misfire of the Revocation.

If, then, the Revocation was a blunder because it was a failure, it behoves us to understand *why* it was a failure; why, in spite of the great power arrayed against the Huguenots, in spite of the enthusiastic popular support of the policy which aimed at their destruction, they survived and, in a certain sense, increased in power; in a word. Why did the Revocation fail as a policy?

It failed because the crown could not, or would not, strike at the heart of the Huguenot strength and the heart of the Huguenot strength was *wealth*.

The crown had tried a fall with the internal Money-power in general, and had succeeded in quite the early days of the reign, as we have seen. Fouquet's ruin was the symbol of that.

The national government tried a fall with the external Money-power in its effort controlling Holland, mastering Amsterdam and preventing the spread of Protestant financial hegemony to London. Here also Louis was to fail. We have seen how and why he failed. The whole story of his wars is the story of how he failed to control the Dutch merchant oligarchy, near as he came once or twice to succeeding. As for saving the Stuarts from the spread of Dutch commercialism, there also, as we shall see, he was to fail in those very years which saw the Revocation, in those critical years of 1685-91, when the policy of Louis would be tested and either checked at its outset or carry all before it. It was checked at its outset.

The great William Cecil, the first Lord Burghley, who stands at the origin of the modern English Protestant State, followed this prime formula: *To destroy a religion it is not enough to persecute its adherents for their creed or for the practice of their liturgy. It is essential to ruin them in their fortunes.*

This Burghley and his successors most thoroughly did, in confiscation after confiscation, fine after fine and capture after capture. The financial basis of English Catholicism being sapped, the whole thing was undermined, until at last it came tottering down. The landed interest passed by direct grant to the enemies of Catholicism whenever supporters of that religion failed in some overt effort to restore themselves. The estates of Catholics were subject to perpetual reduction by enormous fines: then, in the next generation, Catholic wealth was looted wholesale by the promoters of the great rebellion after their victory.

In Ireland that policy was, we know, triumphant and universal. By the middle of the seventeenth century not one acre of land in twenty, much less one pound of rent in twenty pounds, was left in Catholic hands. It is true that the complete and unexampled robbery of the Irish Catholics did not ultimately achieve its purpose, but it nearly did so; and in general the triumph of the anti-Catholic cause in these islands came from the financial policy which William Cecil, Lord Burghley, had preached and practised and handed on to those who continued his mission.

But Louis did not so act in the matter of *his* domestic dissidents. Many of them in emigrating took their wealth with them. Being commercial they could do that by instruments of credit, by purchase of merchandise and bills abroad, to be collected on their arrival. But the great majority of Huguenots remained within the kingdom, and they were in the main left in possession of their superior economic power. For obvious motives the persecution of the Huguenots has nearly always been described in the terms of the poor hill men of the central mountains, among whom were isolated groups of Calvinists. But what counted among the Huguenots was certainly not these. What counted was the great merchants, the prosperous skilled craftsmen, the ship-owners in the Protestant ports (these towns always had a larger proportion of Calvinists that could be found among the landsmen because they had been and still were more open to foreign influences), and most important of all, the moneylenders. Banking and money-lending in general has been, in France, Huguenot at its origin. It is interesting to note how, to this day, the hold of the Huguenot and French banking is firm and dominant.

We all know how the Calvinist philosophy supports such Money-power, how in its eyes poverty has something about it disgraceful, and prosperity is a mark of benediction. How also the denial of efficacy to good works indirectly seeps through the whole Calvinist system and supports the respect for possessions. Wherever you have active Calvinism in the past, wherever you have the air of Calvinism surviving today, there you have mercantile order, mercantile adventure, mercantile foresight, mercantile success; and such order and foresight and the rest are even more developed on the side of finance than on the side of commerce. It is the story of New England, it is the story of Scotland, it is the story of Geneva—and it is the story of the French Huguenots.

There would be no Huguenots today in France, or so few that they would not count, there would have been but a dying despised remnant of them in the eighteenth century, had they been economically ruined with deliberate plan by the great King.

I said that he both would not, and could not, do this. He would not, for such general robbery was opposed to all the morals which he supported. Such action would have been out of tune with the Catholic tradition as well as with the tradition of Caste in Gaul: for it would have meant the ruin of many old families. But even had he desired to ruin them it is doubtful whether he could have done so. He could have diminished their wealth greatly, but that wealth was always so closely in touch with the handling of liquid assets, that is, with banking, that the wealth aimed at, if indeed a policy of confiscation had been attempted, would have escaped.

At any rate, whether he could not or would not, he did not. The Huguenots retained their disproportionate economic power. It was this which gave them their chief strength in creating and defending liberal opinion, and in so preparing—with others—the Revolution. It is this which today establishes them in the parliament, the university, the commerce of France.

What proportion of liquid wealth one would find controlled by the Huguenot body today if a census were taken it is impossible to say. Perhaps a quarter of the mobile wealth of the country, perhaps more. And it is this which gives families still dominantly Huguenot their power in modern French capitalism, although such families are but one in twenty of the population.

After the main action of the Revocation and its failure there are two statements upon it to be examined. They have been widely made and they must be put in their proper position. The first is the statement that Madame de Maintenon was the person who principally inspired the King's action; the second is the statement that the Revocation was an effort to counteract the hostility of the Pope, Innocent, which by this time was thoroughly alarmed at, and aroused against, Louis XIV's general policy, not only at home but in Europe.

Of these two statements it can be roundly asserted that the first is false, and even absurdly false; and that the second, though not absolutely false, is quite out of perspective.

Madame de Maintenon could not in the nature of things have done what this false theory pretends. It was against her character, against all that we know of her and against the circumstances of the time.

Those who have supported this piece of guesswork base their judgment not upon a knowledge of character nor even of surrounding events and their consequences, but on an abstract supposition. Contemporaries who said that kind of thing said it merely as one of the innumerable things which they put forward either as accusations against a woman of whom they were envious, or as ill-informed supposition about a woman whom they knew to have influence with her husband—and deservedly.

Later writers work on another supposition, and of course the least informed and worst in judgment is the inevitable Macaulay. He knew that Madame de Maintenon was devout, he knew that she was herself in youth a convert. He jumped, in his ignorance, to the conclusion, without proof or probability, that *therefore* she must have moved Louis to do what he did. It is a typical judgment of a man who understood neither the woman's religion nor the man's, nor the relations between them, apart from religion, and who had no sufficient knowledge of European things.

It was impossible for Madame de Maintenon to have been, however distantly, responsible for the policy which preceded the Revocation, still more for the Revocation itself, because her whole domestic rule—and she was above all a methodical woman—was based upon the determination never to interfere with policy. This piece of policy, the Revocation, was, of all the rest, the most delicate, perhaps the most hazardous, certainly the most debatable. Only one other decision on the part of Louis was more debatable, more hazardous, and that was his decision, seventeen years later, to support the claim of his grandson to the Throne of Spain.

Madame de Maintenon for reasons already given never interfered in the King's policy. In this case she had another excellent reason for not interfering: her notoriously Huguenot origin: the whole Aubigné tradition. Those who understand neither her character nor that of the time would pretend that she desired by advancing the Revocation to atone for the accusation of Huguenot sympathy that might always be levelled against her. They said she wanted to be "more Catholic than the Pope." But such an attitude was utterly alien to the woman's whole temper and manner. She never exaggerated, and least of all did she exaggerate from a second-rate piece of obvious policy.

The truth about Madame de Maintenon and the Revocation is simply this: that she left all that piece of her husband's policy on one side. Others had approved loudly; the mass of the nation certainly approved; the most intelligent of the Court approved—nearly all of them. *She* neither approved nor disapproved. She stood apart.

As to the theory that Louis acted in order to throw a sop to Innocent, saying, as it were: "You may be angry with me for my Gallicanism but you will admit that I have been right in the matter of the Revocation," those who speak thus do not know what Innocent's attitude was. To say that the Pope agreed with a number of special privileges being granted to an organised heretical body within a Catholic country would be silly, and it would be particularly silly to say it of this particular period, the last years of the seventeenth century. You might as well expect an English Prime Minister in time of war to approve of conscientious objectors. But just as an English Prime Minister might condemn the whole movement of conscientious objection to military service and yet might dislike forcible methods of coercion, just as one not directly responsible—a man important among the public but not in the Government—might deplore conscientious objection and yet feel strongly against using methods of violence to suppress it, so Innocent certainly approved of the general policy of religious unity, but as certainly—which is not so well known—disapproved of the violence used against the Huguenot body, even when that violence was supposed to be exceptional and applicable only to a very small and dwindling minority. There is sufficient evidence that Innocent did take up that position, that he did deplore the forcible means taken for repressing the Huguenots and the pressure used for converting them.

The main motive force governing the official action now taken against the Huguenot body was the desire, or rather the necessity, for national unity, and what set the force to work was the erroneous judgment that resistance to unity was not serious, so that only a slight effort would be necessary to complete the whole task.

Nothing is more difficult than to judge the obscure directing forces at work in a large body of men when that body is in opposition. Men in opposition are always dis-united, and on account of the danger and unpopularity which are continually before their eyes, there will always be among them innumerable degrees of will, from heroic resistance and martyrdom to the very frontier of acquies-cence—and beyond that frontier.

Those who have studied, as I have, the position of the Catholic religion, or rather of the persecuted Catholic minority, in England in the seventeenth century, are thor-oughly acquainted with the phenomenon. To one man who sacrificed his life for the Faith there were a hundred who would run no such risk: for one man who would stand up to increasing poverty there was one other at least who preferred to keep his goods and remain silent. For one man who admitted, perhaps voluntarily, his convictions there was at least one other who conformed. Meanwhile among those who conformed there was every degree of sentiment, from strong (if silent) dislike of the new religion to a somewhat discontented acceptance of it. According to the question which you ask of the historians the figures given in reply are true—yet differ fantastically.

Take such a date as 1625, when Charles I came to the throne. If you were to ask how many heads of English fam-ilies would have been at least favourable to the restoration of the old religion the answer would be at least one-third were still in that mood, but if you ask how many would declare this openly, confess the old religion in the face of presumable poverty and danger, the reply would be barely one-sixth.[1]

We have only to look around us to see that this is true of any public question in our own day. The minority of opponents to some official change already accepted by the bulk of citizens is made up of men in every degree of resistance, from fanaticism to sulky acceptance. So it was with France at the Revocation. But in France the chances of resistance in the minority were at once greater in fact and less appreciated by contemporaries. In England men dreaded a Catholic rising. In France men did not dread a Huguenot rising, and the responsible ministers of the State never saw the difficulty of their task.

For those at the head of affairs who have to judge and who are official directors of a novel National policy will invariably underestimate the resistance to it. Not only will they underestimate the resistance, but they will underestimate its power of survival, and this is especially true of those who have passed the middle of life. They have seen so many fashions change, they have seen so many lost causes abandoned!

If you had asked Louvois, in, say, 1680 or earlier, what proportion of the admittedly Huguenot population would actively resist, he would not have given you a number but he would have told you that the chances of such resistance were negligible and that in any case two or three years would suffice to end the struggle—if struggle it could be called. Mere fanaticism is nearly always neglected in the biased judgment of the administrators, just as wild speech is negligible in the ears of sober men acquainted with their

---

1   The contemporary estimate of Catholic losses among Charles's Cadres was *one-third*.

social worth. "No doubt many will dislike—meaning by many one in twenty or less—the changes to come upon them, but not one in a hundred will raise active opposition, and not one in five hundred will be willing to suffer accordingly." Such would have been Louvois's reply and such was the atmosphere in which the Great King committed the main political blunder of his reign.

28

The Splendour

B EFORE TURNING TO THE NEXT passage of war let us regard that general light which shone upon the whole period and has marked it as a summit in the range of our Western culture. The dates 1681–86, the five years between the entry into Strasburg and the outbreak of the second war—that of the League of Augsburg—is a suitable moment in which to consider the general glory of the reign in the arts and in culture at large: for though the greatest work in letters was done earlier, and some of the greatest works in engineering and building as well, it is this central moment, when Versailles stood much as it now does, when the body of dramatic work had been accomplished, when Bossuet had produced his highest oratory, that what has become the classical type of French action was fixed.

The reign of Louis XIV was specially marked by a certain splendour exactly attached to it throughout and bound in with its dates and duration.

There have been other epochs of which the same might be said. We talk of an "Augustan" Age and a "Victorian," naming the one by a military monarchy acting under republican forms and the other by a nominal monarchy wherein the real government lay in the hands of a wealthy oligarchy. But the reign of Louis XIV had this particularity: that there was bound up together therein the qualities of national glory and the personality of one central will. Anyone arguing the necessity or even the greatness of monarchy as an institution must at once single out the half-century of Louis for his model.

Nor is the reign of Louis XIV splendid by some particular strength only, as was that of English wealth and expansion during the Victorian half-century or that of universal peace and a united world rule under Augustus. The splendour of the great French reign was curiously independent even of the military greatness which enhanced the greater part of it. The splendour of what the nation whereof Louis was king still calls "the great era" was something in the very matter of the time and place. It was a splendour which radiated through the arts and all the civil action of the human mind. That illumination was early recognised by contemporaries, even as it arose, just after 1661. It was dazzling twenty years later in the climax of the reign, but like all great historical things it is seen best from a distance, and today, after such vast and such astonishing vicissitudes in the intellectual fabric of the eighteenth century, the lightning and the thunder, the very magnitude of the Revolutionary and Napoleonic wars, after the great harvest in verse and prose which was garnered by the French until the last generation of the nineteenth century, it is still the epoch of Louis XIV which stands out.

It is like looking back on the lights of a town showing by night against the sky in a wide landscape.

There are many ways in which the greatness of an epoch is apprehended, by its recorded actions, its laws, its campaigns, the fruits of its administration, its institutional foundations, and the rest. It is also sometimes, though precariously, judged by its distant effects. But in two things may always be judged the greatness of an epoch. In the absence of either that greatness is maimed, in the absence of both it cannot exist. These two things are its literature and its architectural monuments.

These two alone remain ever present witnesses whereby posterity may be seized of the time and be compelled to admiration; and, of the two, it is letters which come first.

Other things suffer modification by time; institutions preserved in their name soon come to have another meaning, victories are balanced by defeats; economic prosperity, territorial expansion and the rest, by impoverishment and loss; but the temples of the Gods, and still more, that which the Gods inspire men to write and sing, last long. The letters of a high time and place are so lasting that men have given them the exaggerated title "immortal."

Taste will change; things intense at their first appearance may grow repeated and tedious; but a great body of literature conceived and moulded, cast into form and rendered permanent in one high moment of our civilisation, endures as much as anything mortal can endure. So it was with the prose writers and the rhetoricians, dramatists and poets, of the great reign.

❈　　❈　　❈

Men judging that reign today praise or blame its political effect upon the nation and upon society, according to their mood.

One man will opine that Louis in taming the power of wealth—which is the chief task of monarchy—destroyed the diversity and spontaneity of his people. Another will say that he saved them. One man will call him the original cause of that sterile centralisation which he deplores in the later France, another man will exalt him for the perdurable structure which he gave to the whole realm. But all in their variations of judgment will agree on this article of Splendour.

It was a time of splendour, and the splendour is apparent still in the domes and the palaces, but still more in the dramatic verse, and the prose, and the pulpit oratory of those years.

Not a lifetime ago it was the fashion to deplore what was then done politically, for monarchy was, until lately, receding; today it is becoming the fashion rather to demand the restoration of monarchy or to achieve it in its most extreme form; but while judgment and the effects of judgments rise and fall there is something about the classic beauty of verbal achievement which seems to escape mortality. For when it was said by the wisest of Englishmen that a people were great through their writers, he proclaimed a truth the causes of which are difficult to trace but the manifestation of which is beyond dispute. Dr. Johnson was right. Your writer is no great fellow; he is commonly poor, still more commonly peevish, almost always vain, and so forth—yet by him are nations exalted. *Vixere fortes.*

It is to be remarked that this literary era is not famous for one name nor even for supreme names, nor even for supreme select achievements of the pen. There is one, indeed, the *Misanthrope*, which out-tops the rest; but in the main no single writer or work stand separate and high above their fellows. The Great Time is identified with no isolated renown. Rather is it a moment wherein, to the enrichment of mankind, there coincided as never before or since the matter and the manner of expression.

What men had to say was of closer substance and the vehicle whereby it was conveyed and made permanent was of higher precision and effect, than earlier groups had known. An instinct for perfection inhabited those years, a critical sureness which prevented folly and redundance and dissolved obscurity because it automatically eliminated waste. They had a clarity of perception, a penetration of vision which controlled even high rhetoric and bowed passion under the yoke of order. From the least of the penmen to the mightiest, all moved in one phalanx of achievement wherein they remain.

So much is a commonplace to all who have any general knowledge of Europe. What rather concerns us in these pages is, "How far was the monarch a prime mover in all this?" *That* is the question we have to consider.

In the time immediately following on Louis's own, an enduring voice, that of Voltaire, proclaimed the affirmative: "Not only were great things done in his reign but it was he who did them." Can we agree?

At first it might seem that we cannot; and this for three sufficient reasons: first, that the man himself, Louis, was neither creative nor of any special powers in literary judgment; next, that of the greatest names counted as belonging to his time not a few arose before him, only a certain number are wholly contemporary and none accompany him to his end. Further, it may be justly answered that such constellations of talent have appeared where no monarchy was and even where the essentials of monarchy were most lacking. They have appeared in times of turmoil as under the peace of opulent oligarchies. The glorious body of English lyric verse grew when the national Crown was sinking to nothingness under the end of Elizabeth and was fighting a losing battle for its life under the Stuarts. Our unrivalled treasure of English song, unrivalled in scale as in quality, was gathered when royal power here in England was failing and came to its modern climax when an active monarchy was no longer so much as a memory among the English.

No; monarchy was not a necessity of the part that letters played in the great reign. They have played a similar part when monarchy was dying or dead.

Again, though Louis himself wrote clearly and solidly (not remarkably) he of himself discovered and presented to posterity no writer, though he recognised and justly honoured many. Rather did he inherit his writers. When as a young man he began to rule he found them already awaiting him. Corneille was more than thirty years his senior, the *Cid* was national before the King was born, and its author was already bent towards the grave before the noontide of the reign—even before the first cannon were heard in Flanders. Pascal had blazed out suddenly in the *Provinciales* when the King was as yet in his teens—an awkward silent pupil of Mazarin's. Pascal, the brain of Pascal, failed before the active reign began; he had sunk into death before it had run two years. Molière was nearly seventeen years older than his high patron: he had shown half a dozen plays and grown famous before Louis ruled. He died with the first victories of the Dutch war. The admirable La Fontaine was a year older still. Bossuet was already famous when at thirty-four he was first heard in the Royal Chapel by Louis, eleven years his junior. Racine was a contemporary, but lay dead during all the last sixteen years. Of the first names, Fénelon's alone was that of one junior to Louis. Nor did even he survive his estranged master.

How then can it be said that this master was the maker of such great things?

In this way—that great writing, if not called forth by a right social medium is at any rate fostered by it. Such a social medium may indeed be provided by the active debates of troubled times or may exceptionally arise through the persons and views of a few who indoctrinate their whole society. But, for the classic—"which always says less than it means"—there is needed a certain serenity wherein alone it can breathe. There is needed an air of unity where men can be members one of another. This is the rule of Louis with its discipline and cohesion provided. That was his part in the great result.

When such things are over, when such heights are past and a reaction or decline has set in, the witnesses of this will invariably complain. They will say that the high period sowed the seeds of its own decay: that all blame lies on it for engendering such decay.

The judgment is ill found. Decline of the sort is inevitable. How can anything organic remain at the height of its

powers? To such a height the literature of France did rise
and but for Louis it could not have risen in such majestic
simplicity. Monarchy it was which imposed the stamp of
unity on that day; monarchy it was which put the whole
into its frame.

Though the origins of the great business were well established before the active reign began, still it was those vigorous six years, inspired by the King's own self, which lit the
fires: six years of peace: the years under thirty, the years
of Louise de La Vallière. That fountain of youth, 1661–67,
gave a savour which was never lost. The lights of those
years, the myriad lamps in the undergrowth of the evening
festivals beneath the foliage of Versailles, were symbolic of
that brilliance which was to irradiate the whole lifetime of
the man and to shine over all Europe.

Before the six years closed the masterpiece of our Western
craftsmanship in the expression and discovery of the human
soul had been set down. I mean, once more, the *Misanthrope*.

By this test you may discover whether a man knows not
only the genius of Molière but the nature of human kind.
This, the *Misanthrope*, is indeed creation; the single model:
a symbol and extract of very life. So much a creation is it,
and therefore so superior to the limited genius of human
creator, the Molière did not himself know, I think, how
much he had done. Therefore it is that contesting men
have taken this *Misanthrope* from every angle as they do
the complexity of whatever is at once universal and alive.
Is Alceste sublime or ridiculous? Is his thirst for justice
unassuaged, his challenge of truth, pharisaical, or a vision
and a presentation of reality? Does he indeed drag forth
to the light the falsehood and follies of mankind? Or is
he a victim of his own vanity, exaggeration and unbalanced
reactions? Is he a champion or a man without a skin?

And the foils to Alceste! The criticism which a man
must suffer from his fellows, the sustenance which a man

must derive from himself, the isolation of the human soul and its tenacity and the consequences of such isolation and tenacity. They are all there, in the handful of Molière's puppets upon the stage—puppets whom he fills with more than life, with full perception.

Here we have the man friend; the wise, enlarged and patient wisdom of a woman who would comfort him but is remote from him, as also the wretched insufficiency—or is it the native womanishness?—of another who was too near and broke his heart. And the multitudinous fool is there, a drop from the ocean of fools, as like to all other drops as one drop of water to another, that supreme fool, the literary fool. There they are, but two or three on the stage at once, hardly a hand's count of them altogether—and they are all mankind. Well, this incomparable thing, the *Misanthrope*, was of those years.

So of those years was the fullness of Bossuet, a fullness of body, as in all things Burgundian. Bossuet (I may here be blamed for the violence of the contrast) would seem the pendant to Molière: that other handler of the Word. Bossuet is a deep and broad river always full to brimming over, an infinite wealth. He *saw* passing before him all that he had read, all that he had known, but especially all that he had first come across in youth, notably the Scriptures. Through them I think it was, with his powerful fancy aiding, that he understood the Protestants. He was fitter for that comprehension than any other who has undertaken the task from his side. He understood the Jansenists also and praised the virtues; he understood their limitations and the cause of their limitations. He was combative and therefore lives.

Today rhetoric is lost and the knowledge of it has disappeared, especially in modern England. The more difficult is it for Bossuet to be appreciated just now; but he will outlive all the others, unless perhaps the *Misanthrope* (as I think) should prove the most lasting thing of all.

Of Bossuet this occurred to me when last I stood in his cathedral at Meaux, considering the magnitude of the man. "They say that he no longer suits us. If that is so, it is one more of his titles to fame."

There is no need to go over that list of names, but for the sake of illustrating the multiplicity of their life some few must appear. Thus consider La Fontaine, bringing in during these same years his special note of *Beauty*; the Stag at the Pool, the living creatures moving under so tender a sky. It was a man already in the forties who gave his country so personal a gift, for La Fontaine was already forty-three when the Tales appeared, the exquisite verse for whose character he was so much blamed and which he must repudiate at his conversion in the last years. He was nearly fifty when the Fables were first read, and the war in Flanders was already afoot.

Of the rest, the very great Molière, of whom the best known story well illustrates what he was to those who could best judge but also illustrates the sense of the King. For it has been recorded that the King asking once of Boileau, I think, who would shed most lustre upon his reign, who would by his fame most bring fame to that famous court, he answered him, "Molière, Sire." Louis, surprised, was silent for a moment, but answered: "Molière? I should not have said that! However, it is a matter on which you know more than I."

Molière had reached perfection through a strange apprenticeship of vagabondage following upon an excellent middleclass birth among the tradesmen of Paris, imprisoned for debt, tramping the roads with strolling players, starting his own small theatre and failing, meeting men of every kind, and such are never met save among the poor. In that knowledge he became a master.

He was twenty-seven when Louis first saw and heard his work. For it was two years before the Cardinal's death that there was played before Louis the *Précieuses Ridicules.*

Racine was indeed a contemporary, as was Boileau. It was as a contemporary and almost as a friend that Louis dealt with Racine. It was as a contemporary and almost as a friend that Louis dealt with Boileau. Racine also was made by his own boyhood, when he fell in love with Sophocles.

Very young men, or rather boys, finding high verse for the first time, it is burnt into them, I know not how; it furnishes the rest of their lives. He knew great passages of the Greeks by heart and I think it must have been from Euripides that he caught the taste for the fatal and the warped, for the excess of fate also. The serenity of Sophocles he had not, until the very end, when he was calmed and repentant and understood divine things, but not in any Greek fashion. He himself had passed through the fierce strain of sensuality and discovered how despair is the twin sister thereof; but halting, and a later comer. His discovery was at its height when for a woman of the stage, by whom he had been for the second time captured after his first tragedy, he wrote that *Phèdre* which the Jewish genius of Sarah Bernhardt branded upon the whole of my own generation; a memory as rooted as a personal tragedy might be.

Some power, enchanted by the music of him—he has been blamed for too much music, a thing I should have thought in a poet impossible—some power, I say, hearing such things, rewarded him with the best reward and of the highest future—a woman for a wife, placid, good-natured, ignorant, three things incompatible with uneasy folly: three things of repose. In such an air did Racine rise again after his long silence to the summit of the *Athalie*. Yet all his life, coloured through his early extravagance, this poet of Eros suffered from a misapprehension of what is active in the mind, that is, Will. Corneille is Will: but Racine is Fate. The sense of fate overburdened him.

I will not continue the list though I am tempted to do so. It is a list of what I have called it, "Splendour"; corresponding to the splendours of the new court and of the coming wars. Those splendours it is true were of marble; they were splendours not of nature but of art and of design. Their very greatness was to provoke the reaction of the third generation after, in whom the long past of the nation stirred the Romantic and the sap of the Middle Ages. It is a splendour limited by the worship of order, but also (be it remembered), through this worship of order, imperishable. It is a splendour splendid through proportion—and perfection itself is but a function of proportion.

So much for the Letters: what of the Monuments?

The typical, the central, but not the unique monument under that name and power is Versailles. Nor can a man understand the Great Reign who does not weigh, savour and determine himself upon Versailles. The tradition of that mighty thing has been warped by the French iconoclastic passion for change, by the jealousy and hatred invariably aroused in Europe against any triumph achieved during the rare and vigorous moments of French unity. For the combative nature of the French people and the violent alternations between their declines and their recoveries, their sudden blazes of conquest, then their long periods of eclipse, lead always to intense reaction against their achievements, not only by foreign rivals but by themselves. On the other hand, the peculiar value of these moments when the French are united and go forward is seen by the way in which their deeds during such moments set something more than a fashion, a stamp, marking all around them.

It was so with Versailles. The spirit of Versailles reappears everywhere throughout the West, sometimes almost as though in a mirror.

Its worst drawbacks—such as the chain of open rooms denying privacy, or its great expanse of glass which defies our northern climate and exaggerates both heat and cold, its repetitive grandeur in ornament and lack of domestic detail—all those the rich and the rulers of Europe copied as though by necessity for a century, as they also copied that stamp of majesty (as well as they could) which was never fully and finally imprinted save by the great king.

Human institutions of the principal sort demand strong and exact symbols; each distinct phase of those institutions needs such a symbol, and Versailles is the symbol of the French Monarchy at the moment when it needed no walls and towers to defend its Court and was more powerful than ever it had been before the structural strength it owed to the two Cardinals.

Versailles is further symbolic in this, that Louis made it. Just as he made the great victories, just as he may even be said to have made the great literature which inhabits all the first and middle of his reign, so he made Versailles. Just as he who could not write remarkably nor judge remarkably the writings of others, who could not direct strategy, still less tactics, who certainly could not fortify, or design armament, was none the less at the root of that literature, those victories, and the rest, so was he, who could neither draw nor build, at the root of Versailles. Indeed he made Versailles more than he made any other thing. It was the product of his constant desire and care, of his assiduous application; this Palace corresponded, it exactly rhymed, with what he was in the height of his grandeur. Further, it is this even now in its abandonment, and though silent sufficiently alive with his presence.

It cost what we should call today fifteen million pounds in English money, seventy-five million dollars. No moderns could put up such a thing at all, and certainly an attempt to do so would cost them vastly more. That sum, representing less than £1 a head of the realm, has been exaggerated, and, even when it has not been exaggerated, held up as an example of shameful extravagance, and that by our time which sees nothing strange in the personal and useless extravagance of the mere rich man. The cost of Versailles was not undertaken for a man, it was undertaken for a nation; the man and the nation were indistinguishable. Its gigantic size is the crowd surrounding monarchy. Its continual level lines are the timelessness of monarchy: the claim to be enduring.

Note how curiously Versailles enshrines the landmarks or divisions of that reign.

The old royal palace which he had inherited, which he perfected on his entry into active rule and which retains before our eyes today the delicacy of his father's time, was the scene of his first six years of rule: not an habitation, but the place where the feasts were given and the shining origins of the young reign displayed.

Then comes, almost exactly coincident with the dozen or more years of central maturity, the palace which so greatly overshadowed the original thing.

The Versailles we know starts in 1668. The "Great Gallery" which is its chief feature (it came to be known as the Hall of Mirrors) was designed and rose before the end of the Montespan years—in '78; it took nearly six years to build. The whole thing as you see it now, with its extended wings, was completed just when the decline of Louis's power had begun. It is the moment of the fall of the Stuarts. It grew with the growth of its master, with the slow sinking of its master it ceased to grow. It froze as it were at the turning point.

Stand at the beginning of the Long Water, face eastward, grasp in one view the whole parallel, steep yourself in this view, and you have understood that moment of kingship which was its summit and will not return. But the unity there planned has remained.

What the Monarchy meant in its greatest moment for Paris the fortunes of the Louvre as a building sufficiently show. The Monarchy at its greatest moment in its final triumph abandoned Paris. For this also it has been inordinately blamed, but perhaps could have done no other. Indeed when it returned to Paris (against its will) the Monarchy fell.

The Louvre—the fortress and court of the old kings, standing incomplete, fragmentary, grandeur rising from a mass of the half decayed buildings, slums and narrow streets—the Louvre, lacking plan and completion to the end, reached that end just before it could be called a whole. It was not until the close of the Second Empire that the Louvre with the Tuileries could be presented as one thing. It seems therefore a very part of its character and fate that when this had been achieved the Tuileries should disappear.

The noblest thing in the Louvre and that by which, if it be considered apart, the classic of the great reign most affects the Louvre, is also the thing which has suffered most attack from those who miss its value and meaning—the Colonnade of Perrault, facing east.

It is superb: it has all the strength of that style, all its perfection of proportion, neither too high for its length nor too long for its height, all is *justice* of design. With such a thing to gaze on, the moral chaos of our time has put up the horrors that we know, "Functional Architecture" or what not. Colbert, when he approved the design for additions to the Louvre in the great manner, a nearly perfect classic, spoke, read and thought for men who had forgotten the remote past. The quaint term "Gothic" had become attached to the most native of French things, the ogival architecture and the vision which produced the cathedrals of the thirteenth, fourteenth and fifteenth centuries. So successful was ignorance here that men continued for two lifetimes to imagine that the highest beauty ever achieved in stone was something savage and even something invading and alien, as though Chartres and Rheims were

not in fact from the very heart of Gaul. It is deplorable no
doubt that you cannot have perfection in one manner save
at the expense of killing by total neglect another manner.
The Colonnade of Perrault is not Chartres, it is without
multiplicity, but it is no more without life than is a wide
and calm sea under a noonday sun. There is something as
timeless about it as that other something which we discover
to inhabit the conception of royalty. It satisfies.

Perhaps whenever a generation shall arise (it may be a
remote generation) wherein men shall know satisfaction
again, the Colonnade of Perrault (if some further fury
have not demolished it) will testify to what had also made
the *Phèdre*.

29
The Turn of the Tide

THE RELIGIOUS WORK OF THE reign is the main subject of it, because every society is conditioned by its religion. Next in importance is the Political, including the Military, story. To this, the defensive wars of the decline, 1688-1712, I now turn.

After that change in the mind and soul of Louis, that interior revolution of his which followed on the shock of the Montespan evidence, there is a turn in the tide of his fortunes. It is a common error to ascribe this external political change to this, that, or the other spiritual misfortune. The power of Louis and his people declines (we are told) because he had become regular in his religion and regularly married—two things very contemptible in the eyes of his critics.

Another school puts the whole thing down to a bad illness and operation from which he suffered early in this last phase. That is certainly a wrong conclusion, for he showed the same skill in diplomacy, the same tenacity, and the same industry in public affairs, not only throughout the actual short period of illness but up to the very week of his death.

One may indeed put down a part of his increasing difficulties to the main errors in this period with which we are about to deal, his partial neglect of the Stuart dynasty in England and his leaving the Dutch frontier unmolested in the critical year, 1688. But other errors in policy and strategy he had made without a decline in power following them; such errors are made by all rulers, but they are rarely of general and permanent effect *of themselves*.

No, there was a general cause underlying the decline, and that cause was the gradual exhaustion of the country, which increased under the strain of ten years' war to 1697 and became dangerous during the last and most violent assault of the country's enemies after the year 1702.

This exhaustion of a nation after a great effort, especially when the effort is prolonged, is not easy to analyse. We can see that it roughly resembles the fatigue of an individual with the advance of age, and when the State is one man his old age is the old age of the State. But the direct relation between cause and effect are not so clear as in the case of an individual life.

In general it may be said that there is a deterioration in the service of the State after any summit of success, and this is presumably inevitable from routine, from the exaggeration of past good fortune and either from the consequent disappointment produced by the lessening of that fortune or from the illusion that the better past is still present.

There is also the exaggeration of the main public characters at work during the happier period. They become legendary, and their successors are correspondingly belittled more than they deserve to be: whence lack of confidence in those whom they administer.

Louis did indeed commit three main errors: first the failure to push on to Amsterdam in 1672, the next the *political* miscalculation of the Revocation, and the third, that with which we are about to deal and which I have called the "Turn of the Tide," whereby through faulty strategy he missed his chance of stopping the Dutch influence on England and made it possible for the English Government to become his permanent enemy for twenty-four years. But none of these three errors would have had the effect of bringing the nation to the edge of destruction. That came from no cause more recondite than fatigue.

Happily for the country, it discovered at the very end of its agony, almost in the article of death, a sudden last flash of energy which, accompanied by good luck, saved the commonwealth at Denain.

What we are about to follow is first a defensive war maintained against a coalition stronger than any that Louis had yet had to meet: the League of Augsburg. That war lasted ten years, or nearly ten, from 1688 to 1697. We find Louis surprisingly successful in withstanding such heavy pressure and depending to the end upon that military superiority which continued to attach to the French Army throughout the reign: superiority not of numbers always nor, at the end, of generalship: superiority which did not prevent disastrous defeats; but superiority in the stuff or texture of the military profession during the Great Reign.

This, the beginning of the defensive wars, ends with the treaties known under the name of Ryswick.

The French monarchy emerges from the struggle still on the defensive, shorn of certain outposts, but still the strongest thing in Europe. After a brief interval of peace, a peace that might have seemed permanent, the unexpected[1] crisis of the Spanish Succession lights war again.

This last strain proved to be almost more than the French organism could stand. In seven years of war 1702–09 it suffered, one after the other, defeats which brought the country to its knees. Even after a certain relaxation in 1710 the pressure continued. It might have proved fatal within three years but for the unexpected victory achieved in 1712. By that victory the dismemberment of France and the fall of the monarchy were staved off. The very end of Louis's life, the last two years, are years of peace. He died knowing that the State of which he felt himself to be the restorer was saved.

Let us begin by considering what gave France during the Great Reign that military superiority which first imposed French hegemony in Western Europe and, after this was lost, still proved able to defend what was left.

---

1   The problem had been expected a lifetime, but its solution, the Testament of Charles, was unexpected.

30

The Military Superiority of France

THE MILITARY SUPERIORITY OF France during the whole of Louis XIV's active warfare—1667-1713—is the chief mark of that period. This military superiority accompanied many further glories, but all the other activities of the nation are overshadowed by this principal one of arms. It is the prime mark of the time: and the experience and the memory of it profoundly stamped themselves upon the historical memory of the French people. It was the time when the regimental songs arose which are still familiar to the modern conscript after more than two and a half centuries. It was the time when a number of distinctively French things in the art of war took form. From that time dates the tradition of the French infantry and the bayonet and, in some degree, that special reliance on artillery, the climax of which was reached under Napoleon. Fifty traditions sprang from that period. The idolatry of the flag, the exclusive use of uniforms as the mark of a soldiery; even the slang of the modern French Army has its roots in that later seventeenth century.

The phrase "military superiority" is accurate and just in spite of the vicissitudes of the prolonged struggle. Indeed that superiority in temperament and technique was better seen during the later defeats of the French after 1704 and in their final victorious rally of 1712 than in the easier work of the early years. They further show that the *profession* of arms also rose at this time in France, as there arose in

contemporary England the *profession* of the Royal Navy. In
both cases the earlier form of sea fighting and land fighting
had been sporadic. Military and naval units, and the officers distributed in command of them, appeared in national
conflicts occasionally: officering was something adventitious
to their general life, it was not their occupation.

In both cases the cause of this professionalism was the
length of the wars. A lad, who had got his commission
for the first campaigns in Flanders, 1667, might live on to
serve on the same fields at the end of the reign. Looking
back over his life he would see it as an almost uninter-
rupted experience of camp and marching and fighting. In
the course of such a life men became soldiers by trade.[1]
They were run and hardened into that particular mould
which has since everywhere marked the professional officer
of European armies.

There were two main causes for the military superiority
of the French armies during this reign. The first was the
recovered unity of the French nation, the second was the
fact that the French State was, at this moment, better
organised for war than were its rivals.

The French are by temperament military. It has been
remarked for two thousand years of the men inhabiting this
square of Europe, that not only the practice but the science
of armed conflict has always appealed to them. When this
instinct, habit, or tradition leads them into their favourite
pastime of civil war, or even when it leads them no further
than profound civil dissension without actual fighting, they
are less suited to undertake foreign adventures. They suffer
eclipse, as in the later sixteenth century and again today.

---

1   Villars and Villeroi, the fortunate and unfortunate, nearly fulfil
those conditions. Villars was present in the first Dutch war, com-
mands and is victorious in the very last of the campaigns. Villeroi
came in even earlier, at the very beginning, in Flanders and would
have been present at the end had he not suffered the disaster of
Ramillies only six years earlier.

But when, after one of their recurrent phases of disunion, they find themselves enjoying national unity once more, they invariably prove formidable to their neighbours.

Into such a phase of unity the French had entered with the opening of Louis XIV's active rule. It was to be maintained for a period quite exceptional in length. There is not in all the two thousand recorded years of the continuous French story anything comparable to those one hundred and thirty years between 1660 and 1790, during which the whole French State moved as one thing. Earlier and later not a lifetime passes without heavy fighting between Gallic factions.

The superior organisation of Louis XIV's France is a constant theme of German military historians, and they are right in emphasising it. Europe would not have witnessed the effect of the Great Reign upon history had not this superior organisation been present. France was better equipped for military struggle, by land that is, than England; far better than the Empire and better than Spain, especially in the earlier half of the period, from Rocroi to the Peace of Nijmegen. How the Spanish State had decayed and why, we have seen, as also the special weakness of Austria; but the main contrast lay between the way that German folk as a whole went to work in the later seventeenth century and earlier eighteenth, and the way in which French folk went to work. Today, under the discipline of Prussia, we associate the German name, especially in soldering, with exactitude, co-ordination and every other excellence of organised force. Lack of cohesion, delay in recognising a situation we associate rather with the French. But in those days it was the other way about. It was among the Germans that one found lack of precision, a fatigue of the mind—especially an incapacity for unity, which left the amorphous mass of the Empire open to attack.

The cause is quite clear to us today, though contemporaries sometimes could not see the wood for the trees. That cause was the exhaustion due to the Thirty Years War—the savage, religious struggle of the Germans among themselves. Not only had the miserable business halved the numbers of the Germans, but as its upshot it had left them a welter of small independent powers. The political map of the Empire at the moment when the wars of Louis XIV began is for all the world like a jig-saw puzzle, a crazy patch-work, with only here and there a considerable area of united command, of which the largest is the hereditary possessions of the Hapsburgs, ruling from Vienna. Over and against such a chaos the French block stood in a united strength, for those days quite exceptional.

From the same cause the recruiting field of the French armies was much larger than that of any other sovereign power.

There were no vital statistics in those days. We have to piece together chance scraps of evidence as best we can to make a fair guess at numbers, but we may confidently assume that the French recruiting field—in the middle wars of Louis—lay between a maximum of twenty-one million souls and a minimum of seventeen million. When you compare this with the rivals of France the value of such figures stands out. Spain was reputed to have eight million of total population, contemporary England and Scotland combined had perhaps six and a half to seven million; the Empire not more than seven or at the most eight million all told, and of course nothing like that number for its recruiting field. The numbers upon which the Emperor at Vienna could rely as direct subjects of his whom his own officials could approach were certainly not four million. What he could actually muster depended on what he could pay by way of hire—and his revenue was most insufficient. He had to beg for the alliance of princes and cities nominally under him, really independent: nor did most agree, and some appeared as enemies.

Had conscription been known to the men of that time the contrast would appear at once in columns of national figures. As it was, with armies still everywhere on a voluntary and mercenary basis, we can only conjecture within rough limits, but we have tables of forces which make us certain, for instance, that in the last development of his strength, the King of France commanded first from one-fifth to one-quarter of a million armed men and at last nearly 300,000. No one of his opponents came near such a figure, and only in the general combination against him in the last part of his rule was a hostile numerical superiority established. All through the earlier and main part of Louis's wars the French could put into line numbers superior to any coalition they had to face. On the other hand, the French during this long lifetime of warfare wore themselves out as none of their rivals did. There is a rough parallel here between the French effort in the Great War of 1914 and that under Louis XIV: the numbers mobilised increased to a maximum but the quality did not follow the same curve. It was already declining before the peak in effectives was reached, because the nation was becoming impoverished and the latest classes came from homes that had suffered increasing privation.

The main cause of the defeats which so nearly destroyed French power in the war of the Spanish Succession, and which were only tardily stopped and reversed at Denain, was not ill-choice of commanders through court influence, nor even the multitude of their enemies, but rather the physical and moral decline in *personnel* of troops drawn from a fatigued population.

Their strength thus formidable through numbers and organisation was reinforced by a new and admirable advance in military engineering: the science of fortification and the art of siege warfare.

To speak of these is to recall the high name of Vauban.

The tide of Louis's fortunes turned, not, of course, in a precise moment, but in a group of years which begins with the shock of the Montespan obscure but terrible intrigue, and ends with the battle of the Hogue.

The critical period opens, then, with what was externally, in the eyes of onlookers and in the mind of the King himself, the summit of his fortunes, for immediately after the shock of the Montespan exposure you have the annexation of Strasburg in 1681, which rounds off the defensive frontier and bolts the last door against invasion; and this critical period closes with the battle of the Hogue, after which it was impossible to restore the Stuarts. That "turn of the tide" has, at the beginning of it, the King's gradual conversion, the Queen's death, the private marriage to Madame de Maintenon, which marriage determined and coloured the remaining thirty-one years of his life. It contains the Revocation of the Edict of Nantes, the failure of that policy and, most important of all, the breakdown of the Stuart dynasty and the triumph of the English aristocratic system against the English Crown: the loss to Louis of the English support and the general coalition, which was at last to bring France, just before Louis's own death, to the edge of destruction.

In the long story of this last thirty-one years, much more than half the length of that long reign, the disadvantage of monarchy as an institution appears and must be emphasised. It does not appear disastrously, the monarchy is still glorious and the nation with which it is identified is still very great indeed—far the greatest political thing in the Europe, and perhaps in the world, of its day. Louis first seems to continue the long story of success and glory, stands up to the coalition, which, in the end, he was so miraculously and suddenly to defeat, and proves to his last breath that indeed "Kingship had returned to earth."

But—once more—because monarchy identifies a man with a nation, because the youth of a man and his vigour are the youth of the nation, so also the ageing of a man and the disabilities of age are the ageing and loss of power in a nation. As the man decays the State decays.

This is not true of the alternative Aristocratic form of human government with which, throughout this book, I have contrasted the institution of Monarchy, which the great King illustrates so fully. A class is vigorous at first in government and later slowly declines in power and effect, but its life is far longer than that of a man. A class is always "of its own period." It reflects its own time. It may come to lose its political instincts, it may fall into judgments less sound than those of its vigorous phase, but it remains more or less able to estimate the time and atmosphere in which it lives. This last and long, and, upon the whole, declining, part of the King's reign, found him increasingly at grips with something which he could not understand: aristocratic government, government by an oligarchy. He was at grips first with the unsubdued commercial power of Holland, then with the corresponding new force of an England in which the last of monarchy had been challenged and had been destroyed. And throughout the struggle Louis underestimated the strength of commercial aristocratic government, as he also mis-estimated its character.

The England against which Louis was pitted when the Stuarts fell was an England growing rapidly in strength, numbers, wealth, and of a kind which Louis found it more and more difficult to comprehend. Indeed, all his contemporaries were somewhat tardy in appreciating the change. To Louis in 1688 England was still the England of 1655–60, the England of those years in which a man's motives and character grow permanent; the formative years which introduce a man to his manhood.

The international picture which Louis had formed in his mind as a young man still stood in his imagination. The picture had become fixed, including England's place and character therein.

There is a parallel to this difficulty he had in understanding the new thing, and that parallel is present before all of us today. It is the parallel of our own relations with Italy. We had the advantage of aristocratic government, and yet our government could misunderstand the nature of the Fascist revolution and its enormous effects. So Louis misunderstood the nature of the English revolution when it was brewing, and when at last it broke. To this error in judgment of his we must ascribe that fatal swerve away from the Dutch front and towards the Rhine, which decided the fate of James II, after whose fall France was bound to be soon thrown on the defensive.

The preparations made by the Prince of Orange for invading England mark the true turning point in the fortunes of the French monarchy and of Louis himself. Those who saw the all-importance of the coming struggle in England on the fortunes of the French King and his country, saw the essentials of the day in which they lived. But those men were few, and Louis was not one of them.

In the most critical moment of all, when he had his large forces advancing north-eastward and concentrating along the north-east frontier in the autumn of 1688, he could have decided the future in his own favour by striking directly at the Dutch, or even by menacing them. William of Orange would have been paralysed, unable to act both because the Money-power of Amsterdam would have refused to subsidise him, having its hands full at home, and because he would not have dared to be absent when his opponent was facing him and the United Provinces, with his front towards them. Instead of marching directly on the Dutch Louis swerved half-right and marched on the Rhine.

There are many explanations given for his doing so: Louvois advised it. The Empire had grown formidable since it was relieved of Turkish pressure. Holland was not his main objective, etc. Most of these explanations come from men who cannot see the wood for the trees, and nearly all come from men who, though English, know little of England and her history.

The true cause of the French King's decision was the character of James II: limited, thoroughly straightforward, obstinate and most ill-advised, weakened in its action by those virtues for which such characters are most conspicuous. For James was one of those who think other men as loyal as himself, who believe what they were last told and whom, therefore, treason invariably takes by surprise.

But the particular point in James's character which here undid him and made his cousin turn away in disgust was his violent, uncritical patriotism, coupled with his intense sense of honour.

James II would not have it said that the King of England was dependent upon a King of France. He knew well how his brother Charles had for years maintained the throne by successfully playing French subsidy against Parliamentary treason at home, and against the Money-power of the City of London. Well, his brother Charles might stoop to such things, but he, James, would not. He would claim the arrears of the money actually due under stipulation to the English Crown. More than that he would not do. He would raise a sufficient army of his own. He would prudently economise the reserves of the Crown. He could, and did, depend upon the rising customs revenue he received from the increasing trade of London. He felt sure of his own children, less, of course, of the mentally deficient daughter married to Orange, but quite sure of Anne. He felt sure of Marlborough, whose career he had made, and whom he felt bound to him by every tie of gratitude and decency. He knew that his policy of toleration was just. He believed, as indeed did all right-thinking men, that it would make an end of dissensions, and he was determined to rule on the lines of such justice.

Louis had not only refused help, but had given the strongest private support to the opposite theory. He had implored James not to imperil his position by granting common rights to such of his subjects as were not Communicants of the Church of England.

In particular was Louis anxious that James should not appear too openly upon the Catholic side of the great European struggle. But the King of France underestimated the remaining strength of Catholic tradition in England at that moment. Louis underestimated that large minority. He said that James had only "one-tenth of his people in support of the policy of toleration and of ending the persecution." The numbers were far more than one-tenth, they were more like one-quarter. But anti-Catholic opinion was not only far more numerous than pro-Catholic opinion in England, it was also (what is of greater importance) far more intense, better organised, and above all centralised. It worked from the City of London and through the financial position of the city it worked through most of the great landowners as well. Protestantism had become, in the minds of most *neutral* Englishmen, the national cause.

When Louis saw that his advice would not be taken he determined on the alternative course and swerved off to the Rhine, leaving the Dutch frontier unmolested. That was what determined all that was to follow.

Yet the disaster might have been averted if Louis had been a strategist: and Louis was not a strategist. Strategists are few, and the chances of finding a great king and a great strategist under one skin are small indeed. Here we touch upon one of the principal weaknesses of monarchy as a system of government. It may be said that the monarch need not be a strategist because he can always find a good strategist to serve him. But grand strategy is inevitably part and parcel of politics. And so it was in this case. Louis, instead of facing the Scheldt and the Waal, or even Maastricht on the Meuse (which would have done the trick) committed the strategical blunder from which the future decline of his power proceeds.

What was the nature of that strategical blunder?

It was the failure to perceive that you can hold a hostile force as well, or better, by pressure upon its flank rather than upon its front.

Louis, remaining in the Netherlands and facing northeastward, would not only have paralysed William of Orange and have prevented the States from giving aid to the usurper, he would also have menaced the Emperor, for his forces would have been in a position to change front at will.

I have quoted elsewhere a pregnant five minutes' conversation held by the young Napoleon with the commander of the Savoyard troops who stood between him and Turin in the early days of the campaign of Italy in '96. "If," said Bonaparte, in effect, "you had stood to the east of the road to Turin instead of across it, and still kept in touch with your Austrian allies in the Ligurian hills, you would have prevented my advance on Turin more effectively than you could by losing touch with your Austrian allies and standing a-straddle of the road, in front of me, directly between me and your capital. As it is you have isolated yourself."

It was this principle of threatening from a flank that Louis did not understand. He left the Dutch unmolested; abandoning the threat of advancing against them: therefore was William free to sail. And with him, let it be remembered an army of most varied recruitment, every kind of mercenary raked together for the invasion of England, *but that army mainly officered by French Huguenots.*

345

Here was the backwash of the Revocation—and it swamped the ship.

Would an aristocracy have shown better strategy? Would this weakness of monarchy, because monarchy is personal, have appeared if, instead of Louis, you had had at work a governing class? If, instead of French armies, Carthaginian, or Genoese or Venetian armies had been the weapon in hand? In my judgment the answer, with certain qualification, is in the affirmative. An aristocracy would have used a good strategist and better strategy than Louis used on this occasion.

We all know how frequently and thoroughly aristocracies have failed in the field. I have just written the word "Carthage," and that word by itself is enough. Carthage was defeated by an Italian dictator because Carthage, under class government, did not support its own great strategist. Nevertheless I can but believe that, in such a crisis as 1688, an active governing class would have found a strategist and have done the trick.

I have just said that the superiority of Aristocracy over Monarchy in strategy is dependent upon a certain proviso: this proviso is that the governing class should be fresh and strong, all the better for being new to its job. We know as a fact that the new aristocratic government of England did discover in its ranks for the purpose of the Gallic war as great a strategist and tactician as ever lived: Marlborough. If we ask ourselves why aristocratic government has this advantage I think the answer lies in the fact that, of its nature, a governing class which always surveys a wide field of men, has, when it is still vigorous, an instinct for using the right men. It cannot but be so, seeing how a governing class is composed; how its numbers not only know each other but are compelled by the instinct of self-preservation, when the vitality of their institutions is still strong, to pick out the best instruments not only of administration and rule but of defence. Hence the British Fleet, and, until lately, small intermittent expeditionary forces, sporadically used, often successful and never involving, even in their discomfiture, the defeat of the nation. King Louis, then, left the Dutch alone and ordered his armies to advance on the Germanies.

With the strategical blunder the tide had clearly turned. When the tide thus turns in the fortunes of a State it cannot be reversed. The effect of the change can in part be warded off, the threatened disaster can be mitigated or even neutralised, but the old confidence and security of France will not return.

All that followed showed how right was Vauban when he fixed on Ireland as the critical point in this general war. For on the Continent the wrestling went dingdong: the two sieges of Namur are typical of that. All the odds were against Louis, but his military machine made up for the deficiencies of position and, at places, of numbers.

With the fortunes of William of Orange it was otherwise. He maintained that passionately-desired eminence of kingship, to which his life had been devoted. His falsehoods and treasons had gained the reward that generally follows such practices in the affairs of this world. Though the wealthy English families who had put him where he was were ever ready to betray him, though they taught him sharply that the English King was now their servant, yet King he remained. He was never ousted.

From that position he could act not only as a figurehead but largely as guide to the wars of the League. He meant vastly more to the Dutch as King of England than as Stathouder of Holland, and he lived to see his crown recognised by Louis himself at the next Peace. All this would not have been if Louis had concentrated on Ireland.

William's bungling at the Boyne[2] had left an Irish army intact to continue the struggle. William's Dutch generals were almost as incompetent as he. Ginkel did not take Limerick till the autumn of 1692. The defences of the city were quite insufficient, but the besiegers allowed their siege convoy to be captured and their first siege-train and guns to be taken. A sufficient French reinforcement would have regained Ireland. In England the hostility to the Dutch party as invaders was growing, and, helped from Ireland as a base, its opponents could have overthrown it. But such reinforcement never came.

The old quarrel of Colberts and Le Telliers, the jealousies of the early years were here revived. Colbert's son saw the opportunity in Ireland and urged it. Michael Le Tellier's son, Louvois, urged the opposite policy, the throwing of French force to the east, and Louvois decided the choice. He died in the midst of the debate, in the summer of '98, but not before the harm was done.

It was he who advised and pushed forward the Ravaging of the Palatinate (of which later—it was a great moral asset for the League and a political one as well); it was he who shut the door on the despatch of sufficient troops for the Irish field.

It was not sea-power that prevented the restoration of the Stuarts. It was the failure to send a sufficient force of trained French infantry to support James in Ireland, and later to reinforce the resistance which continued after he had returned to France.

Obviously Louis could not reinforce the Stuart Cause without retiring elsewhere and standing on the defensive. But he would have lost nothing by that in the long run,

2   With a numerical superiority in men of 180 per cent., in guns of 400 per cent., and in *trained* effectives of an overwhelming superiority, he failed to obtain a decision. His opponent got clean away with a loss of but 6 per cent. in men, and of but *one* gun.

for in the end he was back again on the Continent, except for Strasburg and Alsace, to where had been before the high-water mark of Nijmegen, while across the Channel he had allowed his best European asset to be eliminated.

He lost the sea battle of the Hogue in 1692 (after winning at sea the year before), but he lost it because the English Fleet under Russell joined the Dutch and were thereby two to one. With a strong Jacobite force in being, that Dutch undertaking would have failed. The Russells— like most of their equals in that day—were on the fence. As fatal as had been in strategy the "Turn of the Tide" at the opening of the war was, in politics and strategy combined, this failure to lay his stakes upon the cause of James and of the older English tradition. After 1693 it was too late.

I have said that the Ravaging of the Palatinate was under the circumstances of the time a blunder. Let us consider it.

The military thesis underlying the awful policy of devastation in the hereditary lands of the Elector Palatine was the same as that which, on a smaller scale, makes men level buildings and cut down trees over a belt in front of a fortress and destroy or remove stores of provision therein. It was to impede an offensive directed against the French eastern frontier. But the destructive actions accompanying this military policy were on a scale beyond its objects or value.

The peasantry who had done no wrong and were merely defending their homes were hunted in groups. Towns of such great memories and European importance as Spires and Worms were burnt, the former almost entirely. It is lamentable to see in them so little left of what had preceded this catastrophe. The churches, as usual, were spared, and certain other monuments which could give no shelter or sustenance or form centres of residence—but as habitable places they were pretty well destroyed.

It has been pleaded by the apologies of this grave error in policy that German hired bands in the past had been the most barbarous in Europe, and one modern writer on the French side has said: "They would have done worse to our land if they had got through." This is not a full truth. The barbarism of the German and Slav levies for a generation had been a spasmodic barbarism. Orgies of violence and loot, often at the expense of their fellows, the savagery of the Hussite wars and much later the Thirty Years War are examples. But the Ravaging of the Palatinate was deliberate, and it was this character about it which did the most moral harm to our civilisation.[3] It is disputed how far Louis himself was to blame. It is admitted, even by his enemies, that he was appalled before the thing was over and that he put the brake on, too late but still before the worst had been done. But he certainly stood behind the policy as a whole, especially on its inception. He cannot be acquitted of what has left memories operative to this day.

The claims of the second Duchess of Orleans, the heiress of the Palatine, were legitimate. But to attempt their enforcement was to arouse the Coalition to further efforts, and in the upshot what remained? No outpost beyond the Rhine. No accession even to the Defensive power of Louis, but ruins.

When Peace was made in 1697 (the Peace of Ryswick), the French Crown gave up all its conquests of Nijmegen except Strasburg and accepted the garrisoning of a string of fortified places beyond the north-eastern frontier in the Netherlands to secure the Dutch from invasion. But the central thing in the whole batch of treaties was the confirmation of the English Revolution—Louis recognised William as King of England, promised not to allow intrigues against his usurped power, and admitted Anne to be his

---

3   In the same way the horrible Prussian massacre including women and children in Namur, in 1914, has permanently affected German fortunes. In London it is forgotten, but it is remembered on the Continent.

successor, in the place of James II's little son, James III, now in his tenth year and the legitimate heir to the Royal House of England, to the three Kingdoms of England, Scotland and Ireland. *That* was the kernel of the settlement; *that* was the lasting result of those ten years of war.

Next following this third main passage of arms (the war of the League of Augsburg) comes, after a lull, the final war in which the throne of Louis and his country so nearly succumbed: the war of the Spanish Succession.

3 1

The War of the Spanish Succession

HE END OF THE GREAT REIGN IS
filled with a war which might have been disastrous to the French people, which might even
have been the end of the monarchy and conceivably the
disruption of the State. It is known as the War of the
Spanish Succession.

Louis at a critical moment, just on the turn of the century in the November of 1700, accepted the offer of the
Spanish Crown for his grandson the Duke of Anjou: for
a moment the balance trembled between the acceptation
by Europe of so great a claim: its rejection and universal
war. The balance settled finally on the side of war.

What we have to decide in estimating that great affair is
the judgment of the ageing King. Was he right or wrong?
Our answer to that will also be a judgment of monarchy in
human affairs. For this act also was a sharp example of the
strength and weakness of monarchy, of its good and evil.

We have seen that the lingering, wretchedly invalided
life of Charles II of Spain had been prolonged altogether
beyond expectation. His death had been discounted time
and again. More than thirty years before, the Eventual
Treaty had turned upon the anticipation of a sickly child's
approaching end. But that end came not. For half a lifetime it was being privately discussed, tentatively settled
(and unsettled again), what should happen when Charles
II should die. The solution had always been a proposed

partition of those enormous territories, the Americas, the two Sicilies, the Milanese with the other Italian possessions, Spain itself, and the lingering claim to the Netherlands. They were possessions, weakly supported by an insufficient revenue, and possessions hopelessly divided in Europe itself, still more divided by the waves of the Atlantic. Their revenue corresponded in no way to their extent. Still the thing was gigantic. The shadow of the past lay over it and more than a shadow, a certain substance. That substance survives today in the language and social habits, the very cooking, of half a continent whereon Spain has impressed its whole spirit and the ineffaceable memory of ancient glories.

The claims of partition afoot in the last year of Charles's life were, like all the arrangements of the late seventeenth century, a tangle of proposals and counter proposals, of allied interests dissolving and uniting. Something of the final solution—which was to prove not final at all—was achieved by Lady Day of the year 1700. Treaties had been signed between the French Crown, "the Maritime Powers" (as England and Holland were called), the Empire and (what must be distinguished from the Empire) the Austrian possessions ruled directly from Vienna. The main point of these provisions which begin with a treaty as early as June, 1699, were in three groups. The Archduke Charles, the son of the Emperor, was to have Spain and the Catholic Netherlands, but it was stipulated that the latter should never form part of the Empire. The heir to the French King, the Dauphin, should have scattered territories of which the chief were Lorraine (the Duke to be compensated with lands elsewhere) and the Kingdom of the Two Sicilies. The Emperor now free from the pressure of the Turks and Hungarians was to content himself with his son's inheritance.

One after another the terms were signed, the last of them, that concerning the Empire, with a proviso that there should be a delay of three months before a final decision. When this plan of partition was known in Spain there was an explosion. It is by understanding that explosion that we understand what followed.

We tend today—or did tend until yesterday—to underestimate the resisting powers of the Spaniard, and through that resisting power the policy and strength of a united Spain in international affairs. There was fury in the Palace of Madrid of course, but the essential was that there was fury throughout the populace. The Spanish people, for all their differences, for all their rooted provincial antagonisms, were united in this: that their old and glorious inheritance should not be dissipated. England and Holland were regarded as the villains of the piece. France appealed to these ancient enemies because a united French claim at least would preserve unity in the Spanish dominions. Heirship in blood, direct heirship, must go in the line of Philip IV. He was the King whom all men now old could remember. He was the King who had married his daughter all those years ago to young Louis. To the descendants of that daughter and to them alone of right could the united splendour of the unbroken Spanish Empire descend. The gold was old and faded but it was gold.

Now we must keep it clearly in mind that it was this intense national feeling south of the Pyrenees which really determined what followed.

The Spanish Council of State deliberated gravely and with moral strength. They decided for the grandchild of Maria Theresa, for her son's younger son, the Duke of Anjou. Of her son's elder son, the Duke of Burgundy, there could be no question: that would have meant the absorption of all the Spanish realm into the French Crown. But that his younger brother should inherit was the only way to defeat those proposals of partition which Europe had taken for granted and which raised to fever the indignation of Spanish pride. Charles, moribund, as weak in mind as in body, still hesitated. He would consult the Pope, and the decision of the Pope was in favour of the Spanish Council's decision. The Pope has been accused by enemies of so deciding for a mere political motive—because he did not want to have the Empire at his doors in Naples. There was that element, of course, but the moral element is not to be despised in our judgment of the chief of European religion. By all moral traditions the Bourbon inheriting through Maria Theresa could claim what the Spanish people would presumably desire them to claim.

On the 2nd of October the dying King signed a will leaving Spain, the Americas and all, to his great-nephew, the Duke of Anjou as "universal heir." Should he fail, his younger brother, the Duke of Berri, should inherit; should *he* fail, then the second son of the Emperor. Exactly a month later, on All Saints' Day, the King of Spain was dead.

Such was the apple thrown down for the common discord. Within ten days, on the 9th of November, the French Court at Fontainebleau heard the news.

Now let us clearly grasp what the issue was.

Louis was not bound to accept the inheritance for his grandson; no one is bound to accept an inheritance. But if he refused it there would certainly be war and Spain would suffer, for Spain would certainly refuse to accept partition, which was the only alternative to the will. It was either the danger of war with at least the Spanish wealth and ships and people on Louis's side, or the certitude of war with the Spaniards hostile to France and struggling against an unjust and detested settlement.

At 3 o'clock in the afternoon on that day, the 9th of November, the Chancellor, the Governor of the Royal Children and the Secretary for Foreign Affairs met in the room of Madame de Maintenon where the main business of state was always transacted. Opinion was divided. The decision was adjourned. They had twenty-four hours to think it over. On the next day, the 10th, these same men were summoned by Louis again. They were more united: the heir to the throne was as emphatic as his lethargy allowed, the Secretary of State who had hesitated agreed. The King himself, pondering as was his wont all that was said, decided firmly. After four hours of the matter being weighed, at 10 o'clock at night the thing was done. Within forty-eight hours word was sent to Madrid that Louis the King would accept the inheritance for his grandson with all its awful burden of risk. On the 16th in the morning the King received the Spanish Ambassador and privately presented the boy as his King, to whom the Spanish Ambassador gravely made a grave discourse of loyalty in the Spanish tongue. Then the great doors of the Cabinet were thrown open and Louis appeared with the child before the assembled courtiers in the Great Gallery and said to them, "Gentlemen, I present to you the King of Spain."

Now then. Was this on balance an error or a justifiable hazard?

Of the morals of it abroad there could be no debate, for though it meant the repudiation of the partition arrangements so recently made those had in any case disappeared. It was one heir or another to the Spanish King. But was Louis justified in policy? Was he, now approaching old age, running too great a risk for his country, and that country but in part recovered after the strain of those successive wars? If hostilities were to break out could he sustain them? Had he the remaining economic power, the remaining man-power, above all, had he the generalship at his disposal which in happier years had ensured his victories?

These were the elements on which he had to judge. First of all, of the Maritime Powers he could be fairly sure of England; even the new plutocracy which the Revolution had put in the saddle was disinclined for a foreign adventure: it had no love for the dangerous puppet it had set upon the usurped throne of England. Louis could count for the moment almost as certainly on peace with Holland. The merchants of the United Provinces had no desire to strengthen further that man who was now with his wife sovereign of England, whose whole fortune had lain in continual war. William of Orange could not resist this double pressure. On the 17th of April he recognised the Duke of Anjou as Philip V, King of Spain.

The ice had not broken but already it could be heard cracking.

Briefly the issue was this: should the vast Spanish domain, not the Peninsula only, but Italy, the New World and all its future fall into the orbit of the Bourbons or of the Empire: of France or of the German Hapsburgs at Vienna? It would (as it seemed) be necessarily one of the two. If it fell to the latter all the work of a century was undone: the Empire of Charles V had reappeared, and the French Crown and people were once more "encircled." Whoever claimed the Spanish throne there could not but be war.

The last great war of the reign is best understood if we take it as part of a general pattern which marks the political and military story of the time.

There were three main chapters in the military history of Louis XIV. The first was that which we have already described, the early campaign against Holland, of which the preliminary was the claim by inheritance to control the Catholic Netherlands.

The first chapter ended with the Treaty to Nijmegen. Amsterdam was not occupied, the Dutch Money-power was not either broken or absorbed, but on the whole French power had come out of this original struggle greatly increased. Alsace was occupied, the Franche Comté passed to the French throne and—vitally important—a chain of strong places was secured on the north-eastern frontier between the Ardennes and the North Sea, which barred the ancient route of invasion. This first chapter covers the ten years 1667/68–78.

The second chapter, just sketched, was the reaction to other European forces against this extension of French power. The core of that reaction was a league of powers called "The League of Augsburg." This second chapter is commonly called "The War of the League of Augsburg." It also has limits of ten years, beginning in 1688 and ending in 1697 with the Peace of Ryswick. This second chapter was a period far more anxious for Louis XIV and his people than the first had been. They maintained themselves, though with difficulty, against the strain of this second great war, they were at times very hard pressed, but at the end of the struggle they were still within frontiers permanent and continuous, they could still talk as equals to the considerable coalition which had menaced them.

The third chapter, covering that which we shall now deal, was the general assault on France provoked by her King's accepting the Spanish Succession and allowing his grandson to become a King of Spain.

This third chapter of war also lasted ten years, from 1702 to 1712. During its progress the French monarchy and its realm came very near to final defeat and even dismemberment. There was a moment, as we shall see, when Louis would have accepted almost any terms, short of destruction. His offers of peace were refused, he was pressed still harder, then, at the very end, by an astonishing turnover of fortune, the French recovered the initiative after the battle of Denain, and were able to conclude a peace—the Peace of Utrecht—which left them diminished, but still intact and fairly secure for the future. Their candidate for the throne of Spain remained King of that country, the vital fortresses barring invasion on the north-east were retained and so was the frontier of the Rhine, but all the outposts, the "covering works," as it were, which had stood out beyond the frontier were lost, what had been the Spanish Netherlands went to Austria and all French garrisons beyond the Alps and beyond the Rhine were abandoned.

There you have the scheme:

1. The Dutch war of ten years, ending with the Peace of Nijmegen.

2. The heavy and precarious struggle against the general coalition called "The League of Augsburg," ending in the Peace of Ryswick.

3. The desperate struggle for life which all but ended in a final disaster, unexpectedly averted at the very end of Louis's life.

Ten years; ten years; ten years. Triumph; the defensive; then, back to the wall.

Let us return a moment to the second chapter of war and what decided it.

The League of Augsburg had been formed originally not as an offensive, but as a defensive measure. It was not even essentially a military alliance. It began rather as an understanding among the German princes and cities that they would resist any further effort at expansion on the part of Louis. It ended as an attempt to destroy him.

So with the War of the Spanish Succession which followed: it began in a quarrel with the new accession to the House of Bourbon; it ended with a nearly successful effort to destroy that House.

The same cycle is perpetually appearing in all political history on its military side. One state with a long record of danger and invasion has the good fortune at last to be so well organised as to turn the tables and make itself secure by winning great actions against its former invaders, and barring their future menace by occupying their strongholds. Such successful action appears to the victims of it as essentially offensive—in the eyes of many, wanton: mere aggression. At the same time the successful defensive of the state which used to be in peril is led on to an attitude which is really offensive, because not to go forward would mean to go back. By the time this stage is reached each party is convinced of its moral right, but the more successful one is already thinking of renewed expansion and the other side is more convinced than ever that it is fighting justly in defence of its rights.

The scheme of the War of the Spanish Succession is easily to be followed over the areas in which the struggle proceeded, and the dates which determined it were highly separate and defined. First as to the areas. This, the last and most perilous of all, covered the largest surface, and that caused a special strain upon the harassed defensive, because it came just in those years when that defensive was more and more exhausted.

What I have called "the first chapter"—Flanders and the Netherlands and the Dutch war as a whole—had been concerned with the valley of the Rhine and its delta.

What I have called "the second chapter," the war against the League of Augsburg, had covered the base of the Rhine and its delta and part of the Italian peninsula as well.

This, third, chapter, the War of the Spanish Succession, occupied the basin of the Rhine and its delta, and Northern Italy and Spain as well. It was the most universal of the wars, falling just at the moment when Louis and his people could least sustain the effort—but the alternative was the German menace. With the Empire at Vienna taking over the Spanish inheritance, all Europe would once again have been at the mercy of that crown.

The areas in which the fighting fell are four—omitting frills. There was first the external Netherlands business. Next, joined on to it through Luxemburg, the West German and Rhine business.

Days away from this to the south, separated by the whole mass of the mountains, was the North Italian business, and especially the conflicts in the territory of Savoy, removed by the hundred leagues of sea and land from the south and east from this last, which was the Spanish conflict.

In this threefold or fourfold adventure the French had the advantage of interior lines. Indeed, but for that they could not have stood out at all. The advantage of interior lines means that he who possesses it can strike outwards from a centre whether for aggression or for defence, can reinforce himself from one point to another on the inner side of a circle, while those who are working against him on exterior lines work on the outside of the circle with a corresponding increase of distance to be covered, expense and difficulty of communication.

To take one clear example: the French could attack towards the valley of the Danube through Upper Alsace or towards Savoy, through the Alps, 150 miles to the south. The coalition working against the French in the Danube valley could only reinforce their troops in Italy by the long passage through the mass of the mountains. From, say, Belfort to the passes which led to Turin was one hundred miles. From the Upper Danube basin to Piedmont through the Swiss ranges, was at least three hundred miles.

The French also had the advantage of a completely united command and a politically united task. But the allies now had an advantage in financial resources and drafts of men such as they had never had before, and though the Bavarians were supporting France, something of Spain, and notably Catalonia, could be counted on the other side.

Like the areas in space, so in time the dates of this final struggle are clearly defined. Blenheim, in the second year, drives the French to the Rhine. They have no further permanent hold on German territory to the east of that line. That is in 1704. Ramillies, two years later in 1706, is the great master blow under which the French monarchy reels. It drove France out of the Netherlands as Blenheim had driven her out of trans-Rhenine Germany. In that same year, 1706, which was really the critical year of the war, although it did not present so violent a crisis as developed a little later, came the disaster of Turin and the loss of the Italian field by the French.

Thenceforward the only field of partially successful action open to them is Spain. Nor would they even have had this but for two things; the military talent of Marlborough's nephew Berwick, and the strong moral support, and therefore recruiting advantage, of the Spanish populations outside Catalonia. On the vital north-east frontier two years more sees the crossing of the French frontier and the beginning of invasion: Oudenarde, which might have been the final defeat of Louis. Following this you have the hard-fought "blocus" of Malplaquet, very expensive to the allies, but not preventing them from pressing forward still further. Then comes the "last ditch," the lines of Villars. Marlborough in the finest feat of his career so partially turns them that he is able to invest and take Bouchain.

Up to that point all is not only in favour of the coalition but pointing directly towards a complete collapse of French power, when, in the July of 1712, the year after Bouchain, Louis XIV accepted the English government's offer for a separate peace. Even after the elimination of Marlborough's presence and of the small English contingent, the coalition still has somewhat the advantage in numbers on this front and vastly the advantage in material and morale. Landrecies, the last stronghold blocking the way to the coming torrent of invasion, is invested, when, but a week after the French acceptation of the English peace Villars springs the surprise attack of Denain on Eugene. After that all is changed and the realm saved.

If we survey the war of the Spanish Succession as a whole we must decide on the superior importance of the front in Flanders. It outweighed the Rhine, it even outweighed the vicissitudes of the struggle in northern Spain.

There were for this two reasons. First, that the Flanders front was vital to the French monarchy. It might lose its Italian bases of action, it might lose its new claim to overshadow the destinies of Spain and Spain's vast empire. It might fall back to the Pyrenees and even to the Vosges. But if it fell back from Flanders it was retreating along the road which led to its heart. It was opening the gate not so much to defeat as to mortal invasion, to the destruction of the kingship and of the realm itself.

And the second reason was that upon the Flanders front, marching from it and returning to it, was Marlborough.

One might think that because Marlborough is a national hero and because the Flanders fighting in the war of the Spanish Succession stands out so very strongly in the English perspective of history, therefore a right historical judgment should tone it down. But that is not possible. No natural reaction against the over-praise of Marlborough can be admitted, because Marlborough as a soldier cannot be over-praised. Napoleon knew that, and many another has known it before and since Napoleon.

Here was a man commanding large armies for the first time in middle age. He stands forth for nine years, and only eight of real action. In that brief interval he pierces every line, he takes every fortress, he wins every battle, he achieves every decision. And such things are not accidents nor coincidences. It may be said that he was fortunate in not being allowed to carry on to the end, since too long a space of time will defeat the best of luck. Of that we know nothing. He might have done still greater things. He might, as he himself thought he could, after Bouchain have advanced with Eugene into the very heart of the enemies' country and to its capital. At any rate what he actually did is sufficient.

I never hear his name without thinking of Napoleon at St. Helena, pencil in hand as was his custom, annotating his book of Marlborough's campaigns. He offered that book as a legacy to the mess of the English regiment which guarded him and was his jailor. Hudson Lowe thought it improper to receive the gift. Where it is now I do not know, but whenever I read the name of Marlborough I see a picture in my mind of Napoleon in those last months, pencil in hand, marking the margins of the chronicle wherein he followed the action of that other great captain whom he seems to have bracketed with Frederick of Prussia as alone worthy to be his rivals.

Marlborough, after clearing the Netherlands east of Brussels in 1702 by way of preliminary, planned in combination with Eugene a march to the Danube where, in 1704, the first of the great victories against the French power was achieved at Blenheim. When we examine in detail the character of that action we discover the factor present which accounts for the succeeding campaigns: it was the factor of the French exhaustion. Note that in the two-mile front the northern, Bavarian, half remained intact. It was the French in the centre who broke. And why did they break? Through the fault of their personnel. The cavalry there was insufficiently mounted, perhaps insufficiently trained. The infantry support was fatigued. It is true that the fatigue and the too hurried provision of reinforcement were both a function of Marlborough's strategy. He kept his enemy uncertain whether the blow of his advance would fall on the north, the middle, or the south of the line. That enemy had to march round on exterior lines. The troops that fought at Blenheim had been pushed too hard after probably insufficient training, through the Black Forest, and came into action the physical inferiors of those opposed to them.

Blenheim ended the power of Louis to act beyond the Rhine, but it was not decisive. What was decisive was the action, two years later, at Ramillies. Ramillies meant not only the loss of Belgium but the disorganisation of the French army there. It meant not only the abandonment of Brussels and of all the advanced positions in the Netherlands, but the ultimate retirement into France itself; and Ramillies, more than any other of his actions, was the personal, artistic effort of Marlborough. I wish that its eminence were appreciated as it deserves, but unfortunately the succession of victories and the confusion to which that gives rise in the general mind, makes Ramillies but one of a string of names; yet in truth it is the one name worth retaining. Without Ramillies Blenheim would have been of little use; with Ramillies the French power broke. As we shall see, it did not break wholly. It later rallied, but was never to be in these wars what it had been before.

Two years later the disarray of the French army, defeated at Ramillies, had its effect right up to the frontiers of Flanders.

When the third blow fell, at Oudenarde, it might have been the last stroke, had the five columns, which there converged, come upon the field two hours earlier. And here it is that you have perhaps the only exception to the general truth that Marlborough's organisation was always perfect. But though at Oudenarde the French were saved from disaster, they lost their battle and by so much were their opponents heightened.

Next in the story comes Malplaquet, where the French rally begins, and where the French and Bavarians between them did prevent a decision. They stood on the defensive between the two woods covering Bavay, and in the terrible business of that day slaughtered two allies to one who fell on the side of the French marshal. It was a butchery which, had the recruiting of the allies been more exhaustible, might have led to peace. But as it was the succession of Marlborough's triumphs continues. Two years later he pierces the lines of Villars after one of the finest marches in history, a manœuvre which he says himself was his masterpiece. This led to the fall of Bouchain, and from Bouchain it was believed that a further advance would have carried the victories into the heart of France.

Those main dates—Blenheim, Ramillies, Oudenarde, Bouchain—illustrate all that combination which made Marlborough the captain he was. For men of this genius have their standing through three qualities combined: an eye for a situation (and especially an eye for country), power of organisation, and power of command. Ramillies was the eye for country; the battle was won because Marlborough spotted, in the morning mist, even as he arrived on the field before the action, that slight depression wherein it was possible to hide the cavalry upon his left wing. Along this depression he could bring the mounted troops round to his left wing and so, at the decisive moment, appear with a great preponderance of horse, which broke the French Maison de Roi, and so, striking at the flank of the whole of the French army, reduced it to confusion.[1]

The advance at Oudenarde was not indeed a triumph of organisation, for the convergence was not sufficiently well timed. That was why, at the end of the action, when night fell, Marlborough himself said that with another short space of daylight it would have been decisive. But though it was not decisive it at any rate compelled retirement, whereas a similar convergence attempted towards the end of the century at Tourcoing, missed altogether

[1] I know of no life of Marlborough or study of his campaigns which puts at its right value this fold in the ground in front of Autre Eglise on Marlborough's extreme right. Yet it was certainly *this* feature of the terrain and Marlborough's recognition of its value that decided the action at Ramillies, and with it the whole pre-Denain campaign.

and led to the defeat of the British contingent, the flight of the Duke of York, and towards the end of the day, the complete French victory.

As for power of command, it is everywhere present in the calm and exactitude of the decisions, in the driving power communicated by the chief to all his forces, but most of all in the way this man could keep together, and use as a single unit, troops of the most diverse recruitment, troops of all languages and all nations. The great example of that was the piercing of the lines in 1711 and the consequent taking of Bouchain. The piercing of the French lines was only possible through a march of the most exceptional severity, wherein something like half the total of men engaged fell out, and large numbers actually died. But that night march just outdistanced the enemy, surprised him too late for him to prevent the passage of the lines and the consequent investment of the fortress. Though all this was possible only through the exhaustion of France, and though the French successes elsewhere were gained largely with the help of the troops other than of native recruitment, yet it is Marlborough's genius which determines the whole thing. With another commander the peak of the effort would not have been reached, and, indeed, as we shall see in a moment, with Marlborough no longer present, the victories in Flanders came to an end and the French rally reverses the situation at Denain.

How the exhaustion of France affected the campaign is best understood by those who have followed the last stages of any great war. It is not so much the exhaustion of the individual men who have fought, as the result of bad recruitment. New contingents are asked for too rapidly. There is not time to train them properly; they are drafted into units which have felt mortal fatigue and give no expectation of victory to the newcomers. They find officers accustomed to reverses and no longer sure of themselves. They find often among the rank and file either the beginnings of mutiny or that state of mind which is prepared to accept defeat.

In the long succession of French disasters and retreats 1706, the year when Turin (and an army) were lost and when Ramillies was lost is the main moment; but the year of lowest vitality, the year of Despair, was 1709.

Louis in 1709 was ready to offer almost any terms for peace.

The favourable opportunity was missed because the Allies insisted upon demanding of Louis his active aid in expelling his own grandson from Spain and the Spanish soil. The chief, or at any rate the most irreconcilable wills at work in what reads at first sight as a monstrous claim were those of Marlborough and of his colleague Eugene.

But was that claim so monstrous? It has often—until lately, almost universally—been interpreted as something impracticable: a mere desire to humiliate an enemy and register a complete triumph. Why (it is asked) having obtained of the French King all that his opponents could desire, should those opponents have further insisted upon a personal humiliation and so led him to prolong the war?

If that demand had had no military reason behind it, it would indeed have been as wanton as it proved to be in the event fatal to the allied cause. In the end, the desperate struggle over the Spanish Succession ended in the unexpected but sufficient triumph of the French claim; the Bourbon was to remain secure in Madrid; the whole allied effort, in its main purpose, was to fail.

But there *was* a military reason behind so drastic a policy. It was simply this: that without the aid of French military forces it was not certain, it was not even probable, that Philip V would be driven out. The tenacious Spanish there supporting him, the threat of one of those terrible guerilla wars which the Spaniards can conduct better than any other men, the certitude of local resistance everywhere, demanded every ounce of effort available. No one of the allies could support for a long period a sufficient force in so distant a field to make certain of victory. They could barely be certain of it even if the head of the Bourbons did betray the new Bourbon establishment in the peninsula.

Marlborough was not a vindictive man, and what is odd he cared little for glory; he cared still less for scoring verbal odds, but he was certainly a very great soldier, and when he made a military demand it certainly had a military reason behind it. The same was almost equally true of Eugene. Eugene had a stronger appetite for repute and honour, that is for glory, than Marlborough, and he had personal reasons for humiliating Louis, but he also would not have pressed a military demand without a military reason behind it, and the military reason was that necessity for an added force, a French contingent, to turn the scale beyond the Pyrenees.

It should also be remembered that France, even in her present exhaustion, offered a larger recruiting field than was open to any one of the allies single handed. She was the main partner, whether as enemy or ally, in any combination. Further, who could guarantee that French neutrality would be maintained when the pressure against the new King of Spain began? Such are the reasons behind the insistence upon Louis XIV's collaboration in the work of turning out his own grandson and of undoing all the work of his last years with his own hands.

As to the reaction which that demand provoked both in Louis himself and in the nation of which he was the chief—that reaction which was to prove so unexpectedly successful and to end in the triumph of Denain—it was not only personal indignation on the part of Louis at the attempt to bully him, it was also, like everything else he did on the major scale, a piece of policy. Here was an opportunity to rouse the national temper even under its last extreme strain. It was not to be missed. The famous letter which the King of France addressed to his people and which provoked so exalted and sufficient a response was not rhetoric nor indignant protest. It was a calculation—and thoroughly did it do its work.

It was in June, 1709, that the negotiations for peace broke down over this demand for Louis's aid against his own house and blood. On the 11th of September, Villars and Boufflers fought the "blocking" battle of Malplaquet on the frontiers of the Netherlands. The French and Bavarians retired again; but the expense in men to the allies was heavy.

The allied command suffered perhaps twenty thousand, perhaps even higher casualties, on this field: figures insignificant to our more enlightened and humane age, but serious in those days; such a drain on forces recruited with difficulty without forcible enlistment might threaten the future of the struggle. Especially in England was the effect of Malplaquet adverse to the war party. After all, the Netherlands were cleared, the menace of French power there over against the Thames was over. The loss in men from these islands was negligible—for the whole British contingent was but a small fraction of the allied army—but after Malplaquet further English expense seemed called in for the advantage not of England but of foreign powers.

The year 1710 saw some relief in Spain when the Bourbon king returned, an English force under Stanhope had surrendered, and the Imperial Austrian claimant with his army was defeated at Villa-Viciosa, but the salvation or destruction of France lay not there—it lay, as always, on the open frontier between the Ardennes and sea. Here the armies of Louis were on the last line of defence, the artificial line which Villars had drawn up from the sea at Montreuil and the mouth of the Canche up the waterways to the Scarpe and beyond to Bouchain and so to the Upper Scheldt.

In 1711 Marlborough, in what I have already called his greatest military feat, though not his most spectacular (still less the one that had most result), pierced these lines[2] and took Bouchain. It was already autumn. He was for going into winter quarters and proposed with Eugene the "Grand Project" of forcing the last defences and marching on Paris the next year, 1712.

But it was the very moment of the great reversal in his fortunes. In that very winter—in the weeks after Bouchain—the English Government no longer hampered by a Whig House of Commons and relying on one now mainly Tory, began to talk of peace.

Behind the outward change in English policy and the ultimate Tory decision to abandon the war there was a profound national instinct at work. How far it was conscious no man can tell; these deep currents run so far below the surface of things that often they are not perceived even by the men who are carried away by them.

Outwardly and superficially it was a weariness with a protracted struggle which led to no tangible result, at any rate to no result appreciable by the plain man. For though Marlborough, with his unfailing grasp of a military situation, saw that the next phase of the war would leave the allies in the heart of France, those unaccustomed to military planning, those who did not even understand the map, simply thought of the affair as the end of a long and wearisome wrestling in which neither opponent had really touched ground.

Superficially, then, it was tedium and a sense of futility which led to the cessation of the English effort in Flanders. There are explanations even more superficial than this and they were explanations which appealed to contemporaries.

2   It has been disputed whether Marlborough "broke the lines" of 1711 or not. It is a dispute on words rather than on things. The gate was not wide open, but it *was* a gate, and therefore the continuity of defence by lines was shaken. Had Landrecies fallen, later on, nothing lay between the allies and Paris.

Voltaire's solution of the problem is notorious for its absurd insufficiency. *He* would have it that the ending of Marlborough's command and of the English support for the allies was nothing more than the fruit of private quarrel between women, a change of favourites by Queen Anne, and that change provoked by a silly little incident not worth recording. Much more serious an explanation and one appealing specially to us moderns who know the meaning of banking as an economic force in history was the doubt inhabiting those who controlled the new Bank of England and the new English financial machine.

A debt which seemed in the eyes of contemporaries appalling had already been piled up and all that anyone had to show for such hitherto unexampled expenditure was the little fortress of Bouchain. Swift, whose intelligence was far the first of that generation but who was a pamphleteer, writing for a faction, expressed the opinion of the City of London—little as he knew the City—when he put into an epigram the whole grievance: "Bouchain had cost 8 millions of pounds"; and as men read what seemed to them that impossible total they asked themselves, "After all, what was Bouchain?"

Well, Bouchain was an open door for invasion, the breaking of the lines at Bouchain meant the further fall in good time of whatever remaining fortresses might be attempted. Landrecies in particular was, now that the lines were broken, the final obstacle remaining, and after Landrecies should fall the allies could march into the heart of France and threaten Paris itself. But all this was a military calculation, and of military calculations even the instructed public knew little and the mass of the squires in Parliament and of the merchants on 'Change in London nothing.

All these things being admitted, from the most superficial explanation of so great a change to the best reasoned and deepest, there is yet another explanation which can act after a fashion which I have compared to a deep current by which men are borne along without fully understanding what is happening to them. *This decisive factor was the ever present instinct of the English mind that the Netherlands, and particularly the Netherlands in their coast approaching the Straits of Dover, and still more particularly Dunkirk, were the chief issue.*

With the strongest Power on the Continent occupying the Netherlands or any appreciable part of their coast England was not safe. That was a sentiment which had inhabited the English mind for generations, since the fifteenth century at least—and the seeds of it were sown as early as the fourteenth. That England must do her utmost to prevent the presence of a strong offensive Power in the Netherlands was so much taken for granted and for so long and so justly, that even in our own day, when all circumstances have completely changed and when the conditions of war have been transformed by the new art of flying, even in our own day, when the new range of artillery further destroys the meaning of the words "Narrow Seas," this old traditional feeling about the Netherlands has its place in the English political mind. It is a pity, for it weakens us. The all-importance of the Netherlands for England has long ago disappeared: but that importance was real till yesterday and paramount in the early eighteenth century.

Well, the Netherlands were secure from France. Ramillies had begun that. The forcing the French back on the lines of Villars and the turning of those lines by Marlborough at Bouchain left no anxiety as to the immediate future. The French, it seemed clear, would now no longer be able to threaten Flanders and its coast. Therefore England might profitably withdraw from the war: the allied victories had done for her all that she needed.

Marlborough was recalled, attacked by his domestic enemies and superseded. The command in France was given, in early 1712, to Ormonde, but already the English ministry had prepared for a separate peace with France, and were prepared to treat.

The number of men immobilised for the moment on the allied side by the informal truce between France and England was over sixty thousand. Of these sixty thousand one-fifth were from these islands, and the others, principally German, were in English pay. But that very great loss was not sustained by the allies when the French accepted the English offers of peace. They lost the small English contingent, but the rest was taken over by the Dutch financial power, they having refused to follow Ormonde and his cessation of hostilities. The withdrawal of the English was certainly a heavy blow to the coalition. It left the opposed members more equal. But it was not decisive of what followed. It was not so much a blow in the loss of men as in the loss of financial support.

The new banking power of England had provided three millions a year at the beginning of the war, in 1702, to subsidise the campaign against Louis; by the end of 1711 England was providing *eight* millions. The contrast between the financial effort of England now mercantile and the financial exhaustion of agricultural France was very striking. At the worst moment of 1712 the allies had one hundred and thirty thousand men in a united command, and the whole of that great force well appointed. The French could approach only a little more than half that number, seventy thousand, insufficiently munitioned, and with an artillery that had become inferior.

Le Quesnoy was invested by the 8th of June and capitulated on the 4th of July, after which disaster to the defence of the all-important open north-east frontier there remained nothing but the little town of Landrecies at the extreme east of the line.

Eugene began the siege thereof on the 17th of July, the very same day on which Louis had accepted the offer made by England for a separate peace. The odds between the two antagonists were by this time much less. Not only had the English contingent withdrawn, but the Germans and others taken over by the Dutch had not yet been thrown into the field. The allies still had the advantage in mere numbers. They still had, what was more serious, a conspicuous advantage in experience, training and morale. It seemed certain that Landrecies must fall.

There you have the situation a week before that unexpected French victory which was to have so momentous a result.

The scheme of this victory is not difficult to appreciate. Eugene, besieging Landrecies, had for his communications whereby he received munitionment and the rest, the water-carriage of the Scarpe as far as Marchiennes, thence the stuff came overland to Denain on the Scheldt, by a protected road. Eugene had made his general base for material, munitionment and food at Marchiennes: a wise decision, for Marchiennes was central to all the last places he had to capture for the march on Paris, and all of which he had taken by this 17th of July except Landrecies. Marchiennes being on a navigable waterway was suitable for a magazine, as such waterways were to 1712 what railways are today. At Denain another navigable waterway, the Scheldt, was of service. Those communications extended along somewhat higher land another eighteen miles from Denain as far as Eugene's siege lines in front of Landrecies. Marchiennes was garrisoned, of course, and so was Denain: the latter principally by Dutch troops under William of Orange's "friend"—the infamous Keppel.

The praise for what followed has been disputed. The vigour and "spirit of the offensive" in Villars had something to do with it. The recurrent asset of the French in their wars, an elasticity of temperament, had much to do with one of those immediate transformations of which

French military history is full and of which a major example was the Marne. But the modern thesis which has been thoroughly worked out in the best recent monograph is, I think, to be taken at its full value. Denain would not have been what it was but for the information coming from a secret adviser, not a soldier, but a lawyer who was watching the lines: Le Febvre d'Orval, a councillor of the parliament of Flanders. It was he who advised striking, if it were possible, at Denain. But after all, the very difficult work of effecting the necessary surprise at that point was the work of Villars, nor could it have been done but for the marching power of his men.

After any victory, especially after a victory due to surprise, legends arise and extravagant claims are made. It is possible that Villars did not feint towards Landrecies, but seriously intended to attack and then, finding Eugene too strong for him, turned back to effect a decisive manœuvre. It is more likely that the whole thing was intentional, and that the first move of Villars towards Landrecies *was* a feint. Anyhow, what cannot be disputed is the rapidity of action which followed. In the night between the 23rd and the 24th of July, 1712, the French Army, "feeling" the allied lines which invested Landrecies, secretly turned about, and from facing eastward faced westward; then began a night march which changed the story of their country.

Their last elements had to cover twenty miles in the march and countermarch that was before them; even their most advanced elements not less than sixteen. They appeared upon the banks of the river opposite the fortified post of Denain in the early forenoon of Wednesday, the 24th of July.

Villars was not certain whether he were sufficiently well placed to attack. The hours were advancing and there was the river between him and Denain itself. It would take time to get all his strength across the water and during that time Eugene would certainly grasp what was happening, and would send forces pounding up the Denain road and block any effort by the French to cut the lines.

The bolder decision was taken. Fifty-two sleepless battalions were drawn up beyond the stream. Their foremost lines received the platoon fire of the defence and the full discharge of the six guns at point blank range. But the charge, once begun, was not checked. The French poured with fixed bayonets over the earthworks protecting the road whereby Eugene's army had received its supplies. They poured upon Denain, over the works, in numbers overwhelming to the garrison at that one point. They had killed or captured or driven into the river the elements of that garrison in less than the first twenty minutes' work. Eugene's vanguard came up on the far side of the stream only in time to see the rout in the streets of Denain, the fugitives struggling in the water, the surrender of elements cut off upon the bank, and in general the destruction, at its central link, of that line of communications upon which the investment of Landrecies depended.

The effect of thus breaking the chain of communications at its centre was instantaneous, and the ultimate result of that very brief conflict (which contemporary witnesses have called a skirmish, although the forces behind the French charge were so considerable) was to raise the siege of Landrecies at once. With the raising of that siege, and with the severing of the line by which Eugene was munitioned, all the allied army had to fall back. It was what I have called it, a "transformation." The war at this point—and it was the vital point of all—had been turned upside down. The former allied offensive was in retreat, and the French defensive, which had been on its last legs, had now opened a counterattack which moved rapidly forward. Villars was not only ready and able to advance, but manifestly possessed, henceforward, the initiative. Eugene's

great stores of war at Marchiennes were seized at once, Le
Quesny fell to the French, so did Douai, so did Bouchain.
The Dutch hastened to follow England's example and give
up the struggle. Eugene himself went to Utrecht to negotiate. The Empire was ready to treat and nothing remained
but to draw up the treaties of peace.

On that 24th of July, 1712, the War of the Spanish Succession was decided and the French Monarchy was saved.

No general French victory was achieved by Denain. It
was not complete, since the outposts of the Rhine, the
Netherlands, and Italy, were lost to the French; but it
was decisive in the sense that the object of the whole war,
the instalment of the Bourbon monarchy at Madrid, was
determined and the capital point, the throne and authority
of the aged king and his now firm reliance on his own
people was assured.

The General Settlement (the many treaties are conve-
niently grouped under the title "Peace of Utrecht") left
England in possession of Gibraltar and Minorca and the
Protestant succession to the English throne admitted—or,
at any rate, the Stuarts disowned, Newfoundland was ceded
and especially was this country secured in the slave trade,
one of England's most valuable forms of maritime traffic;
the line of "Barrier" strongholds on the Netherland side of
the North-East Frontier was drawn, the French recovered
Lille and drew up a similar barrier on their side. By the
end of 1714 the French frontiers were fixed much as they
stand today, for Strasburg and Alsace had been retained.

Such were the fruits of Denain.

There arises on Denain one last question which the
nationalist historian will too easily answer and indeed
has answered in a hundred textbooks. Was the failure of
the allies to clinch their general victory in 1712 due to
the absence of Marlborough? It is obviously a striking
coincidence that the moment Marlborough had withdrawn

from the field those who had been so successful under his command or his colleague's failed. The immediate conclusion would be that Marlborough was the god of war, the necessary, the inevitable victor, and Eugene was doomed to be defeated in Marlborough's absence and through that absence alone.

The simplicity of such a reply has provoked reaction against it. Our official historians of course make everything depend on Marlborough and will put down the surprising final French victory to the fact that Marlborough was no longer in the field. Against a statement which savours of national vanity those who care for historical reality are naturally on their guard. Now the thing is hypothetical: to say what would have taken place had Marlborough remained can only be guesswork. To affirm the necessity of Marlborough's genius and Eugene's missing of victory from lack of his aid is to provoke a search for almost any other explanation of what happened.

But we cannot dismiss the problem in these terms. Two things remain true and will always be a challenge to those who maintain that Denain did not depend upon the absence of Eugene's great brother in arms. Two plain facts give pause to any just judge of events as much undisturbed by patriotic bias as by reaction against it.

The first of these is the fact that Marlborough had never lost a battle and never failed to take any stronghold he had besieged. Now, in the year after he is withdrawn, a decisive action is lost and through its loss the Bourbon claims are revived. The second is that the French triumph at and after Denain took place on the first occasion when Eugene's unaided judgment was pitted *in open battle* against that of the French command.

It is true that national histories are biased on either side—as is seen in the case of the Boyne and again in the case of the lines of Villars in 1711. But impartial history

379

need not pay attention to such moods: it is concerned only with the truth.

It is true that Eugene continued to conquer and advance for months after Marlborough's withdrawal, taking towns and pressing more and more upon the enemy until, without Marlborough, he had reduced the French to extremity and was on the point of taking their last fortress (Landrecies) and striking through open country at the capital.

But it is also true that, lacking Marlborough, Eugene was at last outmanœuvred.

It is difficult to believe but that historical opinion must finally determine that Marlborough's absence in 1712 made the difference. At Denain Eugene suffered surprise. Would Marlborough have suffered surprise? It may be doubted or even denied, for in all those astonishing nine years Marlborough had never once suffered a tactical surprise.

3 2

The End

HE GREAT REIGN WITH THE GREAT
life were ending. All that life had been the
steady, inflexible Will—but that Will ordered to
its proper end in a governor: the end of Government.

That Will in its persistence and strength, but most of
all in its immobility, may be compared to a flame which,
against all precedent or likelihood, stands fixed in a gale;
as fixed at the height of the storm as in the calm before
and after.

It was this function of the Will, exceptional miraculous
Will, informing the monarch, and through the monarch the
monarchy and the whole conduct of the State, which had
run throughout all that business of sixty-five unceasingly
laborious years, from the first of youth to the last of age.
It was that Will which had forbidden the subordination
of any national interest to any personal tragedy or desire.
It was that Will which was at work when he submitted
without a murmur to the dreadful operation for fistula,
with Louvois firmly holding his wrists; he, the King, silent
throughout the torture and motionless. It was that same
Will which led him through a strain, the like of which you
will hardly find in the whole story of monarchy, I mean
the sudden apparent ruin of the succession.

In that worst and lowest of the valley into which French
fortunes had descended in the years before Denain, which
had seen not only the ruin of armies, the debasement of
the coinage, famine and the mutterings of revolt, one thing
at least did seem secure, the succession. Monarchy need not

be hereditary. The strongest monarchy of our own time, the Presidency of the United States, is elective, so was the military monarchy which saved Vienna and Europe from the Infidel at the hand of John Sobieski. But its hereditary character had been the very making of the monarchy in France.

Monarchy should be hereditary to become a principle sacredly interwoven with the people. The succession had to be secured if the monarchy were to stand well founded and firm, and even in that very issue of life and death for the French people, and therefore for the House of France, the succession seemed among the most secure of mortal things. Monseigneur, the Grand Dauphin, the dull but solid man of fifty, he who should have succeeded to his great father when the time came, was by his apparently unmenaced life a guarantee of the succession. After him there were his sons, the young Duke of Burgundy (since we may not count the young king of Spain) and after those sons again there were the boys, the great grandchildren of Louis, the Duke of Brittany and a child, a little more than a year old and frail, the new little Duke of Anjou—four lives at least between the Crown and any failure thereof. These things standing so, the one prop for a kingdom that was in peril at every other issue, the succession at least being thus undoubted, there fell upon it a hurricane.

On the 14th of April, 1711, the Dauphin died of smallpox, leaving the Duke of Burgundy "pale as death" at the idea that he would have to rule. Within a year—in the following February—that heir to the throne was dead, following his wife who had died a week before, she on the 12th of February, he on the 19th. Within three weeks their child, the Duke of Brittany, was dead, and all that was left of the direct line was a delicate, weak child of whose survival none could be confident, just two years old. He was to live indeed and to succeed to his great-grandfather, as Louis XV, but the last and few remaining years of that ancestor's glorious life lay under this appalling shadow.

But still the Will remained.

Denain with its recoveries; Utrecht with its sacrifices but also its consolidation: a mixture of salvage, resignation and sufficient, recovered achievement. The Bourbon was in Madrid; the final treaties had been signed in an air of successful resistance and even of victory where there might have been only ruins. The task was accomplished. It remained only to die.

There is something so exact in the hushing of the drums and the trumpets, in the Cease Fire coming at a right interval before the human end of the man who had accomplished and defended his heritage, that the onlooker may be pardoned his superstition if he sees in it an exact destiny, a providential conclusion, an ordered drama coming to its appointed close.

Monarchy: the life of the monarch; the life of the State: the age of the monarch: the age of the State.

That sinking into age was not to be denied. The great King lay, before his last coma, the face sunken with the loss of teeth years before, the restrained voice diminished, but the spirit still continuing its function.

Failure through age is not to be denied.

They say that death is kingly. King Louis was to meet King Death, and Death advancing found Louis ready to receive him. The King of France approached Death with an equal majesty.

The last scenes have been too often repeated for me to repeat them here. The gentle courtesy to the servants who wept at his bedside, saying, "Did you think me immortal? I never did." The famous brief commission of duty to the little child who must now succeed.

If men would detach themselves in the contemplation of this from all affection of blood and place and ask themselves what in the sight of those who watch mankind from far above and from far off was the master thing in all that had been done, the right answer to give is that the master thing in all that life had been the fulfilling of a function: kingship.

Now the fulfilling of one's function is called, in older terms of morals, the doing of duty.

Save in one matter, wherein men most frequently fail, Louis had not failed; and even from that private failure he had, with the help of another, restored himself. By the Will had he withstood the intolerable blow at the succession, when loss after loss had suddenly undone the Crown and left but a sickly child and a debauchee between it and extinction. By the Will did he maintain himself into the last hour of consciousness, remaining in his very self the nation until the end.

He might not even—such is monarchy—retain up to the moment of passage that companionship which had been his sustenance for more than thirty years. His wife was not the Queen. Monarchy could not allow her to be present in the pageantry of royal death. She must stand apart, retired. Not even in this did Louis permit any descent from the more than human place assigned to him. On such a height he died.

INDEX

Lightning Source UK Ltd.
Milton Keynes UK
UKHW011057211122
412568UK00001B/144